Library of
Davidson College

COMMUNAL SOCIETIES IN AMERICA
AN AMS RIPRINT SERIES

THE RADICAL PIETISTS

THE RADICAL PIETISTS:

CELIBATE COMMUNAL SOCIETIES ESTABLISHED IN THE UNITED STATES BEFORE 1820

By

DELBURN CARPENTER

AMS PRESS
NEW YORK
1975

Library of Congress Cataloging in Publication Data

Carpenter, Delburn.
    The radical pietists.

    (Communal societies in America)
    Originally presented as the author's thesis, University
of Northern Iowa, 1972
    Bibliography: p.
    1. Christian communities—United States.
2. Pietism—United States. I. Title.
BV4406.U6C35   1975   280'.4   72-13586
ISBN 0-404-11008-8

Published by Arrangement with the Author.

Copyright © 1975 by AMS Press, Inc.

All rights reserved. Published in the United States by
AMS Press, Inc., 56 E. 13th Street, New York, N.Y. 10003

Manufactured in the United States of America

ACKNOWLEDGMENTS

I wish to acknowledge with special thanks the assistance I received from Dr. Glenda Riley McIntosh, Dr. Charles Quirk, and Dr. Ron Roberts. Without their inspiration, encouragement, and technical skill this study would have been far more difficult. Special thanks must also be given to librarians in several states, especially those at the University of Northern Iowa, whose efforts through the Inter-Library Loan Service have made possible the necessary research for this study. Mrs. Beverly Kollman, the typist of this study, also deserves special thanks for her skill and patience.

To my wife, without whose loving care, unstinting faith, and continual encouragement this work would not have been completed, I dedicate this study.

                                                    Delburn Carpenter
                                                    May, 1972

PREFACE

As a group, celibate communal societies have been the most successful communal societies in the United States. There have been many valuable studies of the celibate communal societies as individual societies. Unfortunately, there has been a lack of studies investigating their unity as a religious group, as examples of a particular phenomenon within Pietism. This study, limited to the seven earliest, celibate communal societies in the United States, has attempted to prove that the beliefs and practices of those seven societies gave them a unity within Pietism which was similar to the unity of Pietists within Christianity.

Bohemia Manor, the "Woman in the Wilderness," Ephrata Cloister, the Shaker Society, the Society of Universal Friends, the Harmony Society, and the Separatist Society of Zoar were examples of a special kind of religious group which can properly be called the "Radical Pietists." That conclusion is based on their Pietist heritage, their interrelationships, and their shared belief in direct inspiration, millennialism, separation from the world, asceticism, celibacy, and communism.

The category, "Radical Pietists" was not intended to be limited to the seven societies in this study. The criteria developed in this study as the means for identifying the societies which fit the description, "Radical Pietists," might well be useful in understanding other celibate communal societies.

TABLE OF CONTENTS

	Page
LIST OF MAPS	viii
LIST OF TABLES	ix

Chapter

1. INTRODUCTION 1

2. A COMMON BACKGROUND IN THE BIBLE, THE ROMAN CATHOLIC
   CHURCH, AND PIETISM 5

3. BOHEMIA MANOR 19

   INTRODUCTION 19

   DEVELOPMENT BEFORE FOUNDING 20

   BELIEFS AND PRACTICES 25

   GENERAL HISTORY AND DECLINE 34

4. "WOMAN IN THE WILDERNESS" 37

   INTRODUCTION 37

   DEVELOPMENT BEFORE FOUNDING 39

   BELIEFS AND PRACTICES 43

   GENERAL HISTORY AND DECLINE 58

5. EPHRATA CLOISTER 61

   INTRODUCTION 61

   DEVELOPMENT BEFORE FOUNDING 63

   BELIEFS AND PRACTICES 76

   GENERAL HISTORY AND DECLINE 108

Chapter		Page
6.	THE SHAKER SOCIETY	115
	INTRODUCTION	115
	DEVELOPMENT BEFORE FOUNDING	117
	BELIEFS AND PRACTICES	126
	GENERAL HISTORY AND DECLINE	143
7.	THE SOCIETY OF UNIVERSAL FRIENDS	145
	INTRODUCTION	145
	DEVELOPMENT BEFORE FOUNDING	147
	BELIEFS AND PRACTICES	149
	GENERAL HISTORY AND DECLINE	158
8.	THE HARMONY SOCIETY	161
	INTRODUCTION	161
	DEVELOPMENT BEFORE FOUNDING	163
	BELIEFS AND PRACTICES	170
	GENERAL HISTORY AND DECLINE	187
9.	THE SEPARATIST SOCIETY OF ZOAR	198
	INTRODUCTION	198
	DEVELOPMENT BEFORE FOUNDING	200
	BELIEFS AND PRACTICES	202
	GENERAL HISTORY AND DECLINE	208
10.	COMPARISON AND CONCLUSIONS	214
	INTRODUCTION	214
	COMPARISON OF BELIEFS AND PRACTICES	217
	RELATIONSHIPS	245
	SUMMARY AND SUGGESTIONS FOR FURTHER STUDY	249

Chapter	Page
BIBLIOGRAPHY	253
APPENDIX	260

LIST OF MAPS

Map   Page

1. Main Locations of Celibate Communal Societies   18

LIST OF TABLES

Table		Page
1.	Religious Background of Original Members	215
2.	Main Geographic Source of Members	215
3.	Solicitation of Members After Establishment in America	215
4.	Sabbath Observance	218
5.	Confession	219
6.	Ceremonialism	219
7.	Sacraments	220
8.	Vows	221
9.	Signed Covenants	221
10.	Position of Women	222
11.	Slavery	223
12.	Pacifism	223
13.	Direct Inspiration	225
14.	Millennialism	227
15.	Separation of Believers From the World	228
16.	Economic Separation From the World	228
17.	Asceticism	230
18.	Androgynous God and Adam	231
19.	Androgynous Redemption	232
20.	Relationship of Celibacy to Church Membership	234
21.	Means of Enforcing Celibacy	235
22.	The Church and the Longevity of Celibacy	237

Table		Page
23.	Order of Advocacy of Celibacy and Communism	241
24.	Relationship of Communism to Membership	242
25.	The Church and the Longevity of Communism	243
26.	Longevity of Celibacy Compared with Longevity of Communism	244

Chapter 1

INTRODUCTION

The existence of celibate communal societies in America began in 1683. Since that time there always has been a celibate communal society in America, and one celibate communal society which still exists is older than the Constitution of the United States. The unique way of life of those societies has evoked the curiosity of many historians, as a result most of the celibate communal societies have been well studied as individual societies. Along with other communal societies, the celibate societies have also been well studied as examples illustrating the success or failure of the communal ownership of property. However, the study of celibate communal societies as a particular movement or as a unified group has been relatively neglected.

One good reason for studying the celibate communal societies as a unified group was the degree of success which those practitioners of celibacy have enjoyed as communal societies. One sociologist has described as successful any communal society which lasted 25 years or more and as unsuccessful any communal society which did not last 25 years.[1] On the basis of existence for 25 years as a criterion of success, the record of celibate communal societies in comparison with other communal

---

[1] Rosabeth Moss Kanter, "Commitment and Social Organization: A Study of Commitment Mechanisms in Utopian Communities," American Sociological Review, Vol. 33, No. 4 (August, 1968), p. 502.

societies was astounding. Fourteen celibate communal societies and 117 non-celibate communal societies were established in the United States before 1910.[2] Eleven of the celibate societies and only seven of the non-celibate societies lasted 25 years or more. Therefore, 78 percent of the celibate communal societies were successful, but only 6 percent of the non-celibate communal societies were successful. A total of 18 communal societies were successful, and celibate communal societies formed 61 percent of that total, even though the celibate communal societies formed only 10 percent of the total number of communal societies established in the United States during 1910.

The study of celibate communal societies as a group may have been neglected because studies of each individual society have emphasized the diversity of belief among those societies. Yet, the celibate communal societies obviously held two important beliefs in common, the practice of celibacy and the communal ownership of property. Though some of the societies may have practiced celibacy for other reasons, most of them based the practice of celibacy and the communal ownership of property on their interpretation of certain passages in the Bible. That striking fact of an additional unity of belief among most of the celibate communal societies and their very high degree of success as communists, formed the basis for the attempt in this study to determine if those societies could be better understood as examples of an

---

[2]Ralph Albertson, "A Survey of Mutualistic Communities in America," *Iowa Journal of History and Politics*, Vol. 34 (1936), pp. 375-440; see also Frederick A. Bushee, "Communistic Societies in the United States," *Political Science Quarterly*, XII (1905), pp. 625-664.

inter-related or even unified group within Christianity rather than as separate and distinct examples of communal societies.

Instead of including all 14 of the celibate communal societies established in the United States before 1910, this study was limited to the earliest seven of those societies for several reasons. The source material available on the last seven societies was much more limited than that available for the first seven societies, and most of the later societies were considerably smaller in membership size and longevity than most of the first seven celibate communal societies. The seven earliest celibate societies established in the United States were all founded before 1820, and each of them was religious in origin and purpose. The seven societies can be regarded as free from socialist influence because socialist ideas did not receive considerable publicity in the United States until the mid-1820's when Robert Owen attempted to establish socialist communal societies.[3] The only communal societies known to have been established in the United States before 1820 which were not celibate were Pieter Cornelis Plockhoy's unsuccessful, almost unknown, attempt to start a socialist colony on the Delaware River in 1663[4] and the religious, but non-celibate, communal society formed by Moravians in Pennsylvania from 1743-1763.[5]

Clearly the best opportunity for studying the unity of celibate communal societies was an investigation of the seven earliest celibate

---

[3]Albertson, op. cit., pp. 375-382.

[4]Durnbaugh, Donald F., "Work and Hope: The Spirituality of The Radical Pietist Communitarians," Church History, Vol. 39, No. 1 (March, 1970), p. 73.

[5]Albertson, op. cit., pp. 378-379.

communal societies established in the United States. Those seven societies were Bohemia Manor, Woman in the Wilderness, Ephrata Cloister, Shaker Society, Society of Universal Friends, Harmony Society, and the Separatists of Zoar.

After a preliminary examination of their common background in Christianity each of the seven societies will be studied in an individual chapter. Each chapter will emphasize the development, the beliefs and practices, and the general history and decline of each society. Particular attention will also be given to influences from any other society and to any indications of approval or disapproval of any other societies. A final chapter will present tables comparing the data on all of the societies and the conclusions generated from those comparisons.

In their background, development, and in many of their beliefs and practices the celibate communal societies demonstrated characteristics which identify those societies as part of the Pietist movement. Each society also held certain beliefs and practices which separated that society from most other Pietists. This study will demonstrate that some of the most important of the beliefs and practices which separated each society from most other Pietists were held by all of the seven celibate communal societies. That unity of belief and practice and the interconnections among the seven societies identify them as part of a distinct group which can be called the "Radical Pietists."

Chapter 2

A COMMON BACKGROUND IN THE BIBLE, THE ROMAN
CATHOLIC CHURCH, AND PIETISM

This chapter will briefly indicate some of the development of celibacy and communism within Christianity, discuss the Biblical passages on which the societies based their celibacy and communism, and discuss the Pietist background of the seven celibate communal societies. After this limited discussion of the common background shared by the societies, the individual chapters on each society will explore the above topics with more detail as is appropriate for each society.

All of the seven societies claimed to be Christian and, though many people have regarded some of the beliefs of any of the societies as un-Christian, the original founders and members of each society definitely came from backgrounds within Christianity. Also from within Christianity, according to each of the societies, came the principles of communism and celibacy for which the societies became so famous and, to some people, notorious. In each society both principles were supported by quotations from the New Testament, especially by those passages which indicated celibacy and communism were practiced in the early apostolic church in Jerusalem.

Celibacy and, to a lesser extent, communism may be seen as particular forms of asceticism. As an ascetic practice celibacy may have come into Western civilization through the cultural exchanges with the East fostered by the conquests of Alexander the Great. At the time of Alexander the Great, Buddhism already demanded chastity from its priests and monks and taught, "the nothingness of life . . ., that the supreme good consisted of the absolute victory over all human wants and desires."[1]

An ascetic way of life was followed by the Essenes, a Judaic sect active before and during the time of Jesus, some of whose members practiced celibacy and held property in common. John the Baptist is reported to have been an Essene and James, brother of Jesus, might also have been a member of that ascetic group. Jesus might have been refering to the Essenes when he said in part of Matthew 19:12 "there be eunuchs which have made themselves eunuchs for the kingdom of heaven's sake." That statement of Jesus indicates he was aware some people conceived of celibacy as part of a dedication of one's life to God. Some scholars have believed Jesus was not only recognizing that conception of celibacy but was also recommending celibacy.[2] Matthew 19:12 was not a major Biblical foundation for celibacy among the seven societies, but the conception of celibacy as part of a dedication of one's life to God was very much a part of the Biblical passages which were the most important in encouraging celibacy in the seven celibate communal societies.

Celibacy was not an isolated phenomenon within the seven societies but part of a way of life. Among the Bible passages which were interpreted by some of the celibate societies as encouraging

---

[1] Henry C. Lea, History of Sacerdotal Celibacy in the Christian Church (London: Watts and Co., 1932), p. 6.

[2] F. J. Buckley, "Eunuch," New Catholic Encyclopedia (1967), V, p. 631.

celibacy there are several passages primarily concerned with a way of life which only indirectly encouraged celibacy. The message of Paul in those passages, Romans 8:1-18, Galatians 5:13-26, and Galatians 6:1-10, contraposed the life of the flesh and the life of the Spirit, counseling the reader to live in the Spirit and fulfill not the desires of the flesh,

> For he that soweth to his flesh shall of the flesh reap corruption; but he that soweth to the Spirit shall of the Spirit reap life everlasting (Galatians 6:8).

Paul's contrast between the "Spirit" and the "flesh" was a contrast between a fulfilling way of life dedicated to God and fulfilling a sinful way of life dedicated to one's self. Paul's admonitions to deny the desires of the flesh were admonitions to deny all forms of self-aggrandizement and to avoid earthly concerns.[3] Some of the celibate societies believed those admonitions included a call for celibacy.

For most of the seven societies the most important Biblical reference encouraging celibacy was the advice concerning marriage which Paul gave in I Corinthians Chapter 7. Paul certainly did not condemn marriage, but he practiced celibacy himself and was definitely of the opinion that it was better for Christians to follow his example than to marry. Part of Paul's reasoning was presented in I Corinthians 7:32-34 where he expressed a fear that the concern married people have for each other will distract them from their devotion to God.[4]

---

[3] P. Delhaye, "Celibacy, History of," *New Catholic Encyclopedia* (1967), III, p. 369.

[4] Nolan B. Harmon (ed.), Corinthians, Galatians, Ephesians, Vol. 10, *The Interpreter's Bible* (New York: Abingdon Press, 1953), pp. 76, 86.

Paul's advocacy of celibacy was partially a result of a belief that Christ's second coming would soon occur. That belief was indicated in several verses in I Corinthians Chapter 7.[5] One example was verse 29 where Paul declared, "But this I say, brethren the time is short: it remaineth, that both they that have wives be as though they had none." All of the celibate communal societies hoped or expected that Christ's second coming would soon occur, and Paul's millennial views may have encouraged their celibacy. An even more important Biblical reference which connected celibacy with the second coming of Christ was Revelation 14:4. In that verse those who would be redeemed first when the second coming of Christ occurred were described as "they which were not defiled with women: for they are virgins."

There are fewer Biblical references to communism and all of them occurred in the Book of Acts, specifically Chapter 2: 44-46, Chapter 4:34-37, and Chapter 5:1-12. All of the references concerned the early Christian church in Jerusalem before Paul became a Christian. Perhaps the most basic statement about communism in the Book of Acts was contained in Chapter 2:44-45 which read as follows:

> And all that believed were together, and had all things common.
>
> And sold their possessions and goods, and parted them to all men, as every man had need.

All of the celibate communal societies known to have specifically based their communism on Biblical precedent referred to the verses in Acts Chapters 2 and 4 which have been mentioned.

---

[5]Ibid., p. 84.

Acts 5:1-12 tells the story of Ananias and his wife Sapphira who sold some land and kept part of the money while claiming to have given all of the money to Peter. Peter received some inspiration giving him knowledge of their falsehood and when Peter confronted Ananias and Sapphira with their sin before God both of them died. While none of the sources for this study indicated that any of the societies based their communism on the incident of Ananias and Sapphira, it probably bolstered the societies' communist principles.

Communism was definitely practiced by the early church, yet, unlike celibacy, the statements in the Bible about communal ownership of property are statements of fact and not an exhortation for all Christians to share all property in common. No one clearly encouraged all who could to practice communism, although Paul had done so for celibacy. The different treatment given celibacy and communism in the New Testament may explain part of why celibacy has played a more important role within the history of Christianity than has communism.

Paul's conception of celibacy was important in the development of the Roman Catholic Church's conception of celibacy as a requirement for the priesthood. Those who demanded a celibate clergy and those who resisted such demands have struggled throughout the history of the Roman Catholic Church and are still struggling today. During the first three centuries of the Christian church, vows of celibacy were voluntary, but in 306 an attempt to require celibacy for the priesthood was made in Spain by the Council of Elvira. The final action which made celibacy a requirement for all Roman Catholic priests was taken at the First and Second Lateran Councils of 1123 and 1139 when the marriages of priests were declared invalid.[6] The power of the church to enforce celibacy among its priests varied enough that the church was probably not able to force a real compliance with its demands until around the time of the Fourth Council of Lateran in 1215.[7]

Considering the examples provided by the Roman Catholic Church's celibate priests, and celibate and cloistered monks and nuns, along with the New Testament statements regarding celibacy and communism, the appearance of celibate communal societies among Protestant groups can hardly be surprising. Yet, the seven societies studied in this paper were quite different from their celibate Roman Catholic predecessors and contemporaries. Much of the emphasis on celibacy in the Roman Catholic Church has been on sacerdotal celibacy or celibacy of the priesthood. Though many Roman Catholics have joined the various celibate or communal orders within their church, that way of life was not expected from most Roman Catholics any more than it was from most Protestants. In contrast to the Roman Catholic tradition, the practices of celibacy and communism among the seven societies were intended and encouraged for the whole congregation, even required for the whole congregation in some of the societies.

The different roles of celibacy and communism in the Roman Catholic Church and in the seven celibate communal societies were indicative of the fundamentally different kinds of organizations represented by those seven societies and by large denominations such as the Roman Catholic Church. Ernst Troeltsch in his study, The Social

---

[6]Delhaye, op. cit., p. 373.

[7]Lea, op. cit., p. 277.

Teaching of the Christian Churches, described three main types of religious groups: the church-type which emphasized the objective power of the institution as a storehouse of grace and salvation, the sect-type which, as a strictly voluntary group, emphasized the effect of "re-birth" in the life of the believer and in his practice of Christianity, and the mystical-type which emphasized the purely personal and inward experience of the believer's relationship with God.[8]

The Roman Catholic Church, though it contains all three types defined by Troeltsch, was basically an example of the church-type. All of the seven celibate communal societies were examples of the sect-type. Those societies, particularly during their early years, were strongly opposed to the concept of church institutions as storehouses of grace, and they denied the efficacy of anything the churches could do if church members did not strictly follow Biblical precepts for a Christian life. The seven societies also contained important elements of mysticism, and mystical feelings of closeness with God were important to the founding leaders of at least six of the seven societies.

The title of this study described the seven celibate communal societies as "Radical Pietists." Few, if any, would quarrel with the use of the word "radical" to describe any of those societies, but "Pietism" is a controversial term among those who deal with religious history.

The one movement which has always been identified by historians as "Pietist," occurred within the German Lutheran Church in the 17th and

---

[8] Ernst Troeltsch, The Social Teaching of the Christian Churches, (New York: MacMillan and Co., 1931), p. 993. The original German edition was published in 1911.

18th centuries. One of the most prominent figures of that movement was Philip Jacob Spener, whose book, *Pia Desideria* (Pious Wishes) which appeared in 1675, contained proposals for improving the life of Christians. The essence of Spener's proposals was in his statement, "it is by no means enough to have knowledge of the Christian faith, for Christianity consists rather of practice."[9] Spener called for the formation of devotional groups which became known as "collegia pietatis" or guilds of piety, whose members met under the leadership of ministers to improve their lives as Christians and to worship more frequently. The "collegia pietatis" spread throughout Germany and from their name came the term "Pietism" which has been used by some historians as an exclusive term to describe that movement within the Lutheran Church in Germany.[10]

During, after, and in some cases before the development of German Lutheran Pietism, similar movements emphasizing the practice of Christianity occurred in other denominations and were also known by exclusive terms such as Puritanism and Methodism. Historians studying those similar movements, especially the historians who believed those movements were only part of one movement occurring in all of the denominations, have struggled to find descriptive generalizations and a term which could define the transcending movement common to Puritanism, Methodism, Lutheran Pietism, and other similar movements.

---

[9] Philip Jacob Spener, *Pia Desideria* (Philadelphia: Fortress Press, 1964), p. 95. The original German edition was published in 1675.

[10] Horst Weigelt, "Interpretations of Pietism in the Research of Contemporary German Church Historians," *Church History*, Vol. 39, No. 2, (June, 1970), pp. 236-241.

A term proposed by Donald F. Durnbaugh for that transcending movement is contained in the title of his study, The Believers' Church.[11] Durnbaugh's term would not be confused with the terms identifying any of the individual movements included in the overall term, but his term could be regarded as prejudicial against the church-type organizations for they too claim to be made up of believers. A widely used term covering the movement Durnbaugh calls "the believers' church" is "Pietism."

Ernst Troeltsch believed Pietism belonged to all of the churches and in each Pietist group he found that,

> always there is the same insistence of the New Testament law of morals and on the idea of the Kingdom of God, and the same opposition to all externalism in the ecclesiastical sacremental system.[12]

When Durnbaugh called the same movement "the believers' church," he described its characteristics as: a voluntary profession of faith, separation of believers from nonbelievers and from the world, engagement in benevolent work, living according to Biblical discipline, and acceptance of direct inspiration as tested by the Bible.[13] F. Ernest Stoeffler called the movement "Pietism," and characterized that movement with four terms: (1) experiential--"the personally meaningful relationship of the individual to God;" (2) perfectionist--"the commitment, devotion, and zeal of the choicest souls in Christendom . . ." were to be regarded as the norm; (3) Biblical--"the

---

[11]Donald F. Durnbaugh, The Believers' Church: The History and Character of Radical Protestantism (New York: MacMillan Co., 1968).

[12]Troeltsch, op. cit., pp. 714-715.

[13]Durnbaugh, op. cit., p. 32.

content for the ethical conduct was squarely based on the New Testament;" and (4) oppositive--Pietism was opposed to the formalism and emphasis on doctrine of the churches and extended "the reform principle to the Christian life, a principle which the earlier reformers applied chiefly, though by no means exclusively, to areas of doctrine and polity."[14]

Troeltsch, Durnbaugh, and Stoeffler stressed different aspects of Pietism, but all three basically agreed on its characteristics and on the identity of the groups of which it is comprised. In this study the term "Pietism" will be used to indicate those characteristics or the groups with which those characteristics are identified.

Experiential, perfectionist, Biblical, and oppositive, Pietism developed throughout Protestant Churches, to a lesser extent in the Roman Catholic Church, and in Europe and America during the 17th and 18th centuries. Pietism was certainly not confined to those centuries, nor was Pietism, even Lutheran Pietism, confined to groups operating within church-type denominations. As various Pietist groups developed within large churches their demands for reform within the churches often led to repression from the churches and to the adoption of separatism by the Pietists.

Spener, whose plan for action had given so much impetus to Lutheran Pietism, lived to see the "collegia pietatis" banned in many German cities and to see many church-pietists become separatist-pietists. Spener denounced separatism,[15] and there have been many who have agreed

---

[14]F. Ernest Stoeffler, The Rise of Evangelical Pietism (Leiden, The Netherlands: E. J. Brill, 1965), pp. 13-23.

[15]Spener, op. cit., p. 20. Spener denounced separatism in 1684 in a work entitled, Use and Abuse of Complaints About Christianity.

that Pietism as a whole was primarily a church-oriented movement rather than a separatist movement. Troeltsch believed that Pietism "simply represents the sect-ideal within the churches . . . ,"[16] and he declared,

> The fact that in Pietism the sect-ideal is so closely connected with the Church explains why the few important Separatist movements which took place were not voluntary, but were the result of actual compulsion.[17]

Contrary to Troeltsch's statement, Pietism was neither a church-oriented nor a separatist, sect-oriented movement. That Pietism first existed and developed within churches did not make a continued existence within those churches a necessary characteristic of Pietism any more than a continued existence within Judaism was a necessary characteristic of Christianity. Pietism developed within the churches because most, if not all, Christians belonged to churches. Pietism was in fact opposed to the conception of the church as a storehouse of grace and salvation which Troeltsch considered one of the primary characteristics of the church-type. If in Pietism the sect-ideal was closely connected with the church, it was because the Pietists regarded what Troeltsch calls the sect-ideal as the only true church and because the Pietists attempted to reform the organizations which Troeltsch described as the church-type.

If the Pietist efforts to reform the churches had succeeded, the only kind of churches that survived would have been of the sect-type. Although the Pietists' efforts to reform the churches were not successful, they were not forced to leave the churches. The Pietists were given a choice between conforming to what they regarded as empty

---

[16]Troeltsch, op. cit., p. 714.

[17]Ibid., p. 719.

formalism in the churches, thereby sometimes forsaking their own inner faith, or leaving the churches, thereby keeping their own faith. The failure of the Pietist reform efforts within the churches and the adoption of separatism by Pietists did not signify a fundamental change in the essential characteristics of Pietism or a failure of Pietism. When the Pietists left the churches they did not abandon their reforms or beliefs, they instituted those reforms and beliefs in their own sects.

  The distinguishing features of Pietism were not determined by any one church, by the initial development of Pietism within several large church-type denominations, or by the development of Pietism as a separatist movement. Nor do the definitions of Pietism and Pietist movements given by Stoeffler, Durnbaugh, and Troeltsch identify Pietism with particular doctrines or theological systems. Pietism was not as much a system of beliefs as it was a series of attitudes. Those attitudes, admirably characterized by Stoeffler as experiential, perfectionist, Biblical, and oppositive, led to similar ways of life in all of the Pietist movements, though not necessarily to similar answers on particular questions of theology or on all aspects of daily living. The disagreements among Pietists on certain matters of doctrine and daily life should not obscure the fundamental unity of Pietist movements.

  Within the general unity of Pietism there can be discerned several groups of sects whose particular expressions of Pietism are more unified than that of the movement as a whole. Similar denominational backgrounds are obvious categories in which the individual sects would be expected to be more similar to each other than to the rest of the Pietist movement. One denominational background shared by many Pietist sects was the German Lutheran Church and many of those sects migrated to the United States.

Among the Pietist sects in the United States which had wholly or partially developed from German Lutheran Pietism, Donald Durnbaugh has identified five as "Radical Pietists." In addition to the usual characteristics of Pietists the five sects which Durnbaugh called "Radical Pietists" also emphasized work, believed their leaders to be divinely inspired, were influenced by millennial expectations, owned real property in common, and were founded to some extent on the teachings of Jacob Boehme, whose influence led to another shared characteristic, the advocacy of celibacy. The five communal societies were: "Woman in the Wilderness," Ephrata Cloister, Harmony Society, Separatists of Zoar, and the Community of True Inspiration (also known as the Amana Society).[18]

When Durnbaugh identified those five societies as "Radical Pietists," he was using the term "Pietist" in the limited sense, referring only to groups which had developed from German Lutheran Pietism. If Durnbaugh had been using the term "Pietist" in its larger sense, as it has been used in this study, he might have included in his study three other celibate communal societies, Bohemia Manor, the Shaker Society, and the Universal Friends. Those three societies and four of the societies identified by Durnbaugh as "Radical Pietists" will be studied together in this attempt to prove their unity as a recognizable movement or group within Pietism. The Community of True Inspiration will not be included in this study because that society did not practice communism until after it was established in the United States in 1843.

---

[18]Donald F. Durnbaugh, "Work and Hope: The Spirituality of The Radical Pietist Communitarians," *Church History*, Vol. 39, No. 1 (March, 1970), pp. 85-90.

The seven societies upon which this study focuses were established in the northern and eastern United States as shown on the following map. Only the main location is shown for each society, except for the Shaker Society which is represented by its former headquarters and by the two Shaker communities still in existence near Canterbury, New Hampshire and Sabbathday Lake, Maine.

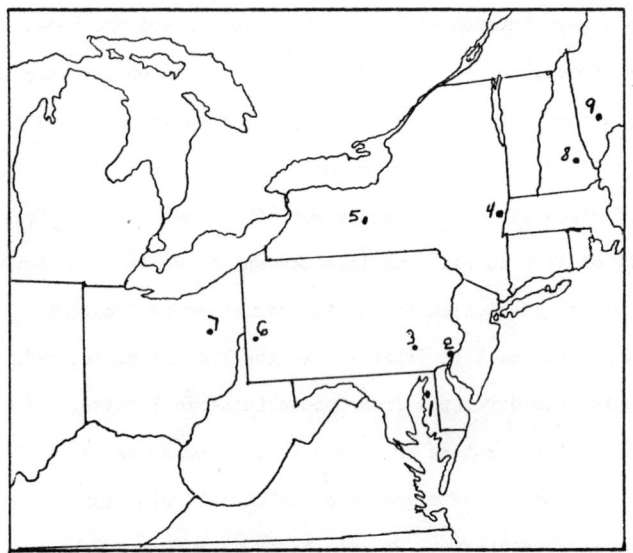

1.= Bohemia Manor. 2.= "Woman in the Wilderness."
3.= Ephrata Cloister. 4.= Shaker Society.
5.= Universal Friends. 6.= Harmony Society
7.= Separatists of Zoar. 8.= Shakers at Canterbury, New Hampshire. 9.= Shakers at Sabbathday Lake, Maine.

Map 1. Main Locations of Celibate Communal Societies[19]

---

[19]Charles Nordhoff, The Communistic Societies of the United States (New York: Dover Publications, Inc., 1966), p. 9. First published in (New York: Harper & Brothers, 1875). The above map is an adaptation of the one published by Nordhoff.

Chapter 3

BOHEMIA MANOR

INTRODUCTION

Though he died before Bohemia Manor was established, Jean de Labadie was the spiritual founder of that society. After a stormy career in both the Roman Catholic Church and the Dutch Reformed Church, Labadie began his own church which he called the "Evangelical."[1] A few years after the death of Labadie, his church decided to send a group of its members to America from the main body of Labadists in Weiward, The Netherlands.[2] Thus, the first celibate communal society in America began as, and remained, a branch of a European sect, the only one of the seven societies in this study that retained membership in a religious group in Europe.

The land on which the Labadists established a branch of their society in 1683 was located on the Bohemia River in Cecil County, Maryland, near the northeastern end of Chesapeake Bay. The Labadists bought their land from Augustine Herrmann and kept the name, Bohemia Manor, which Herrmann had given to the land in honor of his native country. One of Herrmann's sons, Ephraim, had been responsible for

---

[1] No connection with any present church bearing the name "Evangelical."

[2] Bartlett B. James, "The Labadist Colony in Maryland," Johns Hopkins University Studies in Historical and Political Science, XVII (1899), p. 301.

bringing Bohemia Manor to the attention of the Labadists, and Ephraim later joined the society, much to the dismay of his father.[3]

Although a few converts, such as Ephraim Herrmann, were made in America, almost all of the members of Bohemia Manor had previously been members of the Labadist faith and had emigrated together from Weiward, The Netherlands. At its largest, Bohemia Manor had about 125 members including children. The community prospered for a few years, but a partial return to private property in 1698 weakened the society. The death of its leader, Peter Sluyter, in 1722 appears to have weakened Bohemia Manor even further. With a life span of approximately 44 years, Bohemia Manor had disappeared by 1727.[4] The Labadist movement in Europe suffered a similar fate sometime during the middle of the 18th century.[5]

DEVELOPMENT BEFORE FOUNDING

The developments leading to the founding of Bohemia Manor began with the early church career of Jean de Labadie. Labadie was born in Bordeaux, France in 1610. As a young man Labadie studied the works of St. Augustine and began the process for becoming a Jesuit. Instead of finishing the Jesuit training, Labadie was released from the order in 1639 to become a secular priest.[6] Labadie's release from the Jesuits

---

[3]Ibid., pp. 298, 303, 306.   [4]Ibid., p. 310.

[5]Ernest F. Stoeffler, The Rise of Evangelical Pietism (Leiden, The Netherlands: E. J. Brill, 1965), p. 168.

[6]G. Frank, "Labadie, Jean de, Labadists," New Schaff Herzog Encyclopedia of Religious Knowledge (1910), VI, p. 390.

may have occurred because of ill health, or his personal views may have antagonized the Jesuits and led to his release from their order. Labadie was already calling for reforms with the Roman Catholic Church, and he believed he received direct inspiration from the Holy Spirit.[7] Labadie's excellent preaching and his calls for reform earned for him a wide reputation, which resulted in a call to Paris. At first Labadie's reform efforts, which included scathing attacks on much of the Roman Catholic Church, were protected by friends who had some influence with Cardinal Richelieu. By 1645, Labadie's powerful supporters had lost their power either through the death of Cardinal Richelieu or through the death of Louis XIII. Labadie was then tried at court and sentenced to perpetual imprisonment. The Assembly of Clergy appealed the sentence successfully, and Labadie was allowed his freedom with the stipulation that he refrain from preaching for a number of years.[8]

During his enforced silence, Labadie read a copy of Calvin's *Institutes*. Greatly influenced by his reading, Labadie went to Montauban, a Protestant center in southwestern France, and there in 1650 he announced his adoption of the Reformed Faith. Labadie was ordained as a Reformed minister. His previous reputation, which made Labadie's conversion an important event, led to many preaching offers from various cities, including London and Geneva.[9]

Labadie finally went to Geneva in 1659 and preached there for several years. Among Labadie's listeners in Geneva was Phillip Jacob

---

[7]James, op. cit., p. 290.

[8]Ibid., pp. 290-292.

[9]Ibid., p. 292.

22

Spener, a student working on his doctoral degree in theology, who later became one of the foremost leaders of Pietism in the German Lutheran Church.[10] As he had done with the Roman Catholic Church, Labadie found much in the Reformed Church which needed reforming. When Labadie went to Utrecht in 1665 or 1666, his claims of divine inspiration and his insistence on the need for reform were so poorly received by the church leaders and theologians that Labadie soon left and went to Middleburg, The Netherlands.[11]

Success again came to Labadie at Middleburg, but his reforming zeal and his attacks on those who stood in the way of his reforms also produced strong ecclesiastical opposition to Labadie. By 1668, Labadie had applied his belief in direct inspiration to the idea of congregational autonomy, and he published a tract which denied the right of denominational authorities to make laws binding on individual congregations. As a result, Labadie was suspended from the Reformed Church in 1669.[12] Labadie then made the decision to establish his own church, which he did with the members of the Middleburg congregation who remained loyal to him. The civil authorities would not allow the Labadists to meet in Middleburg, so Labadie established the first home for his church at the nearby town of Veere. Since the Labadists were soon forced to leave Veere, the first successful home of Labadie's "Evangelical" church was in Amsterdam.[13]

In Amsterdam the Labadist church grew peacefully for two years until some disorderly services caused the civil authorities to restrict

---

[10]Stoeffler, op. cit., p. 229. [11]James, op. cit., pp. 292-293.
[12]Stoeffler, op. cit., p. 163. [13]James, op. cit., p. 293.

the Labadists' activities so much that the decision was made to leave Amsterdam. From 1670 to 1672 the Labadists were allowed to stay in Hereford, Westphalia, Germany, until disorderly services again forced their removal. Exactly what was disorderly about the services in either case was not made clear in the sources, but some of the emotional outbursts from those under the influence of the Spirit may have been offensive to more ordinary sensibilities. From Westphalia, the Labadists went to Altona, Denmark where Jean de Labadie died in 1674. Following the death of Labadie, the members of his church moved back to The Netherlands, to Weiward in the province of Friesland.[14] Labadie's church remained in Weiward until it ceased to exist in the middle of the 18th century.[15]

Beginning in its early days in Amsterdam, the Labadist church functioned as a communal society with all property owned in common by the church members. Providing sufficient economic support for the members of the Labadist church was often a problem, particularly in the rural environment of Weiward. As a means of relieving the economic pressure on the church at Weiward, branches were started in other cities, such as Rotterdam and The Hague. Following an unsuccessful attempt to start a colony of Labadists at Surinam on the eastern coast of South America, the areas of New York and Maryland were considered as possible sites for a colony of Labadists. In 1679, Peter Sluyter and

---

[14]Ibid., pp. 294-295; see also Frank, op. cit., p. 391.
[15]Stoeffler, op. cit., p. 168.

Jasper Danckaerts were sent to America from Weiward to find a suitable location for the establishment of a branch of the Labadist church.[16]

Economic considerations were not the only reasons the Labadists searched for a site in America. They also hoped to find a place where the Labadist religion could be practiced in peace, and they hoped to be able to convert many of the Indians to Christianity. There was some religious persecution of the Labadists in Weiward, but they did not expect much better treatment in the New World. The first two Labadists who traveled to America in 1679 used false names and did not publicly reveal their intentions in America because they were afraid of religious persecution. Sluyter and Danckaerts were very careful to present themselves in church on Sundays in America, so they would not arouse undue interest,[17] even though Labadists did not regard Sabbath-worship as important.[18]

The mission performed by Sluyter and Danckaerts in America must have been considered a success. They had fulfilled their main purpose in finding a location for a Labadist community, and in private conversations with individuals Sluyter and Danckaerts had converted several people to the Labadist faith. Both Sluyter and Danckaerts were among the approximately 100 Labadists from Weiward who joined with several New World converts to Labadism in founding Bohemia Manor as a celibate society in 1683. Sluyter served as leader of the new Labadist colony until his death in 1722.[19]

---

[16] Jasper Danckaerts, *Journal of Jasper Danckaerts, 1679-1680* (New York: Charles Scribner's Sons, 1913), p. x. (Introduction and editing by Bartlett B. James and J. Franklin Jameson from an 1867 translation by Henry C. Murphy.)

[17] Danckaerts, op. cit., p. 27.   [18] James, op. cit., p. 283.

[19] Ibid., pp. 308-310.

BELIEFS AND PRACTICES

At the center of the faith founded by Jean de Labadie was a particular understanding of the covenants which God had given to mankind. Labadie identified as covenants of the law the three covenants which had been given to mankind through Adam and Moses. The main feature of those covenants was characterized as the promise that salvation would eventually be given to those who followed the letter of the law. In the new covenant given through Christ the promise of salvation was to be fulfilled. Labadie believed that fulfillment came through the sacrifice of Christ, through the active presence of the Holy Spirit in the life of each believer, and in the new life or "rebirth" of each true believer. The new covenant was a covenant of the Spirit and the letter of the law was no longer sufficient for salvation. The Labadists even believed that the law was no longer important. What mattered in the new covenant was the presence of the Holy Spirit in the life of each true believer.[20]

Unlike many other Pietists, Labadie agreed with the established churches that the Holy Spirit was present in and operated through the sacraments of the eucharist and baptism. But Labadie believed the most important way the Spirit functioned was through direct inspiration in the life of the true believer.[21] Receiving the direct inspiration of the Spirit made possible a new life, a rebirth; Labadie insisted that such a rebirth must be visibly present in the life of each Christian. Some of the characteristics which Labadie expected to find in the new life of a reborn Christian were

---

[20]James, op. cit., pp. 280-281.　　[21]Ibid., p. 282.

Evangelical self-knowledge, conversion, hatred and denial
of the world, self-denial, the mortification of all lust,
complete surrender to God, mystical fellowship with God, life
in the presence of God, the Spirit filled life, lowliness,
childlikeness . . .[22]

The Labadists believed that nonbelievers had been able to fulfill the old covenants of the law, but they believed participating in the new covenant of the Spirit was possible only for those who were truly Christian. The Labadist church was supposed to be a pure church with true believers the only members.[23] Several of the other doctrines of the Labadists, including the principles of celibacy and the separation of believers from nonbelievers, may have developed directly from the Labadists' sense of the Spirit-inspired life.

Though the Labadists had expectations that the second coming of Christ would soon occur, their millennial beliefs were not particularly strong.[24] That Christ's second coming did not occur by 1700 or by 1720 or by any other year was not an important factor in the decline of the Labadist faith. Their strong belief that the Holy Spirit was already active within their lives may have made an imminent approach of Christ's second coming less important to the Labadists than to some of the other societies in this study.

What Jean de Labadie actually taught about celibacy was not covered in the sources used for this study. At least some of the Labadists definitely practiced celibacy, and Labadie appears to have encouraged that practice. As a Roman Catholic priest, Labadie had taken a vow of celibacy. There is no indication that he ever renounced that

---

[22]Stoeffler, op. cit., p. 164.   [23]James, op. cit., p. 282.

[24]James, op. cit., p. 279.

vow, and his phrases quoted above about "self-denial" and "the mortification of all lust" indicate that Labadie encouraged celibacy. A visitor to Bohemia Manor in 1721 reported that the sexes were separated in their eating, sleeping, and daily life.[25] A company of Labadists from Denmark visited Ephrata Cloister in 1755. Their leader, Ludovic, was described as having "a pure virgin spirit, and all of his people lived a life of continence."[26] The article by Bartlett B. James, which was the most complete source, did not specifically refer to celibacy, although celibacy probably was included in the "abnegation of the flesh . . ." which James described as one of the principles of Labadism.[27]

The Labadists apparently used the monastic conditions of separation of the sexes as a means to encourage celibacy. Unfortunately, none of the sources indicated whether celibacy was a required practice among the Labadists or when the Labadists had begun to practice celibacy. Nor were there any definite statements regarding the longevity of celibacy in comparison with the longevity of Bohemia Manor. However, the example of the Labadists who visited Ephrata Cloister in 1755 demonstrates celibacy was still practiced among some Labadists at that

---

[25] James E. Ernst, Ephrata: A History, Twenty-fifth Yearbook of the Pennsylvania German Folklore Society (Allentown, Pennsylvania: Schlechter's, 1961), p. 43.

[26] Lamech and Agrippa, Chronicon Ephratense: A History of the Community of Seventh Day Baptists at Ephrata, trans. by J. Max Hark (Lancaster, Pennsylvania: S. H. Zahm & Co., 1899), p. 237. The work was written by two brethren of Ephrata Cloister and originally published at the cloister in German in 1786.

[27] James, op. cit., p. 279.

28

time and is a good indication that celibacy remained as a practice at Bohemia Manor as long as there was a communal society there.

The basis for communism among the Labadists was also not clearly stated in the sources. One author indicated that communism had developed among the Labadists from the small discussion groups which Labadie had instituted as part of his pastoral work in the Reformed Church. Supposedly those groups, which were similar to the "collegia pietatis" associated with Spener, became more and more convinced that believers ought to be separated from the world of nonbelievers, and from that conception they developed a belief in communism as the social ideal for Christians, because the communal ownership of property would enable them to separate believers from the world of nonbelievers.[28] Another author agreed that communism had developed among the Labadists from the principle of the separation of the believer from the world of nonbelievers, but that author also considered the example of the apostolic church and ideas which Jean de Labadie had had for some time as important to the development of communism among the Labadists.[29]

Communism was first established among the Labadists during their stay in Amsterdam. Apparently the communal ownership of property was a required practice among the Labadists until 1692 when the members living in Weiward, The Netherlands returned to a system of private property.[30] However, each branch of the Labadists functioned as a separate communal society, therefore, the return to private property at Weiward did not mean all of the Labadists abandoned communism at that time. A similar

---

[28]Stoeffler, op. cit., pp. 163-165.

[29]James, op. cit., pp. 282, 293, 300.

[30]Frank, op. cit., p. 391.

29

division of property occurred at Bohemia Manor in 1698.[31] However, the evidence from Conrad Beissel's visit to Bohemia Manor in 1721 indicated communal ownership of property continued to be practiced by some of the members of Bohemia Manor.[32] Also, the Labadist group which visited Ephrata Cloister in 1755 still believed in the principle of communal ownership of property.[33]

Much more attention was given in the sources to the Labadists' ideas and practices concerning the sacraments than had been given to the Labadists' ideas concerning celibacy and communism. Two sacraments were observed by the Labadists, baptism and the eucharist. The Labadist doctrines concerning those sacraments exemplified several of the other Labadist beliefs. Jean de Labadie denied the real presence of Christ in the eucharist,[34] but he emphasized the presence of the Holy Spirit in the sacraments and the role of the sacraments as the signs and seals of the new covenant. As a result the Labadists were very careful in the administration of the sacraments and tried to restrict participation to those whose life demonstrated their true belief. Infant baptism was not forbidden, but the beliefs of Jean de Labadie denied any real power to such baptisms. The sacrament of the eucharist was observed only infrequently, partially because the Labadists believed that no one should receive the sacrament if there was any chance even one unworthy person would receive the sacrament.[35]

Though some ceremonies, such as the partaking of the sacraments, were quite important to the Labadists, they believed ceremony was not

---

[31]James, op. cit., p. 310.   [32]Ernst, op. cit., p. 43.
[33]Lamech and Agrippa, op. cit., p. 238.
[34]Frank, op. cit., p. 391.

inherently useful. There was a sharp distinction drawn between
ceremonies which fulfilled the new covenant of the Spirit and ceremonies,
such as the keeping of the Sabbath, which fulfilled the old covenant of
the law. The Labadists did not always observe Sunday as a special day
of worship because such worship was part of the Old Testament law; and,
therefore, not necessary for them.[36] The sacramental ceremonies were
observed by the Labadists because they believed the Holy Spirit operated
through the medium of the sacraments.

    The general attitude of the Labadists against ceremony is a good
indication that oaths or vows of celibacy were not required among them.
For similar reasons the Labadists probably did not require the practice
of confession. The importance attached by the Labadists to the direct
inspiration of the Holy Spirit in the life of each true believer
apparently led the Labadists to regard confessions, oaths, and vows as
unnecessary. None of the sources mentioned whether such practices were
a part of the Labadist faith. Those omissions indicated that such
practices were not a part of the Labadist faith.

    One of the beliefs or practices which separates the Labadists
from the other celibate communal societies was the principle of pacifism.
In the following chapters, pacifism will be identified as a principle
upheld by each of the other societies. The only clear example of the
Labadist position on pacifism demonstrates the Labadists were not
pacifists. In the section about the return voyage to the Netherlands,
Jaspar Danckaerts' *Journal* described his fear and actions when he thought
two approaching ships were Turkish pirates. Believing himself and his

---

[35] James, op. cit., pp. 282-284.

[36] Ibid., p. 283.

companions to be in imminent danger, Danckaerts, along with Sluyter, helped to load the ship's guns. The threatening ships turned out to be friendly but the incident remains a clear example that Danckaerts, Sluyter, and Labadists in general were not pacifists.[37]

One of the principles which the Labadists did share with the other celibate communal societies was the principle of the separation of believers from the world of nonbelievers. Among the Labadists the principle of separation from the world developed from their beliefs that the new covenant of the Spirit required a new life or "rebirth" and that the Holy Spirit would inspire true believers to live that new life. Labadie had described the manifestation of "hatred and denial of the world," and "self-denial . . ." in the life of a believer as signs of the new birth within that believer.[38] An important element in their rejection and hatred of the world was the Labadists' belief that the sinfulness and need for reform which they saw in the churches which professed to be Christian had come from allowing people who were not true believers to become a part of those churches.[39]

The attempt to separate believers from the world of nonbelievers was an important part of the development of communal societies among the Labadists because the communal ownership of property enabled the individual members to separate themselves from the economic system of the world. In some ways the isolation of Bohemia Manor contributed favorably to the Labadists' attempt to separate themselves from the world. Yet, even at Bohemia Manor, a consideration of economic needs led to the same

---

[37] Danckaerts, op. cit., p. 281.

[38] Stoeffler, op. cit., p. 164. [39] James, op. cit., p. 282.

particular compromise with the principle of separation from the world which existed among most of the other societies in this study. Unless a communal society was willing to operate entirely on a subsistence basis, some kind of economic contact had to be maintained with the outside world. Though trade with the outside world was then done in the name of the society as a whole the actual process was carried out by individuals acting in behalf of the society. Therefore, the compromise and the resultant contact with the outside world always threatened to further contaminate the principles of the society.

One of the effects of compromising principles because of economic considerations was manifested at Bohemia Manor in the changing opinion of Peter Sluyter on the issue of slavery. The Journal of Jaspar Danckaerts described both Danckaerts and Sluyter as being against slavery and indentured servitude,[40] but slavery became a part of the production of tobacco at Bohemia Manor and Sluyter even appears to have become wealthy through his private use of slaves following the modification of communal ownership of property at Bohemia Manor in 1698.[41]

Because Bohemia Manor was the first celibate communal society in America, its founding was not influenced by any of the other societies in this study. By 1694, some eleven years after the founding of Bohemia Manor, the "Woman in the Wilderness" was established as a celibate communal society near Germantown, Pennsylvania,[42] about 70 miles from Bohemia Manor. The two societies may have come in

---

[40] Danckaerts, op. cit., p. 192.

[41] James, op. cit., pp. 309-310.

[42] Julius Friedrich Sachse, The German Pietists of Provincial Pennsylvania, 1694-1708 (Philadelphia, Pennsylvania: printed for the author, 1895), p. 11.

contact with each other in 1694, but the only known contact between the two societies occurred indirectly when two men from Germantown, who were intimately acquainted with, but were not members of, the "Woman in the Wilderness," visited Bohemia Manor in 1721.[43] By that time each society was too far developed for any contact to have been important to the history of either society.

There were at least two earlier opportunities for indirect contact between the two societies. Two prominent individuals appeared to have had access to information about both societies before 1700 and may have informed either society about the existence of the other. Those individuals were Benjamin Furly, William Penn's agent in Amsterdam,[44] and Phillip Jacob Spener, one of the leaders of the German Lutheran Pietist movement in the late 17th century.[45] As the younger of the two societies, the "Woman in the Wilderness" was the most likely to have been influenced by contact with another society. For that reason the discussion of the possible contacts which Furly and Spener might have made between the societies will be presented in the next chapter on the "Woman in the Wilderness."

The one celibate communal society which Bohemia Manor undoubtedly influenced was Ephrata Cloister. The founder of Ephrata Cloister was Conrad Beissel, one of the two men from Germantown who had visited Bohemia Manor in 1721.[46] As the chapter on Ephrata Cloister will demonstrate, Beissel was influenced by so many different Pietist and

---

[43] Ernst, op. cit., p. 43.

[44] Sachse, op. cit., p. 46, 170; see also James, op. cit., p. 299.

[45] Stoeffler, op. cit., p. 229.   [46] Ernst, op. cit., p. 43.

mystical groups that pinpointing the particular contribution to Ephrata Cloister of any one of those groups is sometimes difficult. The contribution of Bohemia Manor to Ephrata Cloister was probably one of reinforcing several ideas which Conrad Beissel had already developed from other sources.

GENERAL HISTORY AND DECLINE

Since Bohemia Manor survived 44 years from 1683 to 1727, it must, on the basis of longevity, be considered a success when compared with most other communal societies. In some ways Bohemia Manor was the least successful of the celibate communal societies, although it was neither the smallest in membership nor the shortest in longevity. The conditions which indicate Bohemia Manor was somewhat unsuccessful was the amount of change which occurred in several of the Labadists' beliefs.

Two important organizational changes occurred after the death of Jean de Labadie which did not fit his original conceptions. Labadie had believed that no church organization should have authority over any individual congregation.[47] Yet, when the Labadists began establishing communal societies outside of their headquarters at Weiward, those societies were under the control and direction of the original society at Weiward.[48] The communal ownership of property appears to have been part of the membership requirements when Labadie was still living, but within 20 years after his death that system was abandoned at Weiward in 1692.[49] At Bohemia Manor the communal ownership of property was retained

---

[47]Stoeffler, op. cit., p. 165.   [48]James, op. cit., p. 285.
[49]Frank, op. cit., p. 391.

intact until 1698 when certain modifications were made which apparently allowed members to individually choose between the private ownership of property or the communal ownership of property. Even the leader of Bohemia Manor, Peter Sluyter, chose to accumulate private property. By the time of his death Sluyter had become personally wealthy.[50]

Certain of the other Labadist beliefs were changed at Bohemia Manor. The use of tobacco and the ownership of slaves had been denounced as contrary to the Labadist principles by Peter Sluyter and Jaspar Danckaerts when they visited America in 1679.[51] Those high principles were not maintained. Most of the wealth which was accumulated by Peter Sluyter and other members of Bohemia Manor came from the sale of tobacco which had been produced by slave labor at Bohemia Manor.[52]

Not very much is known about the daily life of Bohemia Manor before or after 1698. The rule of Sluyter has been described as harsh by several outside witnesses and by some former members.[53] Before Sluyter is censured for the hard life which existed at Bohemia Manor during his leadership, the characteristics which Labadie regarded as signs of the true Christian should be considered again. It is quite likely that only a harsh life would have enabled a Labadist to exhibit "hatred and denial of the world, self-denial," and "the mortification of all lust . . . ," as signs of his rebirth.[54]

Each of the seven celibate communal societies in this study had former members who complained bitterly of the hard life within the

---

[50] James, op. cit., pp. 309-310.   [51] Danckaerts, op. cit., p. 134.
[52] James, op. cit., p. 309.   [53] James, op. cit., pp. 286-289.
[54] Stoeffler, op. cit., p. 164.

society, and each society had its share of visitors who afterwards described the society in derogatory terms. Human frailty was as much a part of Bohemia Manor as in any other social organization. But like the beliefs and practices of each of the other celibate communal societies,

>Whatever its defects, and the opportunities for hypocritical pretence which it offered, Labadism was yet a standard of faith and conduct which no one could conform to without at the same time exemplifying high Christian graces.[55]

---

[55]James, op. cit., p. 284.

Chapter 4

"WOMAN IN THE WILDERNESS"

INTRODUCTION

The name for the celibate communal society known as the "Woman in the Wilderness" was an ironic choice because that society excluded women from its membership. The name had not been chosen by the members but was given to the society by the people who lived near them. The name, "Woman in the Wilderness" which refers to the "woman" mentioned in Revelation 12:6, 14, had been given to the celibate brethren in response to their preaching about the need for repentance and their frequent quotations from the Book of Revelation.[1] The brethren considered themselves nonsectarian and used their own name for their society, "The Contented of the God-Loving Soul," as infrequently as possible.[2] Though "Woman in the Wilderness" was slightly derisive in origin and the brethren would not acknowledge it as their name, that is the name by which the mystical society has been known to history.

In 1694 the group of German pietists who became known as the "Woman in the Wilderness" settled near Germantown, Pennsylvania in a

---

[1] Julius Friedrich Sachse, The German Pietists of Provincial Pennsylvania, 1694-1708 (Philadelphia, Pennsylvania: printed for the author, 1895), p. 81.

[2] Lamech and Agrippa, Chronicon Ephratense: A History of the Community of Seventh-Day Baptists at Ephrata (Lancaster, Pennsylvania: S. H. Zahm & Co., translated by J. Max Hark, 1889), p. 15.

rough, wooded area which is now contained within the northern half of Philadelphia's Fairmount Park, part of which still looks much like it did in 1694. The society built a large communal hall where the members lived and worshipped, but after 1708 and the death of the group's leader, Johannes Kelpius, most of the members lived as hermits in individual cabins. Certain land transactions indicate the community had ceased to exist by 1741, seven years before the death of the last known leader in 1748.[3]

At its beginnings in 1694 the "Woman in the Wilderness" was composed of forty men who had traveled from Germany to America in one group. Throughout its short history the society received not more than forty more members, most of whom also came from Germany. The original immigrants who came from Germany in 1694 had been members of "collegia pietatis" in various cities and many of them were university graduates or university students. Perhaps each of the original immigrants was well known to one of the group's leaders before emigration, but most of the members did not know each other until they came together as a group in 1693.[4] Even though the most active period in the history of the "Woman in the Wilderness" was only a brief fourteen years, the legacy left by that communal society, especially in the founding and development of Ephrata Cloister, lived on much longer.

---

[3]Sachse, op. cit., pp. 206, 399.

[4]Ibid., p. 11-12.

DEVELOPMENT BEFORE FOUNDING

The most important impetuses for the founding of the "Woman in the Wilderness" came from two sources: the attempts made in many German cities in the early 1690's to suppress the "collegia pietatis" and the millennial calculations formulated by Johann Jacob Zimmermann in 1684. More than any other single man the credit for the existence of the "Woman in the Wilderness" belongs to Zimmermann, but credit must also be given to leading pietists such as Phillip Jacob Spener and Augustus Herman Francke whose work in many instances paved the way for Zimmermann.

Johann Jacob Zimmermann was born in 1644 in Vaihingen on the Entz River in Wurttemburg; he graduated from the University of Tubingen in 1664; he became the diaconus of Beitigheim in Wurttemburg in 1671. Zimmermann became a noted mathematician, publishing six books on that subject before 1680. The appearance of comets in Europe in 1680, 1681, and 1682 apparently changed Zimmermann's interests for his next three books concerned comets.[5]

Sometime in 1683 or 1684 Zimmermann fell ill and was attended by Dr. Louis Brunquell who introduced Zimmermann to the works of Jacob Boheme, a mystical philosopher whose belief that God was androgynous had led to the advocation of celibacy. Zimmermann combined his astronomical observations with the ideas of Boehme, and in 1684, under the pseudonym, Ambrossii Sehmanni, Zimmermann published Mundus Coperinizans, which prophesied that Christ would come again before or during 1694. The book also asked certain questions of the local Lutheran consistory; when

---

[5]Ibid., pp. 119, 469-462.

the consistory produced answers which were not satisfactory to him, Zimmermann publicly preached against the consistory, denouncing the church as a part of Babel. After being tried and convicted of heresy, Zimmermann was ordered to leave Wurttemburg, which he did, but not without predicting dire calamities for that duchy on account of his exile. Shortly thereafter, Wurttemburg was successfully invaded by the French which Zimmermann claimed as a fulfillment of his prophecy.[6]

Probably because of his reputation as a mathematician and astronomer, Zimmermann was able to find employment as a mathematics professor at the University of Heidelberg. He lost his professorship in 1689, and his history from then until 1693 is mostly unknown. Zimmermann is known to have worked during part of that period for a book publisher in Hamburg, who had many contacts in Pietist circles. Through the publisher, Zimmermann became acquainted with Johann Heinrich Horbius, the brother-in-law of Phillip Jacob Spener, with Dr. Johann Wilhelm Petersen, a leader of the Philadelphian Society in Germany,[7] and with Johann Gottfried Seelig, who once served as secretary to Spener[8] and later sailed to America as one of the original members of the "Woman in the Wilderness." In 1690 or 1691, while in Nuremburg, Zimmermann met Johannes Kelpius, his future successor.[9]

---

[6]Ibid., pp. 463, 467-472. Sachse gives a reprinting and translation of "Proceedings of the Ducal Government of Wurttemburg versus Magister Johann Jacob Zimmermann" which Wurttemburg printed in 1708 as a small pamphlet.

[7]Ibid., p. 60.

[8]Julius Friedrich Sachse, Justus Falckner: Mystic and Scholar (Philadelphia, Pennsylvania: printed for the author, 1903), p. 33.

[9]Sachse, Pietists, p. 223.

By 1693 Zimmermann was living in Erfurt and planning to form a "Chapter of Perfection" with forty men who would migrate to America to be present there when the millennium began.[10] The "collegia pietatis" in Erfurt had been investigated by local authorities in 1691; Augustus H. Francke was then exiled for his activities in the "collegia," but the Pietist meetings continued unabated, although more secretly. In the early 1690's edicts forbidding the sale of Pietist literature and forbidding the meetings of the "collegia pietatis" were issued in many German cities; in Erfurt, those meetings were banned on July 20, 1693. The relationship, if any, between Zimmermann's plans and the Erfurt ban against the Pietists, is not known; but it appears likely that some of those who formed the "Woman in the Wilderness" did so because of the worsening political climate in Erfurt and other cities. The use of Magdeburg and Halberstadt as the final meeting places in Germany for the "Chapter of Perfection" was a result of the ban in Erfurt.[11]

None of Zimmermann's followers were wealthy; so, being in need of assistance, they applied for help from a wealthy Quaker in Holland, saying they desired, ". . . to depart from these Babilonish Coasts, to those American Plantations, being led thereunto by the guidance of the Divine Spirit."[12] A generous contribution of money was given to the group along with an equally generous arrangement on land usage in

---

[10]Ibid., p. 60. An explanation of their ideas about mystic numbers and the significance of "40" as the "number of perfection" will be given at the beginning of the section on Beliefs and Practices.

[11]Ibid., p. 258.

[12]Ibid., p. 46. Quoting from Gerard Croese's *Historia Quakeriana* II (London, 1696), p. 262. The original Dutch version was published in 1694.

Pennsylvania; the total contribution from that wealthy Quaker is what actually enabled the group to migrate to Pennsylvania and establish the "Woman in the Wilderness." The Quaker benefactor chose to remain anonymous, but circumstances indicate that Benjamin Furly, William Penn's agent in Holland, was the man responsible for helping Zimmermann's party. One of Zimmermann's followers, Heinrich Bernard Koster, had a brother living in Amsterdam who was personally acquainted with Furly; and, it appears likely that this connection was important, either in generating a contribution from Furly or in contacting another wealthy Quaker through Furly.[13] It is possible that whoever gave the contribution did so partially because of the threatening situation which faced Zimmermann's followers in Germany.

In the late summer of 1693, the future members of the "Woman in the Wilderness" walked to Rotterdam, where Zimmermann fell ill and died at the age of 49. His widow and four children remained with the group, although they were not an integral part of the "Chapter of Perfection." Johannes Kelpius, then only 20, became the leader of the group, and the journey was continued. They sailed first to England where they waited for a protective convoy because the War of the League of Augsburg was in progress. During their stay in London they became acquainted with the Philadelphian Society of London; Kelpius corresponded with the London Philadelphians for several years after his arrival in Pennsylvania. The final sailing from England to America was begun in February, 1694; the group led by Kelpius arrived at Bohemia Landing in the Chesapeake Bay on June 19, 1694. The company of pilgrims reached

---

[13]Sachse, *Pietists*, pp. 47, 258.

Germantown a few days later, June 24, 1694, in time to celebrate St. John's Eve near the wooded area which was to become their home.[14]

Kelpius and his followers lived with various German families in the area until arrangements were made to purchase a 175 acre tract on Wissachickon Creek. The land included steep, wooded ravines where, even today, in the midst of the bustle of Philadelphia, the lush vegetation holds off the outside world with an aura of solemnity and silence. On a level area at the top of one of the hills was erected a communal building, forty feet square, which contained a worship hall, a schoolroom, separate cells for the members, and an observatory on the roof. On cleared ground, a large garden was cultivated for the support of the members with particular attention given to raising medicinal herbs.[15]

BELIEFS AND PRACTICES

In the previous section on the developments which led to the founding of the "Woman in the Wilderness," the emphasis, like the available information, has been on the Pietist background of the brethren with scant mention of an equally significant mystical background. Except for Zimmermann's introduction to the works of Jacob Boehme through Dr. Brunnquell, and the group's relationship with the London Philadelphian Society, hardly anything is known about the development of mystical knowledge among the brethren before the founding of "Woman in the Wilderness." Even knowledge about their mystical beliefs is limited;

---

[14]Ibid., pp. 11-12, 15-16, 61.

[15]Ibid., pp. 70-75.

the few items they published were intended for the general public and do not contain expositions of any mysticism. What is known about their mystical beliefs has come mainly from a few books of mystic lore which were owned by members of the community and which have been studied by Dr. Sachse, whose books are the best and largest available source of information on the "Woman in the Wilderness."

The brethren of that mystic community were not just a band of Pietists, but also "a company of Theosophical Enthusiasts . . .;"[16] students of the ancient books of the Kabbala;[17] followers of Jacob Boehme who wooed the Virgin-Sophia with their celibacy;[18] and Rosicrucians[19] who found mystic significance in ancient symbols and in having forty men for a "Chapter of Perfection."

The significance of having forty men for a "Chapter of Perfection," is somewhat explained by a consideration of mystic numbers. For various reasons, which will not be discussed here, the number "4," known as the "equal perfect number," has been viewed by many religious cults as a symbol of the Deity. In almost all languages, except English, "God"

---

[16]Ibid., p. 37.

[17]The Kabbala (also spelled with a "C" and with several variations of "b's" and "l's") appears to have been written in medieval times and was probably of Jewish origin. Its books give strange, mystical interpretations to the Old Testament.

[18]The Virgin-Sophia was the divine, female-half of androgynous Adam, which was lost to mankind when Adam fell by desiring the separation of the sexes like the animals. Ultimately in the redemption of mankind, the Virgin-Sophia was supposed to be restored as part of man's androgynous nature.

[19]The Mastery of Life (Official publication #19, Ancient and Mystical Order Rosae Crucis, 21st ed., no author or date given), p. 17. The "Woman in the Wilderness" is described as the first Rosicrucian group in the Western hemisphere.

45

has been represented by four letters, such as the German, Gott, or the French, Dieu. "40," the decade of the perfect number, was ". . . known as the number of perfection." Within the Bible the number "40" was used in many significant episodes: the Flood was produced from 40 days and nights of rain; the Israelites wandered 40 years in the desert; Christ, like unto all men, was carried in his mother's womb 40 weeks; He fasted in the desert 40 days and nights; and Christ, from his resurrection to his ascension, spent 40 days upon the earth. There are other examples; and for those who found religious significance in symbolic numbers, the Bible gave reason enough to venerate the number "40."[20]

The actual benefits, which the brethren of the "Woman in the Wilderness" intended to derive from putting together a "Chapter of Perfection," are not known. They might have intended by their presence together to grasp some power or magical property inherent in the creation of a "Chapter of Perfection," or having forty men might just have been a symbol representing and reminding the brethren of a revered belief. It may be significant that in most of the Biblical episodes where "40" is an important number, the number denotes a time of cleansing from sin or a time of preparation in the wilderness for a prophet before he returns to the world. The brethren believed that Christians might pass through three stages of wilderness, which Kelpius described as: the barren, the fruitful, and the ". . . Wilderness of the Elect of God."[21] Whatever kind of help may have been expected from the formation of a "Chapter of

---

[20]Sachse, Pietists, pp. 40-41.

[21]Ibid., p. 184. Quoting from a letter written by Kelpius to Hester Palmer of Flushing, Long Island on May 25, 1706. Sachse prints the letter in full, pp. 180-191.

Perfection," part of its purpose was to help its members progress through the three stages of wilderness to reach the highest state of holiness and to become the ". . . Elect of God."[22]

Along with a personal desire to be prepared for the millennium, Kelpius and his followers also wished to prepare others. In their letter to the Quaker in Amsterdam, from whom they requested funds for the journey to America, they promised to show their faith and love for God by converting people.[23] Daniel Falkner's letter to Germany in August, 1694, speaks of plans to provide moral instruction for children, ". . . otherwise there will be only mending and patching of the old people."[24] Their plans for converting others to prepare for the millennium did not call for conversion to a particular religious denomination, but only for repentance.

The following passage from a letter by Johannes Kelpius indicates the brethren's attitude toward other religious groups: ". . . I love them (Quakers) from my inmost soul, even as I do all other sects that approach & call themselves Christ's, the Paptists (sic) even not excluded."[25] Kelpius did not regard all other sects as having the "truth," but further explained his attitude saying, ". . . I hope to become one in God through Christ both with those who do not yet see as I do, and with those that see much better and farther than I."[26]

---

[22] Ibid., p. 81. [23] Ibid., p. 46, see footnote #12.

[24] Ibid., p. 74.

[25] Sachse, *Pietists*, p. 229. Quoting from a letter of Kelpius to Johannes Fabricius, Kelpius' former professor, July 23, 1705. Sachse printed the letter in full, pp. 229-233.

[26] Ibid., p. 232.

47

Often the sectarians which are most contentious about the truth of their beliefs do so because they believe they have been directly inspired by the Holy Spirit. While the mystic brethren did not emphasize beliefs in direct revelation, their sectarian modesty did not come from any lack of "direct inspiration," for they believed they had been led "by the guidance of the Divine Spirit . . ." in their decision to migrate to America.[27]

The mission to prepare settlers for the millennium was carried out, as much as possible, in ways which did not violate the nonsectarian beliefs of the "Woman in the Wilderness." Immediately after discovering that Germantown was without regular church services, H. B. Koster began to hold regular services to which all were invited. Koster's services were held according to German Lutheran ritual and were well attended by the German Protestants in the area; they were also attended by a group of "Keithian" Quakers, who adhered to the seventh-day Sabbath. Koster held services in Philadelphia as well. Other members of the mystic community conducted twice daily services in their communal hall, known as the "Tabernacle," to which all were invited. Religious instruction was available for anyone who wished it. The brethren were even ready to travel to anyone's household whenever they were called.[28]

The brethren could not be everywhere, so Kelpius distributed small boxes full of cards on which moral cuplets were printed. Whenever immoral acts were committed, such as cursing or blasphemy, the offender was to be given one of the cards, which he was to read; and, by

---

[27] Ibid., p. 46, quoting from Croese, see footnote #12.

[28] Ibid., pp. 66-68, 78-79, 126.

following the moral directions, he was to mend his ways. In order to increase both public and private devotion, Kelpius also wrote and published a pamphlet entitled, A Short Easy and Comprehensive Method of Prayer.[29]

While their mission to the settlers around them was important, the brethren of the "Woman in the Wilderness" also spent much of their time away from the world. They sought seclusion and solitude in which they could improve their own religious condition through contemplation, asceticism, and mystical studies. All of their efforts were part of a preparation and striving for "the Prize of the first Resurrection. . .,"[30] which would come at the beginning of the millennium.

Following Zimmermann's calculations, the mystic brethren had hoped and expected the millennium would begin soon after their arrival in Pennsylvania. From their observatory, with the use of telescopes and other scientific instruments of the day, they studied the heavens for indications of the approach of Christ's second coming. The millennium did not arrive in 1694, but the brethren continued their watchfulness and did not give up hope. When the Barbadoes plague (yellow fever) ravaged Pennsylvania in 1699, the brethren regarded the plague as a sign, the millennium was about to begin. In 1701, an apparition like an angel appeared once during the community's traditional celebration of St. John's Eve and once three nights later; both visions were taken as signs that the millennium was nigh, but nothing further happened.[31] The

---

[29] Ibid., pp. 100-101.

[30] Sachse, Pietists, pp. 129. Quoting from a letter by Kelpius to Steven Momford, Long Island, December 11, 1699. Reprinted in full pp. 129-136.

[31] Ibid., pp. 139, 152.

rapid decline of the mystic community after the death of Kelpius in 1708 might have been hastened by the continued disappointments regarding the millennium.

The sources for the beliefs of the "Woman in the Wilderness," regarding the millennium, are well known; unfortunately, the reasons for the adoption of communism by the mystic brethren are not known. Communism was not mentioned in Zimmermann's book about the approaching millennium, and communism is not mentioned in any of Kelpius' letters which have been reprinted by Sachse. It is likely that communism was adopted by the brethren for the purpose of following the early church as described in Acts 2:44-45. It is also possible that because necessity forced them to share their goods in order to migrate to America, they may have simply continued the communal ownership of property. Whatever their reasons for adopting communism, the decision must have been made before or soon after they arrived in America, because the communal building built by the brethren provided living quarters for each member.

Kelpius developed a habit of retiring by himself to a secluded cave in the woods. After his death in 1708, communism appears to have been modified or partially abandoned as the brethren also began living in separate cabins on various parts of their land. The land and tabernacle remained a common possession, but all other property was held privately. When Johannes Seelig died in 1745, he left a will giving his possessions to a friend, and not to Conrad Matthai, the last surviving member of the "Woman in the Wilderness."[32]

---

[32]Ibid., pp. 196-197, 339.

50

More is known regarding the sources for the mystic community's beliefs about celibacy. Considering their beliefs concerning the imminent approach of the millennium, the Book of Revelation must have been an important influence in the decision of the brethren to adopt celibacy. Kelpius once described himself as striving to be "among the Virgin waiters . . ." who would partake in the first resurrection.[33] A letter by Daniel Falkner indicated that Paul's advice in I Corinthians, Chapter 7, was also part of the brethrens sources of ideas about celibacy. That letter described the first brother who succumbed to the allurements of marriage as not being true to his vow "to remain free according to the better advice of St. Paul."[34] Ludwig C. Biedermann, the first brother to break the vow, married Zimmermann's daughter soon after the community's arrival in America. Several others also broke their vows of celibacy within the first few years. According to the chroniclers of the later Ephrata community, after Kelpius died, temptation again became successful among the mystic brethren and many of those "who had been most zealous against marrying now betook themselves to women again . . .," which so shamed the solitary state "that the few who still held to it dared not open their mouths for shame."[35]

Another of the early dividing forces within the "Woman in the Wilderness" was disagreement concerning the sacraments of baptism and the eucharist. The disagreement was not about the manner in which

---

[33]Ibid., p. 129. See footnote #30.

[34]Ibid., p. 85. Falkner's letter was published in Germany and Holland in 1695 and 1696. Sachse did not print the full letter.

[35]Lamech and Agrippa, op. cit., p. 14.

sacraments were given or their meaning, it centered on how often the sacraments were to be given. Kelpius and most of the brethren favored very few observances of the sacraments, while Heinrich B. Koster and a few others wished to observe the sacraments more frequently, according to the custom of the German Lutheran Church. The disagreement was one of the reasons which led to Koster's withdrawal from the mystic community. The infrequent observance of the sacraments also led some to charge Kelpius and his followers with having embraced the doctrines of the Quakers.[36] Other than their infrequent observance, the ideas of the mystic community about the sacraments did not acquire any attention and little is known about their actual sacramental practices.

While the brethren of the "Woman in the Wilderness" objected to meaningless ceremony in the form of too-infrequent observance of the sacraments, they were not simply against the use of ceremony; they apparently practiced many mystical ceremonies. Part of the desire for a "Chapter of Perfection" may have come from a desire to practice mystical ceremonies requiring the presence of forty men. On June 24th, their first night in Germantown, and on each anniversary thereafter, the brethren celebrated St. John's Eve with the performance of mystic rites around a large bonfire. There are traditions which indicate that local people went to the mystic brethren to acquire magical charms known as zauber-zettle and wunder-siegel and to have the brethren cast horoscopes.[37] Kelpius and his followers undoubtedly believed that heavenly bodies could influence their lives, but the letters of Kelpius show clearly that he

---

[36]Sachse, Pietists, pp. 87, 148.

[37]Ibid., pp. 151, 112, 120-123.

did not trust his salvation to mystical numbers or to magical charms, but to the grace of God.

In regard to ceremonies not so mystical, it is known that each brother gave a vow of celibacy,[38] but whether those vows took the form of oaths sworn on the Bible is not known. There is also no information in any of the sources regarding the attitude of the mystic brethren toward confession. On the question of pacifism the position of the brethren is clearly described in Daniel Falkner's account of a sea-battle which occurred on their voyage to America in 1694:

> The passengers were given the choice to fight or not. We, of course, abstained of carnal weapons and taking the shield of faith, sat down between decks behind boxes and cases, prayed and invoked the Lord . . .[39]

One other area of mystery concerning the beliefs of the "Woman in the Wilderness" is the question of which day they observed the Sabbath. When the mystic community arrived in Germantown, the seventh-day Sabbath was observed by a group of "Keithian" Quakers who followed the ideas of George Keith. There are several indications that observing the seventh-day Sabbath became the custom followed by the "Woman in the Wilderness." H. B. Koster, who left the community because of disputes about the sacraments, is known to have observed the seventh-day Sabbath. There was a warm relationship between Kelpius and Steven Momford, the founder of the first Sabbatarian church in America, and also with John Rodgers, a Sabbatarian from Connecticut who visited the community on the

---

[38]Ibid., p. 85. See footnote #33.

[39]Ibid., p. 23. The battle was a very minor part of the War of the League of Augsberg. The ship which carried the mystic brethren was on the winning side in that battle.

Wissahickon in 1700. There are some indirect references to the "Woman in the Wilderness" as Sabbatarian in a few manuscripts from Ephrata Cloister, which was Sabbatarian.[40] Unfortunately, there is no unequivocal evidence which clearly marks the "Woman in the Wilderness" as a community observing the seventh-day Sabbath. The ordination of Justus Falckner, who left the mystic community in 1701 to become a minister of the Swedish Lutheran Church, was attended by the mystic brethren and is an indication that the community observed the first day Sabbath.[41] As nonsectarians and as men who had devoted their lives to worshipping God, the mystic community might have observed either or both days.

The attitudes of the "Woman in the Wilderness" toward the world appear to have been paradoxical because the two basic principles regarding the mystic community's relationship with the world were service to the world and separation from the world. Yet, the two principles were not so different. The brethren believed the greatest service that could be performed for worldly people would be to separate them from worldly sinfulness and convert them to a life of preparation for Christ's second coming. As a collective group, the mystic brethren remained true to the principle of separation from worldliness, and, even after 1736, they reportedly would not "engage in any occupation for profit or gain."[42]

---

[40] Ibid., pp. 125, 129, 161-162.

[41] Sachse, Falckner, p. 63. Daniel Falkner and Justus Falckner were brothers. The different spelling of Justus' last name apparently came from his ministry to the Swedish Lutheran Church in New York.

[42] Sachse, Pietists, p. 199. Quoting from a report made in 1736 by Rev. August Spangenberg to the Moravian Church at Herrnhut after he had visited the "Woman in the Wilderness." Sachse reprinted part of the report.

Some of the brethren were not successful at following the principle of separation from the world. Daniel Falkner was the most prominent example. He had been sent to Europe in 1698 to inform people there of the society's well being and to recruit more members to make up for those who had already left. Falkner returned in 1700 with new members and with a letter of attorney giving Falkner, Kelpius, and a new member, Johannes Jewart, power over the lands of the Frankfort Land Company. Falkner also brought back a similar letter from Benjamin Furley giving Falkner power of attorney over Furly's lands in Pennsylvania. Kelpius maintained his separation from the world and refused to exercise his authority in any way except to execute a document which passed his authority to Jewart and Falkner, and which, in effect, declared Kelpius to be civilly dead.[43] Falkner exercised his authority and drifted more and more away from the "Woman in the Wilderness" until he ceased to be a member. The wide variance between the actions of Daniel Falkner and of Johannes Kelpius in regard to the power of attorney, when Falkner was still a member of the mystic community, indicated the community allowed widely divergent beliefs among its members and did not insist on a discipline as strict as that maintained within most of the other celibate communal societies in this study.

The beliefs of the mystic brethren regarding slavery are shrouded in mystery. In at least one old Pennsylvania family, there was a story which told of a disagreement between William Penn and Kelpius about

---

[43]Ibid., p. 170. Sachse reprinted the whole of Kelpius's renouncement of his power of attorney. From a copy in the papers of Daniel Francis Pastorius, the agent of the Frankfort Land Company who was replaced by Falkner, Jewart, and Kelpius.

slavery. Kelpius is supposed to have questioned Penn's religious integrity on the grounds that Penn's slave-holding was wrong. Although the chances are good that Penn and Kelpius did meet sometime during Penn's visit to Pennsylvania from November, 1699, to October, 1701, there is no concrete evidence of such a meeting. The will of Dr. Christopher Witt, who had left the membership of the mystic community in 1720, provided for the manumission of his slave upon Witt's death, which occurred in 1765.[44] If Kelpius actually questionned Penn about Penn's slave-holding, it was probably done more for the purpose of saving Penn's soul than for the purpose of freeing Penn's slaves.

Considering their nonsectarian acceptance of other religious groups and their communications with other far-away groups, it is strange that there is no record of any direct communications between the "Woman in the Wilderness" and Bohemia Manor. When the mystic brethren came to America in 1694, they landed at Bohemia Landing, Maryland, a few miles from the celibate communal society of Bohemia Manor.[45] During their years of simultaneous existence in America the two societies were less than seventy miles away from each other. The only known instance proving that each society knew of the existence of each other occurred in 1721 when two men from Germantown visited Bohemia Manor. Both of the men had once considered joining the "Woman in the Wilderness;" one of the men had relatives in Bohemia Manor and the other man was studying under the tutelage of the leader of the "Woman in the Wilderness."[46] In 1721 when that visit took place both of the societies were already seriously

---

[44]Ibid., p. 417.   [45]Ibid., p. 11

[46]James E. Ernst, Ephrata: A History, Twenty-fifth Yearbook of the Pennsylvania German Folklore Society (Allentown, Pennsylvania: Schlechter's, 1961), pp. 36-38.

declining, therefore, if that visit was the only instance of communication between the two societies then neither society seriously influenced the development of the other.

There were two prominent individuals, Phillip Jacob Spener and Benjamin Furly, who might have been able to inform the members of the "Woman in the Wilderness" of the existence of the Labadist celibate communal societies. After listening to Labadie preach in Geneva, Spener could have followed Labadie's career through the publicity given to Labadism in Europe, and Spener could have informed the "Woman in the Wilderness" of Labadism through his secretary, Johannes Seelig, who became one of the original members of the "Woman in the Wilderness."[47] Benjamin Furly, a Quaker who served in Amsterdam as the agent of William Penn, must have known that Penn twice asked the Labadists to merge with the Quakers.[48] It is therefore very likely that Benjamin Furly informed the "Woman in the Wilderness" of the existence of the Labadist societies because Furly was familiar with the "Woman in the Wilderness" before that group sailed to America, and because his trust of Daniel Falkner as his American land agent in 1698 also indicated a close communication with and knowledge of the "Woman in the Wilderness."[49]

Unfortunately, there is no substantial evidence that either Spener or Furly actually gave any information concerning the Labadists to the "Woman in the Wilderness." Nor is there any substantial evidence

---

[47] Sachse, Pietists, p. 60.

[48] Bartlett B. James, "The Labadist Colony in Maryland," Johns Hopkins University Studies in Historical and Political Science, XVII (1899), p. 299.

[49] Sachse, Pietists, pp. 46, 170.

that the "Woman in the Wilderness" was influenced by any other communal societies. The only definite connection between Bohemia Manor and the "Woman in the Wilderness" is their joint influence on the founding and development of Ephrata Cloister.

The two men who visited Bohemia Manor from Germantown in 1721 had both originally migrated to America for the purpose of joining the "Woman in the Wilderness," which they had heard about from members of the Philadelphian Society in Germany. One of those two men, Conrad Beissel, studied under Conrad Matthai, who was then the leader of the "Woman in the Wilderness."[50] By 1735 the combined influence of "Woman in the Wilderness" and Bohemia Manor, along with influence from several other Pietist groups, had borne fruit in the founding of Ephrata Cloister by Conrad Beissel. Before the founding of Ephrata Cloister as a monastic community some of Beissel's followers emulated the last members of the "Woman in the Wilderness" by living as celibate hermits. The mystic brethren also gave at least one important form of economic assistance to Ephrata Cloister. In the early 1740's several members of Ephrata Cloister were instructed by Johannes Seelig, one of the last members of the "Woman in the Wilderness," in the art of book-binding, which helped the cloister become an important publishing center.[51] Long after the last of the mystic brethren had died, some of the beliefs and practices of the "Woman in the Wilderness" continued to exist through the mystic community's influence on Ephrata Cloister.

---

[50] Ernst, op. cit., pp. 36-38.
[51] Sachse, *Pietists*, p. 337.

GENERAL HISTORY AND DECLINE

When Johannes Kelpius became the leader of the men who were to form the "Woman in the Wilderness," he was only twenty years old and his youth may have contributed to the problems of retaining members which the group later faced in America. Yet, the other two men, Heinrich Bernard Koster and Daniel Falkner, who were probably the most capable of leading the group, were not sufficiently loyal to the "Woman in the Wilderness" to remain within it as members. After about a year in America, Koster, with a few of the mystic brethren and with some "Keithian" Quakers, formed his own communal society, which he called, "The True Church of Philadelphia or Brotherly Love."[52] Koster and his followers owned all property in common, but their community-house, called "Irenia or House of Peace," soon became a house of dispute, and they disbanded sometime in 1697.[53] Daniel Falkner was sent to Europe to recruit more members so that a "Chapter of Perfection" could again be attained, a task at which he was successful; but after he returned to America, his new power and influence taking care of the lands of the Frankfort Land Company drew him away from the "Woman in the Wilderness."

By 1704, after ten years in America, many of the original members had left the mystic community; however, new immigrants had continued to arrive from Europe, and the "Chapter of Perfection" was nearly complete, if not actually so. Unfortunately, Kelpius spent much of his time in a small, natural cave which he enlarged and called, "Laurea." In its damp chillness, aggravated by his fasting, Kelpius contracted consumption,

---

[52]Ibid., p. 87.   [53]Ibid., p. 266.

an illness from which he suffered during the last two years of his life. Kelpius died on or shortly before March 1, 1708; the exact date is unknown.[54]

At first Johannes Seelig, the former secretary of Phillip Spener succeeded Kelpius, but he soon decided he preferred being an ordinary brother, and the title of Magister went to Conrad Matthai. Matthai led the community until he died as its last member in 1748. Not too long after the death of Kelpius, communal living was abandoned by the brethren of the "Woman in the Wilderness," because most of the brethren already lived in separate cabins as hermits except for their worship together. For the sake of marriage or to seek their fortune, members continued to leave, until by 1720, potential new members were advised not to join. There were so few members that the land was sold in 1741, and the last two members, Seelig and Matthai, died, respectively in 1745 and 1748.

Today, perhaps the only group with any claim to the spirit of the "Woman in the Wilderness" is the Ancient and Mystical Order Rosae Crucis, which proudly describes Kelpius and his followers as the first Rosicrucians who came to the western hemisphere. In a serenely secluded section of Philadelphia's Fairmount Park, next to the entrance of Kelpius' cave, the Rosicrucians have erected a stone monument which reads as follows:

    Johannes Kelpius, Ph.D. AD 1673-1708
    The Contented of the God-Loving Soul

---

[54]Ibid., p. 156, 192, 244.

Magister of the first Rosicrucian AMORC
colony in America which arrived in Phila
delphia, June 24, 1694, then known as the
Monks of the Ridge. Fra Kelpius used this
cave as a shelter and as a sanctum for
his meditations. Lovingly erected to his
memory by Crane Lodge, Rosicrucians
A.D. 1961 in cooperation with
The Supreme Grand Lodge
AMORC

Chapter 5

EPHRATA CLOISTER

INTRODUCTION

The founder of Ephrata Cloister deserved a place in religious history before he founded any religious groups. In his quest for a satisfying faith, Johann Conrad Beissel had worshipped with, or studied with, at least twelve different Pietist and mystical groups between 1710 and 1725. The twelve groups are listed here in the order in which Beissel is believed to have come in contact with them: German Reformed Pietists, the Philadelphian Society, the Rosicrucians, German Lutheran Pietists, Roman Catholic Quietists, German Baptist Brethren (Dunkers), the Community of True Inspiration, the "Woman in the Wilderness" Quakers, Labadists, English and Welsh Sabbatarians, and Mennonites. By themselves none of the groups were satisfying to Beissel, but he found something different and valuable in each group; they all contributed to the unique institutions founded by Beissel.

Ephrata Cloister was influenced by almost all of the groups which were important influences in the development of each of the other celibate communal societies. Also, more of the celibate communal societies received influence from Ephrata Cloister than from any other celibate society. If the unity of belief among celibate communal societies was to be studied in the history of just one society, the best society to study would be Ephrata Cloister.

The present small city of Ephrata, Pennsylvania, located about halfway between Reading and Lancaster, owes its name to Ephrata Cloister, whose 220 year old buildings can still be seen at the edge of the city. Ephrata Cloister began as, and remained, an integral part of the Seventh-Day German Baptist Church, which had been founded by Johann Conrad Beissel in 1728. The first cloister members had been part of a small hermitic community centered around Beissel. The group of celibate hermits, which had begun in 1733, was gradually transformed until, by the end of 1740, it had become the monastic community known as Ephrata Cloister. Although Ephrata Cloister declined rapidly during the last quarter of the 18th century, there were still a few members at Ephrata in the early 19th century. The spirit of the cloister also lived on through a branch, which had begun in 1814 at Snow Hill in Franklin Co., Pennsylvania, until the last celibate member died in 1895. The Seventh-Day German Baptist Church, which had preceded the cloister, also succeeded it until 1934 when the congregation was dissolved by the last few members.

The membership of both the church and Ephrata Cloister was drawn mostly from German settlers already in the area; only a few are known to have come directly from Germany to join the cloister. Within the cloister in 1740 there were about 35 celibate brothers and about as many sisters. At its high point around 1750, there may have been 100 celibates within the cloister and about 200 in the secular congregation. In 1770 there were only 42 celibates living in the cloister, and by 1835 there were only a few sisters carrying on the celibate tradition at Ephrata.

DEVELOPMENT BEFORE FOUNDING

The founder of Ephrata Cloister, Johann Conrad Beissel,[1] was born at Eberbach in the Palatinate about 15 miles east of Heidelberg on March 1, 1690. His father had died a few month's before Conrad's birth, and his mother died when he was seven. Conrad was raised in the Reformed faith and learned to read and write in the parish school before he was apprenticed to a baker to learn what had been his father's trade. As a young man serving his apprenticeship, Beissel experienced a religious awakening within himself, and he began to attend a pietist conventicle in Eberbach. Although his religious awakening did not yet entirely rule his life, Conrad stopped attending the Reformed Church, and by the time he left for his journeyman travels in 1710 or 1711, he was being threatened by the authorities in Eberbach for breaking the church attendance law.[2]

Beissel attended the meetings of pietists in various cities during his travels as a journeyman baker, but he had not yet dedicated his life to God; he fluctuated between a pious and a worldly life. On a worldly level, Beissel was successful, and he became a master baker in Heidelberg in 1715 or 1716. Beissel also gained enough respect from his fellow bakers to be made the treasurer of the baker's guild. At that

---

[1]Sometime during his early life, Beissel dropped the use of his first name. The change may have occurred because of the prevalence in Germany of Johann as a first name. The founder of the Harmony Society, George Rapp, also had Johann as a first name but did not use it.

[2]James E. Ernst, <u>Ephrata: A History</u>, Twenty-fifth Yearbook of the Pennsylvania German Folklore Society (Allentown, Pennsylvania: Schlechter's, 1961), pp. 9-13.

time, Beissel's pietist tendencies did not hamper his social acceptance; although he continued to attend secret pietist meetings, he also attended church in Heidelberg. Nor at this time did Beissel's pietism stop him from enjoying the worldly entertainments given at the banquets of the baker's guild.[3]

During 1716 Beissel's life abruptly changed. He stopped going to church, became more active among pietists, and he rebuked the bakers for the worldliness of their banquets. Why Beissel suddenly changed his life is not definitely known. Beissel had learned that a company of bakers with whom he had once tried to enlist were all killed in a battle with the Turks. From that circumstance Beissel might have concluded God had saved his life for a particular purpose.[4] Whatever the reason for the change in Beissel's life, his scolding of the bakers' guild led those whom he had rebuked to have Beissel arrested for breaking the church attendance law. At the end of his trial before an ecclesiastical court, Beissel was given the choice of leaving the area or formally joining one of the three established churches in Heidelberg (Lutheran, Reformed, and Roman Catholic). Beissel chose to leave. Therefore, he was banned from the Palatinate and his wandersbuch, without which Beissel could not work as a baker, was revoked.[5]

---

[3]Ibid., pp. 13-19.

[4]Julius Friedrich Sachse, *The German Sectarians of Pennsylvania, 1708-1742: A Critical and Legendary History of the Ephrata Cloister and the Dunkers*, I (Philadelphia, Pennsylvania: printed for the author, 1899), pp. 37-39.

[5]Ernst, op. cit., p. 20.

During the period before his complete conversion to pietism in Heidelberg, Beissel had been in contact with at least four pietist groups: those from the Reformed Church, from the Lutheran Church, the Philadelphian Society, and the Rosicrucian Brotherhood. Other than Beissel's early training in the Reformed Church, the most important of those four groups to the history of Ephrata Cloister were the Philadelphians and the Rosicrucians. Beissel was first introduced to members of the Philadelphian Society in Strassburg, who were then under the leadership of a Professor Haug, one of the men who later edited the Berleburger Bibel.[6] In Heidelberg, the members of the Philadelphian Society were also Rosicrucians; and while he was in Heidelberg, Beissel became an adept in the Rosicrucian Brotherhood. Through the Philadelphians and the Rosicrucians, Beissel became acquainted with the works of many mystical writers, including supporters of Jacob Boehme (if not Boehme's own works). Many of Beissel's mystical ideas appear to have come from his associations with the Philadelphians and the Rosicrucians.[7]

After his banishment from the Palatinate, Beissel stopped briefly at his home in Eberbach and then fled north toward Wittgenstein. The rulers of the two counties of Wittgenstein had, since shortly before 1700, exercised a large degree of religious toleration.[8] In 1712,

---

[6]The Berleburger Bibel was published by members of the Philadelphian Society in Berleburg, Wittgenstein, Germany in 8 volumes from 1726 to 1742. It was a new translation and contained a mystical and symbolic commentary. The commentary was important to the development of the millennial views of the Harmony Society and will be discussed in the chapter on the Harmony Society.

[7]Ibid., pp. 14-19.

[8]E. Ernest Stoeffler, Mysticism in the German Devotional Literature of Colonial Pennsylvania, Fourteenth Yearbook of the Pennsylvania German Folklore Society (Allentown, Pennsylvania: Schlechter's, 1949), p. 41.

Count Casmir of Wittgenstein-Berleburg had even announced complete religious freedom for anyone who would settle in his lands.[9] While their religious toleration may have been motivated by a desire to increase the population in their sparsely populated domains, some of the rulers of Wittgenstein were also pietists, including one member of the Philadelphian Society, the ruler of Wittgenstein-Schwarzenau from 1698-1724. Wittgenstein became a haven for pietists, mystics, visionaries, religious outcasts of all kinds, and it was the main center for the Philadelphian Society in Germany.[10]

Among the Philadelphians whom Beissel met in Wittgenstein were: Dr. Horch, who taught that celibacy was a higher state than marriage; Charles de Marsay, a hermit who emphasized asceticism and introduced Beissel to the ascetic writings of Madame Guyon, a Roman Catholic Quietist (1648-1715) who believed in severe asceticism; and Ernst Christian Hochmann von Hochenau, an ascetic who revered celibacy above marriage.[11] Horch, Marsay, and Hochmann later participated as editors in the production of the Berleburger Bibel by the Philadelphian Society. From the Philadelphians in Wittgenstein, Beissel heard about Johannes Kelpius and the mystic community in America, "Woman in the Wilderness," to which Beissel later traveled.[12]

Beissel studied for a time under Hochmann, whose ideas about celibacy and other matters were important to the founding of the German

---

[9]Ernst, op. cit., p. xx.

[10]Ibid., p. 26.

[11]Ibid., pp. 27-35.

[12]Stoeffler, op. cit., p. 31.

Baptist Brethren. Also known as the Dunkers, the German Baptist Brethren had been founded in Schwarzenau in 1708 by Alexander Mack, a former disciple of Hochmann. The Dunkers believed in adult baptism, separatism, congregationalism, and pacifism. For their first seven years the Dunkers were also celibate and held property in common, but they returned to marriage and private property in 1715, about a year before Beissel came in contact with them. Beissel did not become a member of the Dunkers in Schwarzenau because he believed them to be entirely too sectarian. About eight years later, after both he and most of the Dunkers had migrated to Pennsylvania, Beissel did join the Dunkers.[13]

After leaving the Dunkers in Schwarzenau, Beissel walked the countryside as a peddler until he was taken in by a baker who belonged to the Community of True Inspiration.[14] By this time, the fasting and mortification of the flesh which Beissel's asceticism had led him to practice was bringing him near death. The physician attending Beissel's physical ills advised him to stop meditating so much on the evilness of man, and Beissel did modify his ascetic practices. After his recovery, Beissel spent time in Marienborn with the Community of True Inspiration, whose chief distinction, as indicated by their name, was their belief in direct revelation. They believed God spoke through the mouths of his "inspired instruments," the community's leaders. One of those leaders, Johann Friedrich Rock, was also a member of the Philadelphian Society. Beissel's previous training in mysticism with Philadelphians and

---

[13] Ernst, op. cit., pp. 28-30.

[14] Throughout the United States this group is more widely known as the Amana Society, which is now located in Iowa in seven villages known as the Amana Colonies.

Rosicrucians helped him to become Rock's assistant and to learn the trance-ecstasy and other motions of an "instrument." Beissel did not stay long with the "Inspired." After a misunderstanding, he was reduced in position and a short while later he left their company.[15] "He (Beissel) has, nevertheless, borne favorable testimony concerning the spirit of the Inspiration, namely, that it was a pure, clean, virgin spirit . . . and . . . none could escape its judgment."[16]

Beissel again became a peddler and later a spinner of wool, while he continued his search among the pious. In 1720, a friend named Michael Stuntz offered to loan Beissel the money for passage to America; Beissel accepted the offer. Together, with three others, they sailed to America for the purpose of joining the hermits of the "Woman in the Wilderness."[17] When Beissel and his companions arrived in the Germantown area, only a few members of the mystic community were left,[18] and they had been so demoralized by the defections from their midst that Beissel and his companions were advised to not join the "Woman in the Wilderness." The five companions separated, and Beissel apprenticed himself as a weaver to Peter Becker, one of the leading men of the Dunkers in the Germantown area.[19]

---

[15]Ernst, op. cit., pp. 30-34.

[16]Lamech and Agrippa, Chronicon Ephratense: A History of the Community of Seventh-Day Baptists at Ephrata, trans. by J. Max Hark (Lancaster, Pennsylvania: S. H. Zahm and Co., 1889), pp. 9-11. Lamech and Agrippa were members of Ephrata Cloister and their work was first published by the cloister in 1786.

[17]Ernst, op. cit., pp. 36-38.

[18]Lamech and Agrippa, op. cit., p. 14.

[19]Sachse, Sectarians, I, pp. 42-47.

During 1721, Beissel's religious inquisitiveness again brought him in contact with a variety of religious thinking. He had many religious conversations with Peter Becker; he studied under Conrad Matthai, then leader of the "Woman in the Wilderness," and he attended the meetings of Mennonites and Quakers. Beissel visited Bohemia Manor with one of his original sailing companions who had relatives at Bohemia Manor. Peter Sluyter, leader of the Labadists at Bohemia Manor, gave several books to Beissel, including some by Labadie.[20] Beissel then visited the English and Welsh Sabbatarians west of Philadelphia, and at various times, he helped Peter Becker hold services among the scattered Dunkers.[21]

Before his trip to Bohemia Manor, Beissel had begun the life of a hermit with Machael Stuntz. By the end of 1721 they were joined by two of their former sailing companions. The four hermits lived in a secluded area and held all property in common. At Beissel's insistence they also celebrated the Sabbath on the seventh day and worked on the first. Along with an ascetic life of fasting and praying, Beissel and his companions conducted a school for children from nearby farms and walked to various homes in the area, proclaiming the word of God. Sometime during 1722, they adopted the plain dress of the Mennonites.[22]

Only things of the spirit mattered to Conrad Beissel. Often when it was his turn to provide food, the four hermits went hungry. Beissel frequently forgot to get food or gave it away to some needy person. Throughout the next year, each of the other three hermits left

---

[20]Ernst, op. cit., pp. 42-43.   [21]Sachse, Sectarians, I, pp. 60-72.
[22]Sachse, Sectarians, I, pp. 71-72, and Ernst, op. cit., p. 46.

the group, including Michael Stuntz who sold the cabin to get back the passage money he had advanced to Beissel. So, in the fall of 1722 Beissel was alone and homeless. He moved further into the forest where he built a cabin and lived alone until he was joined by Michael Wohlfarth in the spring of 1724.[23]

Due to several factors, including the isolation of many pioneer farms and factional disputes among the Dunkers, religious life for the German settlers in and around Germantown was very disorganized when Beissel arrived. Beissel tried to awaken the dormant religious spirit of the people, especially in the Conestoga valley north of Germantown where he held revival meetings in the years 1722-1724. Beissel was successful as an evangelist, but he was not yet the sect-founder he would become. Many of those whom he "awakened" accepted baptism in the Dunker church, which was also experiencing a revival under the leadership of Peter Becker. The first Dunker baptisms in America were held near Germantown on Christmas Day, 1723. Early in November in 1724 a second Dunker congregation was formed in Coventry; and on November 12, 1724, Peter Becker established a third congregation by baptizing seven people, including Beissel, in the Conestoga valley. Because Becker left the new Conestoga congregation of Dunkers without a leader, they chose Beissel to lead them.[24]

During the four years of Beissel's leadership from 1724 to 1728, the Conestoga congregation of Dunkers grew in numbers, and their beliefs grew away from those held by other Dunkers. Beissel's religious ideas

---

[23]Sachse, *Sectarians*, I, pp. 81-83, and Ernst, op. cit., pp. 47-48.

[24]Sachse, *Sectarians*, I, pp. 90-104, and Ernst, op. cit., pp. 48-55.

were not controlled by any allegiance to the Dunkers, and as he grew stronger, he became more bold. At worship services, Beissel spoke without a prepared text, often putting himself into a trance, and speaking as though he was divinely inspired. Beissel exhorted his hearers to follow Mosaic dietary laws, adopt celibacy, and observe the seventh-day Sabbath.[25]

A split developed within the Conestoga congregation, and Beissel decided to leave the Dunkers to form his own congregation. A special ceremony was performed sometime in September, 1728, during which seven people, three brethren including Beissel and four sisters, were re-baptized. The three brethren symbolized the triad, the four sisters symbolized the square, together their two sexes symbolized Adam's original androgynous nature, and as a whole they symbolized the seventh-day Sabbath; thus began the Seventh-Day German Baptist Church.[26]

While he led the Conestoga congregation, Beissel had continued to live as a hermit and his spiritual strength drew others to live around him in a similar fashion. The hermits around Beissel were known as the "Solitary," and two women had joined their ranks by the summer of 1728. After the founding of the Seventh-Day German Baptist Church, the "Solitary" continued to increase in number, as did the number of married "householders" following Beissel.[27]

The numbers of the Solitary were increased even further after Beissel published a book called _Ehebuchlein_ in 1730 which denounced

---

[25] Ernst, op. cit., pp. 55-70.   [26] Ibid., p. 71.

[27] Ibid., pp. 69-75.

marriage and praised celibacy.[28] The vigor with which he attacked marriage led some women to leave their husbands and led many of Beissel's married followers to pledge themselves to celibacy, though they continued to live in the same house. Partially as a result of the fervor for celibacy at that time, Beissel's followers were organized into three orders: one of the male Solitary, one of the female Solitary, and one of the married householders.[29]

The life of the ascetic Solitary was a hard one and several of the members suffered mental breakdowns. To those common people who lived in the area but were not of Beissel's following, the spectacle of a few insane Solitary, of single women living in the woods near single men, and of wives leaving husbands, was reason enough for wild rumors and accusations to fly throughout the countryside. Beissel and one of the sisters were even brought into court on the charge of producing an illegitimate child. The information, when traced from one gossip to another, proved to be based on a misunderstanding.[30]

Along with the strains of celibacy and an ascetic life, Beissel also had to provide leadership for his followers and contend with their problems. Once there was a discussion of the idea of going further into the wilderness and building a communal church made up strictly of the Solitary, but Beissel rejected the idea because of his responsibilities to the householders.[31] Even without proposals which would split Beissel's

---

[28]Sachse, Sectarians, I, p. 167.   [29]Ernst, op. cit., pp. 82-83.
[30]Sachse, Sectarians, I, pp. 174-175, and Ernst, op. cit., p. 79.
[31]Sachse, Sectarians, I, p. 181.

small sect, there were tensions between the householders and the Solitary because of their different religious interests. The congregation of Seventh-Day German Baptists was dramatically changed on February 8, 1732 when Beissel appointed three new leaders, one for each part of the congregation (male Solitary, female Solitary, and householders). Then, for reasons which he never explained, Beissel resigned his office and walked into the wilderness.[32]

Beissel journeyed about eight miles to Cocalico Creek and joined Emmanuel Eckerlin, a hermit already living there, in the life of the Solitary. Beissel might have been content to live the life of a hermit; but his "flock" needed their shepherd, and many of them went to visit him with their problems. By the end of May, 1733, three of the male Solitary and two female Solitary had even built cabins near Beissel's. During the next two years the area around Beissel's camp was rapidly filled with the homes and farms of the married members of his congregation, and with the cabins of the Solitary. Beissel soon returned to his position of leadership and to preaching throughout the area. His missionary efforts, undertaken especially in the Tulpehocken area, brought in more members, both for the married householders and for the Solitary, including Peter Miller, Beissel's eventual successor.[33] Other developments before 1735 included the establishment of a common storehouse and a common bakehouse which were the first aspects of communism introduced into the camp on the Cocalico.[34]

---

[32]Lamech and Agrippa, op. cit., p. 63, and Ernst, op. cit., p. 88.

[33]Sachse, Sectarians, I, pp. 245-246.   [34]Ernst, op. cit., pp. 91-95.

In May of 1735 those Solitary not already living near Beissel were called upon to leave their scattered hermit cabins and to live at the camp on the Cocalico. Although many of the Solitary did not move to the Cocalico until that fall, those who did respond early that summer added significantly to the already existing problem of not enough room at the worship services of the Seventh-Day German Baptists. In July, construction was begun on a building named Kedar, which was to be used as a place of worship for the entire congregation.[35] Sometime before Kedar was ready for use, the Solitary began to meet for midnight worship services each night. They also adopted regulations, which strictly governed every hour of their lives.[36]

Shortly before the dedication of Kedar, one of the housefathers gave his daughter to Beissel, ". . . with the request that he should bring her up to the glory of God."[37] The girl became one of the founding members of the Order of Spiritual Virgins. With three others, she pledged herself to celibacy and a communal life. The Spiritual Virgins took the second story of Kedar as their quarters and there they became the first group at Ephrata to practice monastic communism.[38]

Even with the established example of the Spiritual Virgins, monastic communism was not adopted by the male Solitary, who became known as the Angelic Brethren, until 1740. During the intervening five years, several other features were added to the life of Beissel's celibate followers, which brought them closer to the particular

---

[35]Sachse, Sectarians, I, pp. 247-249.

[36]Ernst, op. cit., pp. 109-110.

[37]Lamech and Agrippa, op. cit., p. 76.   [38]Ibid., p. 77.

monasticism that characterized Ephrata Cloister. Weekly confession was made a requirement in 1736. Monastic garb was adopted by the Spiritual Virgins in 1737 and by the brethren in 1738.[39] The use of a special monastic name for each celibate member was introduced either in 1737 or 1738.[40] All of the celibates began eating at a common table in 1737, and vows of fasting, prayer, charity, chastity, poverty, and obediance were given by each of the celibates in 1739.[41] Kedar was given completely to the use of the sisters, after the construction in 1736-1737 of Bethaus, a new place of worship for the householders and the celibates. The gradual adoption of monastic life by the brethren was given further impetus by the building of Zion-Saal in 1737-1738, which became a convent for the brethren.[42] In August, 1740, the last of the brethren who lived in private cabins moved into Zion-Saal, and all private property was given up by the brethren.[43] The camp on the Cocalico had been called "Ephrata," since the name had appeared in a hymnal which Benjamin Franklin printed for the community in April, 1736. After the events of 1740, the community of celibates became known as Ephrata Cloister.[44]

---

[39] Lamech and Agrippa, op. cit., pp. 81, 88-90.

[40] Sachse, Sectarians, I, p. 305.

[41] Ernst, op. cit., p. 136.

[42] Sachse, Sectarians, I, pp. 256, 353.

[43] Lamech and Agrippa, op. cit., p. 121, and Ernst, op. cit., p. 165.

[44] Sachse, Sectarians, I, p. 264.

BELIEFS AND PRACTICES

Many books and pamphlets were published, especially during Beissel's lifetime, which proclaimed some of the beliefs held by members of Ephrata Cloister, but there was never any attempt to present in a single document or in a series of documents a complete confession of faith. According to Michael Wohlfarth, one of Beissel's staunchest followers, the lack of such a statement of faith was due to a conscious decision. In response to a question from Benjamin Franklin regarding a statement of faith, Wohlfarth reportedly said,

> . . . we fear that if we should once print our confession of faith, we should feel ourselves as if bound and confined by it, and perhaps be unwilling to receive further improvement, and our successors still more so, as conceiving what their elders and founders had done to be something sacred, never to be departed from.[45]

One practical consideration which weighed against producing a confession of faith was the diversity of opinion which existed among Beissel's followers. Each of the orders within the Seventh-Day German Baptist Church exercised a large degree of autonomy; their divergent interests were not always complementary, the relationships between the orders were often strained, and developing a confession of faith that pleased all of them would have been difficult. For instance, within the Angelic Brethren was a group known as the Zionitic Brotherhood, which emphasized Rosicrucian and other mystical rites and to which most of the

---

[45] Felix Reichmann and Eugene E. Doll, *Ephrata as Seen by Contemporaries*, Seventeenth Yearbook of the Pennsylvania German Folklore Society (Allentown, Pennsylvania: Schlechter's, 1952), p. 139. Quoting from Benjamin Franklin's, *Autobiography* (ed.) Max Farrand (Berkeley, California: University of California Press, 1949), pp. 141-142.

Angelic Brethren did not belong.[46] Yet, practical considerations were probably not given too much weight. Beissel was not a man guided by practicalities, but by his faith. Part of that faith was a belief that he would and did "receive further improvement" or divine revelation. Even though the major tenets of the Seventh-Day German Baptists did not change after 1740, there were many significant and sometimes costly policy changes after that date which indicated Beissel's willingness to follow the dictates of what he believed was new divine revelation.[47]

Because a confession of faith was not produced by the Seventh-Day German Baptist Church, the agreement of the secular congregation with any given belief known to be held by the cloister members can only be surmised. In view of the intimate relationship between the secular congregation and the cloister, it can be assumed that most, if not all, of the beliefs held by the cloister members as a whole were also held by the secular congregation. Yet, the different ways of life practiced by the householders and by the celibates indicated that profound differences in belief might have existed. Therefore, the reader should be aware that the following discussion of the beliefs of Ephrata Cloister does not necessarily apply to the secular congregation of Seventh-Day German Baptists.

The name "Ephrata" appears to have been chosen by Beissel sometime in 1734 or 1735 before the camp on the Cocalico had really begun to develop as a communal organization. The Biblical references to that name

---

[46] Ernst, op. cit., pp. 97, 133-136.

[47] One of the major changes occurred when Beissel switched the cloister from a commercial to a subsistence economy in 1745.

provide important indications of what Beissel hoped his camp on the Cocalico would become. Within the Old Testament, there are references which connect both the people known as "Ephrathites" and the area, "Ephratah" with Bethlehem.[48] Ephratah, apparently, was another name for Bethlehem or for the area around or near Bethlehem. Among those cited as Ephrathites are David and his father, Jesse;[49] therefore, Jesus must also have been an Ephrathite for he was to come from the lineage of David. Such a prophecy is given in Micah, 5:2 which reads

> But thou Bethlehem Ephratah, though thou be little among the thousands of Judah, yet out of thee shall he come forth unto me that is to be ruler in Israel; whose goings forth have been from of old, from everlasting.

Whether Beissel and his followers aspired to be of the lineage of David and Christ, or whether they hoped to form a place and a group out of which Christ would make his second coming, their view of themselves may have been somewhat elevated because of their beliefs regarding the imminence of Christ's second coming.

Beliefs about the second coming of Christ and expectations that it would soon occur were much more important in the early history of Ephrata Cloister than in the years after 1750. In 1728 in the preface to his book on the Sabbath, Beissel said, "the Time is near at Hand, wherein God the Truth, will set on the Candlestick again, and that whore . . . shall be destroyed . . ."[50] An address to Quakers by Michael Wohlfarth, which was printed in 1729, contained the words, "the Light of God shineth very clear in these latter Days . . .," and "O happy are they

---

[48] Genesis, 35:16,19; Ruth, 1:2; Ruth, 4:11; I Samuel, 17:12; Psalms, 132:5-6; Micah, 5:12.

[49] I Samuel, 17:12.   [50] Sachse, *Sectarians*, I, p. 146.

that take Notice of the Signs of these Times . . . ."[51] The worship services at midnight, which were made a part of life at Ephrata in 1735, were instituted partially because the hour of judgement was expected to come at midnight. Two comets, which respectively appeared in February, 1742, and December, 1743, were considered signs of the second coming of Christ. The belief that the days of judgement were near was spread throughout the countryside as is indicated by the example of Christopher Saur, a Germantown printer and friend of the cloister, who described the comet of 1743 as a plain sign that the "destruction of the religious Babylonian governmental order is near at hand."[52]

After the passing of the comets, expectations of an imminent second coming lessened considerably and soon ceased to play any important role in the affairs of the cloister. It appears that even before the comets had arrived, the beliefs about an imminent fulfillment of the prophecies of Revelation were not as strong or as important at Ephrata as they were in some other societies in this study. Yet, the intense belief in the imminent approach of Christ's second coming might also have influenced other aspects of the cloister life. The belief of Beissel's followers that they may have been among the members of the last Christian church might have helped to center their attention on the actions of the first Christian church and, as such, may have been

---

[51] Ibid., pp. 151-152.

[52] Julius Friedrich Sachse, The German Sectarians of Pennsylvania, 1742-1800: A Critical and Legendary History of the Ephrata Cloister and the Dunkers, II (Philadelphia, Pennsylvania: printed for the author, 1900), p. 95. The comets are also mentioned in Sectarians, I, pp. 416-420, and in Ernst, op. cit., pp. 193, 223.

instrumental in the adoption of communism and other features of Ephrata Cloister that were conscious imitations of the early church.

As mentioned previously, communal ownership was adopted gradually, first by the Spiritual Virgins in Kedar in 1735 and finally by all of the Brethren in 1740. There were many precedents known to Beissel which might have influenced the decision to require property to be held in common in Ephrata Cloister: the original Dunkers had held property in common from 1708 to 1715, the hermits of the "Woman in the Wilderness" had once held all of their property in common, communism was part of life at Bohemia Manor, and Beissel had tried communism with three others in 1721-1722. The most important influence was probably the belief that the first Christians had held property in common.[53] When the communal life was completely established in 1740, "all private ownership was declared to be an Ananias-sin . . . ."[54] Eventually, in the last part of the 18th century, private property was again allowed in small matters but real property was always held in common among the inmates of the cloister.[55]

From the very beginning of the institution of communal property it had been agreed "that anyone who should leave . . . should forfeit

---

[53]Reichmann and Doll, op. cit., p. 56. From an account of Ephrata in Israel Acrelius, A History of New Sweden, translated by Wm. M. Reynolds, in the Memoirs of the Historical Society of Pennsylvania (1874), p. 373-401. Acrelius visited Ephrata Cloister in 1753 when he was Provost of the Swedish Lutheran Church in America. His whole account appears in Reichmann and Doll, op. cit., pp. 50-77.

[54]Lamech and Agrippa, op. cit., p. 138. The reference to Ananias comes from Acts 5:1-11. Ananias and his wife Sapphira gave part of their property to Peter under the pretense that they had given all of it; when Peter confronted them with their falsehood both Ananias and Sapphira died.

[55]Ibid., p. 121. See also Ernst, op. cit., p. 167.

whatever he had contributed . . . ."[56] Yet, in actual practice, those who could not stand the cloister life were not entirely cut off. As long as they attended worship services at the cloister, they kept their right to a share in the products of the community.[57] The married householders, also, had a share in the products of the community, even though they had their own private farms, because they had shared the costs of building both religious and manufacturing buildings at the cloister. Also, before the economy of the cloister was strong, the tithes of the householders were an indispensable source of food for the Solitary.[58]

There are several indications that celibacy had more religious significance than did communism at Ephrata Cloister. Celibacy had been a part of the belief system of the Seventh-Day German Baptists before the cloister and the practice of communism had begun. After the Revolutionary War, when communism was partially abandoned, celibacy was still an important part of cloister life. Although Beissel is not known to have written any books or pamphlets about communism, celibacy was a significant subject in at least three of his works.[59] Part of the following discussion on celibacy will also show that it was an important part of Beissel's ideas about the fall and ultimate redemption of man.

According to Chronicon Ephratense, Conrad Beissel renounced any desire for earthly women, following an unfortunate personal experience

---

[56]Ibid., p. 121.   [57]Ernst, op. cit., p. 331.

[58]Ibid., p. 177.

[59]Celibacy was an important subject in Beissel's book about the Sabbath, Mysterion Anomias (The Mystery of Lawlessness), 1728, in Euhebuchlein (Book on Matrimony), 1730, and in Mystiche Abhandlung... und des Menschen Fall (A Dissertation on Man's Fall), 1765.

when he was a journeyman baker in Mannheim in 1715.[60] Beissel traveled to America in 1720 and his plans to join the hermits of the Woman in the Wilderness reaffirm his espousal of celibacy. Whichever of the many influences acting upon Beissel was the most decisive in convincing him to become celibate, the decision was definitely made before he arrived in America. The best source for understanding Beissel's early ideas about celibacy would be his Ehebuchlein (Book on Matrimony), which was printed by Benjamin Franklin in 1730. Unfortunately, no copies are known to exist. The best knowledge about the work is contained in a comment from Chronicon Ephratense, which said the book, ". . . declares matrimony to be the penitentiary of carnal man, and fully exposes the abominations committed therein under the appearance of right."[61] It is known that Beissel's views at that time aroused some people to renounce matrimony and espouse celibacy, including a few who were already married.[62]

Celibacy was never required for the secular congregation of Seventh-Day German Baptists, but it was exalted while marriage was made suspect, which led a number of the married householders to join the cloister as celibates in 1743. A building called Hebron had been built especially for the former householders, and ceremonial letters of divorce were exchanged to make as official as possible the celibate state of the new cloister members. The divorces were completely illegal, and they provided a target for some of the cloister's enemies who began legal proceedings against the "divorced" householders. The legal action was never carried through, but the grand experiment began to fail anyway in

---

[60] Lamesh and Agrippa, op. cit., p. 5. [61] Ibid., p. 58.
[62] Ernst, op. cit., p. 80.

the fall of 1744. Unlike the other cloistered celibates, the former householders were also parents and most of their children had remained on the farms. The ties between parents and children proved to be stronger than the householder's belief in the cloister life, and by the middle of 1745, all of them had returned to their children, their farms, and to marriage.[63]

Not all of the regular members of the cloister were able to lead celibate lives. Several of the members left the cloister to become married. Once in the late 1740's, one of the brethren asked for permission to marry one of the sisters. Their wedding was performed within the cloister walls with most of the celibates in attendance, including Beissel.[64] Among the people of the area who were not Seventh-Day German Baptists, there were constant rumors of illicit sexual activity at the cloister; not even Beissel was free from suspicion. Beissel's actions often created suspicion, for he spent most of his time with the sisters; he even lived in their first convent, Kedar, from January, 1739 to June, 1741.[65] Regarding Beissel's life in Kedar,

> it is easy to imagine what temptations he had to endure in his natural body, in reference to which he once declared that he had really first learned to know his Father in his fiftieth year.[66]

Whatever Beissel's reasons for exposing himself to temptation, his reason for not succumbing to that temptation--his reason for upholding celibacy--is made clear in his statement,

---

[63]Sachse, Sectarians, I, pp. 468-474.

[64]Lamech and Agrippa, op. cit., p. 215.

[65]Ernst, op. cit., p. 184.

[66]Lamech and Agrippa, op. cit., p. 80-81.

if any body will be Partaker of the true Rest and Peace
with God . . . the same must truly repent, and withdraw
. . . from all Worldly and carnal or fleshly desire
whatsoever, and turn with his whole Heart and Mind to
God.[67]

Some of the ideas about celibacy which brought Beissel to make that statement came from Paul's advice in I Corinthians, 7:32-38, and from the Revelation of St. John the Divine, 14:3-4. It was believed that the primitive church had followed Paul's advice to be celibate if possible.[68] The hope of the cloister members to be among the 144,000 virgins, the "first fruits" redeemed in Revelation, 14:3-4, is indicated by one of the ornamental writings which hung in a worship hall at the cloister: "we are numbered among the flock of pure Lambs, Who by the immaculate Lamb espoused, are redeemed from the world . . . ."[69]

Celibacy at Ephrata was not based entirely on Paul's and John's comments in the New Testament. Perhaps the most important, and certainly the most distinctive foundation for the practice of celibacy at Ephrata Cloister, came from certain beliefs about the fall and ultimate redemption of man, such as those presented in Beissel's short book, A Dissertation on the Fall of Man.[70] Although Beissel's Dissertation was not written

---

[67] Sachse, Sectarians, I, p. 148. Quoted from the preface to the 1729 English version of Mysterion Anomias (1728) which had been translated by Michael Wohlfarth. Sachse reprinted all of the preface, pp. 145-148.

[68] Reichmann and Doll, op. cit., p. 56. From account by Israel Acrelius. See footnote #52.

[69] Sachse, Sectarians, I, p. 412.

[70] Translated and published in 1765 by Peter Miller who was prior of Ephrata. The work may have been published in 1745 under the title, Mystiche Abhandlung uber die Schopfung und des Menschen Fall und die Wieberbringung durch des Weibes Samen. Beissel himself referred to it as Die Wunder-Schrifft.

until 1745 or later, the opening paragraphs indicated the ideas had come to Beissel when he was a young man. Since Beissel was 45 in 1735 when the first monastic order was founded at Ephrata, it can be assumed that the ideas present in his Dissertation were already part of his teachings when Ephrata Cloister was just beginning. It is likely that most of those ideas were at least partially developed in Beissel's mind before he came to America, because the ideas expressed in Beissel's Dissertation strongly reflected the distinctive ideas and terminology of Jacob Boehme. It is likely that Beissel came in contact with Boehme's works or the works of his followers while Beissel was still in Germany. Johann Georg Gichtel (1638-1710) had published the first collection of Boehme's writings in 1682,[71] and Beissel is known to have studied under a man in Heidelberg who had corresponded with Gichtel.[72] Beissel is also known to have studied under members of the Philadelphian Society, a society whose major purpose was the study of Boehme's works.[73] It is quite improbable that Beissel had as much contact with Philadelphians as he did without also coming into direct contact with the writings of Boehme or those of his most important followers, Gichtel and Gottfried Arnold (1666-1714). Yet, if Beissel had not yet absorbed Boehme's ideas by the time he arrived in America, he had another opportunity to do so from his contact with the members of the Woman in the Wilderness, who had several complete sets of the 1682 edition of Boehme's collected works published by Gichtel.[74]

---

[71] Julius Friedrich Sachse, The German Pietists of Provincial Pennsylvania (Philadelphia, Pennsylvania: printed for the author, 1895), p. 48.

[72] Lamech and Agrippa, op. cit., p. 5.

[73] Sachse, Pietists, p. 15.   [74] Sachse, Pietists, p. 48.

However historians think Beissel came in contact with Boehmist ideas, they generally agree that Boehme was an important force in the mysticism of Ephrata. The most prominent evidence of Boehme's influence is the use at Ephrata of certain terms, "such as <u>Tincturen</u>, <u>Magia</u>, <u>Sophia</u>, and <u>Temperatur</u>."[75] Those terms are used throughout Beissel's <u>Dissertation</u>, and will be explained when they come up in the discussion of that work. Before proceeding with the discussion of Beissel's book, it should be noted that much of the somewhat erotic imagery which Beissel used is more likely to have come from the work of Gottfried Arnold than from Boehme.[76]

According to Beissel's <u>Dissertation</u>, God was both male and female, and his properties or "tinctures" were in divine balance or "temperatur;" thus the male properties of fire, dominion, and strength were balanced by the female properties of water, meekness, and wisdom. Beissel blamed Lucifer for upsetting the divine balance and causing the separation of the "tinctures," the male and female properties. Lucifer had somehow aroused and exalted his fiery male property, breaking the balance within himself. By attacking God, Lucifer would have been able to subject God to his will, if God had not also broken the divine balance of dominion and meekness by arousing the godly maleness. God was, thereby, able to withstand Lucifer's attack, but the rest of creation would not have been able to repulse the aroused dominion of Lucifer. Therefore, God separated the balanced properties of the whole creation into male and female, and he made the female subject to the authority of the male so that,

---

[75] Stoeffler, op. cit., p. 46.

[76] Ibid., p. 47.

the fallen angel might find no female location empty and unoccupied even in God or any other creatures which he might govern as a male in his fiery property and wrathful exaltation.[77]

Beissel believed that Adam was created to fundamentally change the situation, for Adam was created not like the separated animals, but both male and female in the image of God. Beissel said, Adam's role was to "reduce all creatures subordinate to him from the separation of tinctures to the Godly harmony and union, for he had within him the temper or balance."[78] Unfortunately, instead of restoring the divine balance in all creatures, Adam "caused the completion of the apostacy" by his own lusting after the separation of the tinctures.[79] According to Beissel, Adam's female half, the Virgin-Sophia, was taken from him and preserved for that day when the divine balance would again be restored in mankind. God then created a new femalety, Eve, like unto the separation in the animals. Supposedly, if Eve had remained innocent, part of God's original plan for Adam might have been fulfilled; but Eve also acquired part of Adam's corrupt self-will, and she, too, fell.[80]

Beissel believed that since the exalted self-will of maleness had caused the separation, only a man would provide a suitable sacrifice for the restoration of the balance, but until Christ appeared no man could overcome his exalted maleness enough to make himself a sacrifice for all of mankind. Though there were martyrs who had previously sacrificed themselves, none had been able to make atonement for and to love their enemies, none had sacrificed themselves for all mankind; but

---

[77] Beissel, op. cit., p. 7.   [78] Ibid., p. 8.
[79] Ibid., p. 10.   [80] Ibid., p. 11.

Christ performed all of his ". . . <u>sacerdotal</u> function, which consisted in yielding himself for a sacrifice and interceding for his enemies."[81] Christ was able to fulfill his role for he was a second Adam;[82] another androgynous man who had within him the divine balance of both male and female. Instead of seeking to dominate with his fiery male will, Christ, "by sinking down into the soft quality of water, became female . . .,"[83] and was able to live "in subjection and obediance even to the death on the cross."[84] Through Christ's sacrifice and death on the cross the "justice of God is avenged upon the male image of Adam, and sin is atoned."[85] Beissel said Christ's sacrifice could not have been done without "the fountain of heavenly waters or the heavenly femalety in Christ."[86]

Since the fall of Adam, the Virgin-Sophia, the heavenly female half of Adam, having been deprived of her husband, had been waiting for an opportunity to restore the divine balance; but according to Beissel, such an opportunity was not offered until there came the purity of the Virgin Mary, "who had a will not to know a man in the animal separation."[87] Beissel believed Christ could not have fulfilled his role had he been born of the polluted intercourse of those who hunger after the separation, as did Adam and Eve; only the chastity of one such as the Virgin Mary would have allowed Jesus to be born with the divine balance or "temper," without being polluted by mankind's fiery self-will. Both the sacrificial

---

[81]Ibid., p. 19.
[82]Ibid., p. 4.
[83]Ibid., p. 26.
[84]Ibid., p. 18.
[85]Ibid., p. 20.
[86]Ibid.
[87]Ibid., p. 25.

atonement of Christ and the chaste purity of Mary were necessary for the restoration. Beissel summed it up by saying,

> as Lucifer and Adam by their self-elevation in their fire-will have introduced separation, so on the contrary, by the sinking down will of Christ and through the pure will of the Virgin Mary all is to be reinstated into the Holy unity to the very last . . . .[88]

The restoration of the divine balance was not immediate or inclusive in all things, "for as in Adam all die even so in Christ shall all be made alive, but every man in his own order . . . ."[89] Beissel goes on to say that none of Adam's race (male or female) are brought to that final restoration unless they suffer with Christ on the cross, because "wrath must be atoned by wrath and the female water quality, though ever so godly, is not able to mitigate that, above itself exalted, fire . . . ."[90] Repentance was not enough. If the wrath was to be atoned, if the union with the Virgin-Sophia was to produce heavenly fruit, Beissel said, "I must first have suffered beyond the gate with the body of Christ . . . ."[91]

To humble oneself and willingly suffer, to be burdened with a cross of self-denial, and to fast and otherwise discipline the body were all part of the asceticism practiced at Ephrata. That asceticism was grounded in beliefs about the means for attaining redemption. In Schwester Chronicon, the example and teachings of Christ are given as the source for those beliefs. The stated purpose for disciplining the body was,

---

[88]Ibid., p. 26.   [89]Ibid., p. 23.   [90]Ibid., p. 26.

[91]Stoeffler, op. cit., p. 50. The quote is from a translation by Stoeffler on page 27 of Beissel's Dissertation. The same line in Peter Miller's translation read as follows: "I needs must on that body wherein I am dressed suffer with Jesus before the city gate . . ."

So that our whole life and conduct be that of a suffering and dying pilgrim upon earth, for which reason we have divorced ourselves from the ways and customs of this world, and daily and hourly learn the manner and laws of our crucified Jesus, who instructs us in all things and taught us abnegation of self, and to take up the cross and follow him.[92]

Unlike their ascetic beliefs, the beliefs of Beissel's followers regarding the sacraments were very much like those of the German Baptist Brethren (Dunkers), the sect which had unwillingly supplied so many of the members of Ephrata Cloister. The sacraments of baptism and the Lord's Supper were very important in the religious lives of Beissel's Seventh-Day German Baptists. Participation in both sacraments was limited to adults. Partaking of the two communion elements in the Lord's Supper was part of a longer service known as a <u>Liebsmahl</u> or love-feast. Love-feasts were held in the evening and usually followed an afternoon worship service. During the love-feast, appropriate Bible passages were read and interpreted, and hymns were sung; foot-washing ceremonies, the passing of the kiss of charity, and a full meal preceded the Eucharist.[93]

At the love-feast the sexes were separated, sitting either on opposite sides of the room or sometimes just on opposite sides of the table. An elder and the oldest female would begin the foot-washing by washing the feet of the person on their right, who then washed the feet of the next person; each continued to do the same for his neighbor until

---

[92]Sachse, <u>Sectarians</u>, II, p. 194. <u>Schwester Chronicon</u> was written by the sisters of the Order of the Roses of Sharon and contained a history of the order along with a discussion of their way of life. The book was found in manuscript form by Sachse and portions of it were translated and included by him in <u>Sectarians</u>, II. <u>Schwester Chronicon</u> was probably written in the late 1740's.

[93]Sachse, <u>Sectarians</u>, I, pp. 107-110.

it had been done for all. The full meal which followed was eaten in silence, and when it was over the kiss of charity was passed from one to another as had been done with the foot-washing. Then after an appropriate reading, the communion symbols were blessed, and the bread was passed among both sexes. Beginning with the elder, each man broke off a piece of the bread for his neighbor, and the bread was passed to each one in that manner; but among the women, whose sex was counted as having had no part in the original breaking of Christ's body, the bread was broken and given to each by the elder. The same manner of distribution was used in passing and partaking of the wine.[94]

Within Ephrata Cloister, love-feasts were not held at scheduled intervals, but whenever the mood arose. Sometimes in the cloister they were held by just one of the sexes, although they were often held with all of the orders present including the Householders. Love-feasts were held at Ephrata to celebrate the consecration or dedication of new buildings, and other special events such as revivals, but they were probably most often held in conjunction with baptisms. The baptism of new members at afternoon services would be followed by a love-feast in the evening.[95]

Even though they may have originally been used as epithets, the names of Beissel's sect, the Seventh-Day German Baptists, of their immediate predecessors, the German Baptist Brethren or Dunkers, and of their spiritual ancestors, the Anabaptists, reflect the importance of the sacrament of baptism to each group. While he was still more of a separatist than a sectarian, Beissel accepted baptism into the Dunker

---

[94]Ibid., p. 108.   [95]Ibid., pp. 107, 109.

church in 1724 because he believed baptism was necessary for salvation.[96] The method of baptism used by the Dunkers and by Beissel's followers was complete immersion as the baptizer dipped the supplicant's face into the water three times. When the break occurred in 1728 between Beissel's followers and the Dunkers, Beissel chose baptism as the means to express that division. Beissel gave the baptism back to the Dunkers by having himself and six others baptized backwards. Then in the usual manner, they baptized each other into membership in Beissel's new sect, the Seventh-Day German Baptist Brethren.[97]

Perhaps because of the precedent set in 1728, re-baptism occurred quite often among Beissel's followers. In 1738, "the custom came into vogue to have one's self baptized for the dead . . .," for parents and relatives who "in their life time received their divine calling, but had not attained unto the covenant of God."[98] When the Order of Spiritual Virgins was reorganized in July, 1745, into the Order of the Roses of Sharon, all of the sisters were re-baptized as a symbol of their new membership.[99] Later in the fall, after the Prior, who had been elevated above Beissel, was deposed, the cloister brethren who had been baptized by the Prior, were baptized out of his baptism and then baptized into Beissel's baptism. The re-baptisms also occurred again in the fall of 1745 among all of the sisters.[100] It is possible that the two female Solitary, who had been part of the original group

---

[96] Ibid., pp. 102-104.   [97] Ibid., pp. 138-139.
[98] Lamech and Agrippa, op. cit., p. 122.
[99] Ernst, op. cit., pp. 249-251.   [100] Ibid., p. 279.

of Seventh-Day German Baptists, were baptized seven times on four different occasions.

The ceremonial use of the sacrament of baptism is indicative of the frequent use of ceremony and ritual at Ephrata Cloister. Special ceremonies were used in the mystic rites of the Zionitic Brotherhood, for the cutting of the tonsure, for honoring the special positions of the Prior and the Prioress, for the giving of monastic names, and for the dedication of newly erected buildings. The self-denial and simplicity which guided most aspects of life at Ephrata Cloister did not rule out ceremony, nor did it rule out creative expression. Inventiveness, originality, and some degree of artistry were all evident in the Frakurschriften (ornamental writing),[101] in the writing of hymns, in the special style of music and singing, and in the historical and religious works written at Ephrata. Though sensual pleasures and even certain mundane physical comforts were proscribed at Ephrata, creative expression and its aesthetic pleasures were encouraged. Not all of life at Ephrata was dull, drab, harsh, and self-sacrificing.

One of the controversial questions about Ephrata Cloister concerns monastic vows. William Fahnestock, one of the leaders of the Seventh-Day German Baptists at Antietam, Pennsylvania, wrote in 1835 that members of Ephrata Cloister did not take any monastic vows.[102] He was certainly familiar with the cloister known as Snow Hill which had developed from

---

[101]Some examples of Frakurschriften are given in the Appendix.

[102]Reichmann and Doll, op. cit., p. 170. A reprint of William M. Fahnestock's, "An Historical Sketch of Ephrata; Together with a Concise Account of the Seventh-Day Baptist Society of Pennsylvania," which appeared in Hazard's Register of Pennsylvania, XV, January-June, 1835, pp. 161-167.

the Seventh-Day German Baptists at Antietam, and it is likely that Snow Hill, as a direct descendant of Ephrata Cloister, would have had practices similar to those of Ephrata. However, two later historians, Sachse and Ernst, both stated that celibate members of Ephrata Cloister gave monastic vows.[103] In Chronicon Ephratense, the description of the founding of the Order of Spiritual Virgins says the four original members "were the first who bound themselves by a pledge to a communal life."[104] Considering the regular use of ceremony at Ephrata and the precedent established by the founding members of the Order of Spiritual Virgins it can be concluded that some sort of promise, pledge, or vow was given by those who became members of the orders within Ephrata Cloister.

The vows mentioned above were not part of life at Ephrata until the establishment of the celibate, communal orders, but the confession of sins to Beissel was a practice which had begun among the Seventh-Day German Baptists soon after the sect had been founded in 1728. Confession became required among the celibate members in 1736, and they followed a unique system of confessing. Each week on the evening before the Sabbath, every member of the cloister was required to "examine his heart before God, in his own cell, and then hand in to the Superintendent (Beissel) a written statement of his spiritual condition . . . ."[105] The statements, called Lectiones, were read by Beissel on each Sabbath at the congregational meeting, and a collection of them was published at Ephrata in 1752 under the title, Theosophische Episteln.[106]

---

[103]Sachse, Sectarians, II, p. 201, and Ernst, op. cit., p. 136.
[104]Lamech and Agrippa, op. cit., p. 76.
[105]Ibid., p. 81.   [106]Ernst, op. cit., pp. 115-116.

Ephrata Cloister was not always able to maintain its high principles; one of the lapses occurred in its strictures against the use of force. In regard to armed force, Beissel's followers held on to their pacifism, even during the French and Indian War in 1755 when a bloody Indian raid came within thirteen miles of the cloister.[107] During the Revolutionary War, the American cause was favored by the members of the cloister but no active support was given because of their beliefs against force and violence. Several accounts written during the cloister's history also mentioned an abhorrence of the use of legal force and stated that the members of the cloister would not sue at law for any reason.[108] Near the end of Beissel's life, the principle of avoiding lawsuits was disregarded as the cloister became entangled in a long series of court battles over the title to the cloister land.[109]

One of the oldest and one of the most venerated customs of Beissel's followers was the seventh-day Sabbath. After his return from Bohemia Manor in 1721, Beissel had attended the meetings of Sabbatarians in Chester County just west of Philadelphia. He began to question which day was the true Sabbath, and when he became convinced that the seventh day was the proper day rather than the first, Beissel persuaded his companions to adopt the seventh-day as the Sabbath.[110] Beissel's first book, Mysterion Anomias (The Mystery of Lawlessness), which was published in German in 1728 advocated the seventh-day Sabbath, and led directly to

---

[107]Ibid., p. 306.

[108]Reichmann and Doll, op. cit., p. 83. Similar accounts given on pp. 87, 114, 118, 137, and 150.

[109]Ernst, op. cit., pp. 325-328.   [110]Ibid., p. 44.

the adoption of Saturday as the Sabbath day by the Dunker congregation which Beissel headed. The adoption of the seventh-day Sabbath by that congregation was followed soon after by their secession from the Dunkers and the founding in September, 1728, of the Seventh-Day German Baptist Church.[111]

Along with advocating the Seventh-Day Sabbath, Beissel's Mysterion Anomias also advocated celibacy and the adoption of Mosaic dietary laws.[112] Presumably, Beissel's study of the Old Testament, when he was questioning which day was the proper Sabbath, also led him to adopt other Mosaic laws. Some of his followers are known to have adopted Mosaic dietary laws at that time.[113] In the preface to Beissel's "Treatise on Music," which was printed as part of the hymnal Turteltaube in 1747, he went even further than Mosaic law and admonished singers to avoid eating meat, saying, "for it is certain that all meat dishes by whatever name known, quite discommode us, and bring no small injury to the pilgrim on his way to the silent beyond."[114] In the early years of the cloister, the diet was restricted. According to Israel Acrelius who visited Ephrata in 1753, "At first they regarded it as a sin to kill any animal, and still more so to eat flesh."[115] The prohibition against

---

[111]Sachse, Sectarians, I, p. 142. The 1729 version was entitled, The Mystery of Lawlessness; or Lawless Antichrist discovered and disclosed... by Cunrad Beysall, translated out of the High Dutch by M. W., Philadelphia, 1729.

[112]Ernst, op. cit., p. 44.   [113]Ibid., pp. 57-58.

[114]Julius Friedrich Sachse, The Music of the Ephrata Cloister (New York: reprinted by AMS Press, 1970), p. 67. Sachse reprinted all of Beissel's "Treatise on Music."

[115]Reichmann and Doll, op. cit., p. 73. See Footnote #52.

killing animals came from the cloister's interpretation of the Biblical commandment, "Thou shalt not kill." As explained by Peter Miller, Beissel's successor, that commandment meant not only thou shalt not kill men, "but no creature whatsoever, for a law spoken in so general terms might be extended so far, as the sense will permit."[116] Acrelius said that by 1753 each cloister member was free to eat what he wanted to eat, "but what liberty is there in eating what is not found in their storehouse?"[117] Even when the religious prohibition against eating meat was relaxed, the poverty of the cloister continued to limit the consumption of meat.

The beliefs affirmed by the Seventh-Day German Baptists included a renouncement of the world, and that was particularly true for the members of the cloister. The attention and efforts of the cloister members were focused on preparing for a life in the kingdom of heaven with God's church. They believed, "so far as consolation is sought in the amusements of the visible world, so far we lose communion with the Church . . . ."[118] The extent of the cloistered celibates' rejection of the world can be seen in the following statement from Schwester Chronicon concerning the way of life of the Order of the Roses of Sharon:

> Our life and conduct cannot agree or conform to the world, whether it be in eating and drinking, --sleeping or waking, --in clothing or other requisite things pertaining to the natural life . . . .[119]

---

[116]Ibid., p. 197. Quoting from a letter by Peter Miller written in 1790 and which appeared in Hazard's Register of Pennsylvania, XV, July-December, 1835, pp. 253-256, under the title, "Letters to a Gentleman of Philadelphia."

[117]Ibid., p. 73.

[118]Sachse, Music, pp. 55-56. From the Forward to the Turtelaube.

[119]Sachse, Sectarians, II, p. 193.

Members of Ephrata Cloister renounced their worldly names, dress, and living habits in exchange for monastic names, dress similar to the Capuchin Order, restricted diets, the Jewish method of counting days from evening to evening, six hours of sleep and six hours of worship, prayer, or contemplation each day, and one meal a day.[120] For those who could not limit themselves to one meal a day the rule was not enforced.[121]

At least for the Order of the Roses of Sharon, there was even a rule against visits to the outside world, "except such as are called for by an urgent necessity, and if it were possible to be relieved entirely, it would be to our pleasure . . . ."[122] When the Roses of Sharon did venture forth from the cloister it was usually for evangelistic purposes in an attempt to convert others from the sins of the world. In comparison with other celibate communal societies, the attempts made by Ephratans to convert the world were surpassed only by the Shakers. Books and pamphlets written by Ephratans were important in bringing converts to the community and even more important were the revival meetings personally conducted by cloister members. Along with the local successes, Beissel's followers also established three distant churches: one in Amwell, New Jersey, one in Nantmel, Pennsylvania, and one in Antietam, Pennsylvania. The church at Antietam, the only distant church with any lasting success, became the foundation for the cloister known as Snow Hill, which carried on the Ephrata tradition from 1814-1870.[123]

---

[120]Ernst, op. cit., pp. 120, 129, 254.

[121]Sachse, *Sectarians*, II, p. 194.

[122]Ibid., p. 196.

[123]Sachse, *Sectarians*, I, pp. 364-376, and II, pp. 255-273, 360-371.

In the area of economic activity, the policies of the cloister changed considerably during the period from 1741 to 1745. The guiding principle of separation from the world was for a time almost entirely disregarded in favor of intense commercial activity. The economic developments, which transformed the cloister into what has been called an "industrial commune,"[124] occurred as a result of two other changes in the life of the cloister: the rise to power of Israel Eckerlin and a loss of income.

As the cloister grew, the administrative problems of running the community increased, and under Beissel's superintendency two lesser offices, of prior and prioress, became positions of power within the celibate orders. Under Beissel's leadership, the cloister would probably have always been poor, but in 1741 the death of the first prior, Michael Wohlfarth, who had been one of Beissel's staunchest supporters, brought to the office of Prior Israel Eckerlin, who was both able and willing to develop the economic power of the cloister.[125] A large portion of the economic support of the cloister had been provided by the tithes and offerings of the Householders; but after a separate place of worship, known as Peniel-Saal, was completed for them in December, 1741, their support of the cloister dropped to a lower level.[126] The drop in contributions from the householders made some expansion of economic activity necessary, and Prior Eckerlin responded to the challenge with startling and somewhat unbecoming success.

---

[124] Ernst, op. cit., p. 266.
[125] Ibid., pp. 180-183.
[126] Lamech and Agrippa, op. cit., p. 137.

A grist-mill on the Cocalico, which had been purchased in July, 1741,[127] was expanded and within four years the mill-site included, "a sawmill, a flaxseed oil mill, a fulling mill . . . ," and a bark mill used for making paper.[128] The mills were a valuable asset to that pioneer area, and a clear financial success for the cloister. Prior Eckerlin also speculated in grain, by purchasing grain at harvest time when the prices were low and storing it until the market went up. Commercial agents who bought and sold for the cloister on a commission basis were retained in Philadelphia and Germantown; wagons carrying goods owned by the cloister were constantly traveling between those cities and the cloister.[129] Prior Eckerlin has even been accused of instituting the Hebron experiment as a means of acquiring the farm land of the householders so that the industrial nature of the cloister could be balanced with a large agricultural base.[130]

During the first half of the 1740's, while Prior Eckerlin was increasing his prestige, his power, and the economic status of the cloister, Conrad Beissel's control over the cloister was declining. In the spring of 1744, Beissel, by his own choice, gave up all power over the celibate orders to Prior Eckerlin. In January, 1745, Beissel also withdrew from his position as spiritual leader to the householders in Hebron and gave that position to the prior. Although Beissel never acted

---

[127]Ernst, op. cit., p. 187.

[128]Eugene E. Doll, The Ephrata Cloister: An Introduction (Ephrata, Pennsylvania: Ephrata Cloister Associates, Inc., 1958), p. 9.

[129]Ernst, op. cit., p. 216.

[130]Ibid., pp. 268-269.

101

like an ordinary brother, he was reduced in power to the state of an ordinary member of the cloister. Beissel did not long remain in that lowly state. In the summer of 1745 there began an open revolt against Prior Eckerlin which culminated in August, 1745, with the expulsion of the prior from the cloister and the restoration of Beissel to the position of overseer or superintendent.[131]

Prior Eckerlin had made mistakes or failed in several areas: he was never able to bring the sisters under his control; he was unable to make the Hebron experiment a success; and he antagonized the brethren by his penchant for delivering sermons of several hours duration and by the changes in values which accompanied his economic changes. Beissel did not confront the prior directly, but Beissel appears to have worked for Eckerlin's downfall: Beissel encouraged the housefathers to leave Hebron; he helped to reorganize the Order of Spiritual Virgins into the Order of the Roses of Sharon, which was done in the spring of 1745 without Eckerlin's approval or cooperation; and Beissel, in the summer of 1745, encouraged the revolt among the brethren which succeded in deposing the prior.[132]

The overthrow of Prior Eckerlin went to excess as books he had written, along with records which he had kept were cast into a fire. Ten brethren who had been baptized by Prior Eckerlin were re-baptized by Beissel, and soon all of the celibates were re-baptized by Beissel; the Zionitic Brotherhood was dissolved, and the brethren were reorganized into the Brotherhood of Bethany, for which a new brother-house called Bethania was built; and an orchard of a thousand trees which had been

---

[131]Ibid., pp. 227, 267, 273.   [132]Ibid., pp. 229, 268-269, 271.

planted under Prior Eckerlin's direction was uprooted. The most far-reaching changes occurred in economic policy as the mills were temporarily closed, all contracts were canceled, and the cloister announced that henceforth they would not produce goods except for the use of their congregation.[133]

So in 1745, what may have been the largest single industrial unit at that time in Pennsylvania closed its doors to outsiders and turned its back on commercial success and financial rewards. Those financial rewards which had already been accumulated through the business shrewdness of Prior Eckerlin were dissipated in about three years by Beissel's open, and sometimes foolish, generosity. After Beissel had spent most of the legacy left by Prior Eckerlin, the brethren removed the control of economic affairs from Beissel; but there was never any return to the economically acquisitive policies followed by Prior Eckerlin. Ephrata Cloister began as a poor institution and, with the exception of the Eckerlin years, remained poor.[134]

The printing establishment was the only part of the industrial enterprises which Prior Eckerlin helped to build, which remained an important part of the Ephrata Cloister. The first products of the Ephrata press were struck in 1743, and for most of the remaining 18th century, Ephrata Cloister was an important printing center in Pennsylvania. At that time, the cloister was unique in the printing business because,

> Ephrata had the only complete publishing unit in the colonies--a paper mill with its own watermark, a press with trained printer, a tannery, ironworks and cabinet-makers,

---

[133]Ibid., pp. 273, 278-280, 284.

[134]Ibid., pp. 266, 283, 291-293.

materials for ink, bindery, sales department and men and women capable of writing.[135]

Along with works such as hymns and devotional writings produced by their own members, especially by Beissel, materials for the general public were also printed, including a German edition of John Bunyan's Pilgrim's Progress and an edition of the Mennonites' Martyr's Mirror, which was "the largest book printed in Pennsylvania before the Revolution."[136]

The outpouring of religious literature from the press at Ephrata Cloister can be viewed as an indication of a concern for the world; but one historian, in reviewing the contents of writings authored at Ephrata, has criticized the morality of the cloister on the grounds that its separation from the world and its emphasis on an intense personal relationship with God produced "ethical sterility" in regard to the world outside the cloister.[137] In comparison with the many social concerns expressed by religious organizations today, Ephrata Cloister might appear to have been ethically sterile in some ways, but the aforementioned historian has concentrated too much on the devotional literature of Ephrata without adequately concerning himself with the actual practice of Christianity at Ephrata Cloister. As the following paragraphs will show, the earnest attempts of the cloistered celibates of Ephrata to separate themselves from the sins of worldliness did not separate them from a concern for mankind.

---

[135] Ibid., p. 220.

[136] Doll, Cloister, p. 11.

[137] Stoeffler, op. cit., p. 64.

104

The concern of Ephrata Cloister for the rest of mankind was expressed in ways which cost the members their time, their collective possessions, and even their lives. The successful efforts undertaken by members of the cloister to establish churches in distant areas demonstrated their concern for souls other than their own. At Ephrata travelers were always given food and a night's lodging; the cloister was a haven for many people of the area during the threat of Indian raids in 1754-1756.[138] When space became available, widows and orphans were given quarters within a cloister building.[139] After 1739, a school was maintained for children in the area; what may have been the first Sabbath-school was opened in the 1740's to accommodate those children who could not come to school during the week.[140] A large portion of the riches acquired under Prior Eckerlin was given to beggars and other indigents by Beissel.[141]

The most significant example of the Christian spirit at Ephrata is the way in which the cloister responded to the several hundred wounded soldiers which were brought to the cloister after the battle of Brandywine in 1777. Cloister buildings became hospitals where the suffering of wounded men was eased by the devotion of the brothers and sisters. The wounded soldiers brought typhus with them and many died, including both male and female members of the cloister. Several of the original communal buildings which had been used as hospitals were burned to destroy the

---

[138] See footnotes #106 and #122.

[139] Sachse, *Sectarians*, I, p. 495.

[140] Doll, *Cloister*, pp. 12, 21.

[141] Ernst, op. cit., p. 283.

typhus. Membership in the cloister had been declining and the lives sacrificed for the wounded soldiers, foreshadowed, and perhaps sealed, the fate of the cloister.[142] As for official compensation or recognition, the brothers and sisters did not ask for any, and none was given, only the words of a soldier who had been there,

> Until I entered the walls of Ephrata, I had no idea of pure and practical Christianity. Not that I was ignorant of the forms, or even of the doctrines of religion. I knew it in theory before; I saw it in practice then.
>
> . . . Many a poor fellow, who entered there profane, immoral, and without hope or God in the world, left it rejoicing in the Saviour.[143]

The particular interpretations of Christianity followed at Ephrata Cloister came from many different sources, including the celibate communal societies of Bohemia Manor and the "Woman in the Wilderness." Some of the contributions of its forerunners may have lived on in the contributions which Ephrata Cloister gave to the developments of other celibate communal societies. One of those later celibate communal societies, Snow Hill, was a direct descendent of Ephrata Cloister. That society will be discussed in the section on the general history and decline of Ephrata. Two other celibate communal societies, the Society of Universal Friends and the Harmony Society, also appear to have been influenced by the example of Ephrata Cloister. Evidence is lacking with which to _prove_ that Ephrata Cloister substantially influenced those

---

[142]Doll, Cloister, p. 23.

[143]Ibid., p. 31, and Reichmann and Doll, op. cit., p. 115. From an account by an American officer who had been wounded at the battle of Brandywine and cared for at Ephrata Cloister. His account was first published in 1784.

societies, although circumstantial evidence in both cases indicated strong possibilities that such influence existed.

The possibility that a relationship even existed between Ephrata Cloister and the Society of Universal Friends is wholly based on Christopher Marshall of Philadelphia and his friendship with both societies. Marshall's relationship with Ephrata was quite extensive: he served as a business agent in Philadelphia for the cloister in the early 1740's; in 1765 he helped to sell the English translation of Beissel's Dissertation on the Fall of Man; he corresponded with Peter Miller, Beissel's successor; in 1777, according to Marshall's diary, he prepared an English translation of Chronicon Ephratense, which unfortunately has never been found; and he is known to have stayed at Ephrata during part of the Revolutionary War.[144] Marshall's relationship with Jomima Wilkinson, the leader of the Universal Friends, began in 1782 during her first visit to Philadelphia, and during her second visit to Philadelphia in 1784, Jemima Wilkinson stayed at the home of Marshall's son.[145]

There is no concrete evidence that Ephrata Cloister was ever discussed by Jemima Wilkinson and Christopher Marshall, although they are known to have had many religious discussions. Circumstances do indicate that Ephrata was discussed because two important aspects of life at Ephrata Cloister, the seventh-day Sabbath and communal ownership, became part of the life of the Universal Friends after Jemima

---

[144] Ernst, op. cit., p. 214 and Reichmann and Doll, op. cit., pp. 116, 195.

[145] Herbert A. Wisbey Jr., Pioneer Prophetess: Jemima Wilkinson, The Public Universal Friend (Ithaca, New York: Cornell University Press, 1964), pp. 82-83, 94-96.

Wilkinson's discussions with Christopher Marshall. The Universal Friends adopted the seventh-day Sabbath after Jemima Wilkinson's stay in Philadelphia in 1782, and the first mention of plans for a communal society for the Universal Friends was in 1785, after Jemima Wilkinson's second visit to Philadelphia.[146]

There is no doubt that the Harmony Society was aware of the Ephrata Cloister. Their hymnal, Harmonische Gesangbuch, which was printed in 1820, contains 60 hymns from an Ephrata hymnal written in 1766.[147] None of the sources indicated when or how the Harmonists acquired those hymns. It is possible and even probable that the Harmonists had heard of Ephrata before the Harmonists migrated to America. A list of books owned by the Harmonists in 1830[148] includes two books which contained relatively accurate accounts of Ephrata Cloister.[149] Both books were about life in the United States, and both were published in Germany before 1800. It seems very likely that those

---

[146]Ibid.

[147]Karl J. R. Arndt, George Rapp's Harmony Society, 1785-1847 (Philadelphia, Pennsylvania: University of Pennsylvania Press, 1965), p. 253.

[148]John Archibald Bole, The Harmony Society (Philadelphia, Pennsylvania: Americana Germanica Press, 1905), p. 148.

[149]Reichmann and Doll, op. cit., pp. 135-138. A reprint of the section on Ephrata from Johann David Schopf, Reise durch einige der Verienigten Staaten, Erlangen, Germany, 1788. It was translated by Alfred J. Morrison and published in 1911 by William J. Campbell, Philadelphia, Pennsylvania as Travels in the Confederation. Volume III, pp. 15-19 has the section on Ephrata and on pp. 155-156 there is a reprint of the section on Ephrata from Christoph Daniel Ebeling, Erdbeschreibung und Geschichte von Amerika, Carl Bohn, Hamburg, Germany (1797), IV, pp. 331-334. The section concerning Ephrata was translated by Reichmann and Doll. Both books appear on the list of books owned in 1830 by the Harmonists as compiled by Bole. See footnote #146.

two books were purchased in Germany as part of the Harmonists' preparations for migration to America, and that the Harmonists were therefore aware of Ephrata Cloister before arriving in America. The Harmonists might also have come in contact with Ephrata Cloister in their travels from Philadelphia to their first settlement in western Pennsylvania near Pittsburgh.

GENERAL HISTORY AND DECLINE

In many ways the history of Ephrata Cloister was as strange and unfathomable as some of Beissel's mystical beliefs. From 1735 to 1745 changes were a constant occurance: celibate orders were organized and then re-organized; the cloister became an industrial power and then changed to a subsistence economy; buildings were erected, occupied, and then abandoned; Beissel went from being the most powerful to being almost powerless to being most powerful again; new religious ceremonies were introduced many times; and the relationships among the orders of the church were always changing. The period after 1745 was more stable, but Beissel's penchant for following the inspiration of the moment remained an important factor at Ephrata until his death in 1768.

The largest number of members in Ephrata Cloister was reached around 1750, when there were about fifty male and fifty female celibates with approximately 200 supporting householders.[150] Some of the householders included in the above figure had arrived from Germany in 1750; many of those moved to the Antietam area and later formed a congregation

---

[150]Ernst, op. cit., p. 347.

there.[151] By 1770, membership in the cloister and the congregation at Ephrata was only half of what it had been in 1750, and by 1794 the cloister had dropped to about twenty members.[152] While longevity of membership is an important factor in any organization, eventually all institutions rise or fall commensurate with their ability to acquire new members. From the children born to the Seventh-Day German Baptist congregation, Ephrata Cloister might have had a continuing flow of new members, but as the population of the area grew and other opportunities became available to the children, the cloister became an anachronism and less appealing to its potential members.

One sequence of events which began with bright hopes for the cloister may have cost the celibate orders the affections of many of the children, who might have later become members of the cloister. A pietist awakening in 1749 at Gimsheim on the Rhine in the Palatinate, and attempts by government authorities to suppress that awakening, brought a group of those awakened to migrate to Ephrata under the leadership of Peter Beissel, Conrad Beissel's brother.[153] The new influx of members to the cloister produced a rise in morale at Ephrata, which also led to the establishment of a new celibate order known as the Society of Succoth.[154]

The Society of Succoth, or the Society of Youthful Celibates, occupied a newly constructed convent in January, 1750, with twenty-two

---

[151]Sachse, Sectarians, II, pp. 360-364.
[152]Reichmann and Doll, op. cit., pp. 94, 151.
[153]Lamech and Agrippa, op. cit., pp. 218-219.
[154]Ernst, op. cit., p. 297.

members. Apparently most of the members were teen-agers, because their baptism into the Society of Succoth aroused many of the householders to complain about the baptism of children. Some of the householders even left the congregation because of the youthful baptisms. More disasterous than the loss of those householders was the manner in which the Society of Succoth was organized. Like the other celibate orders, the Youthful Celibates were virtually autonomous; unfortunately neither the leader, Conrad Beissel's nephew, nor the members were mature enough to handle their responsibilities, and within eighteen months the Society of Succoth had disbanded.[155] It is likely that most of the Youthful Celibates, who might otherwise have grown up to become adult members, were forever lost to Ephrata Cloister either as celibates or as householders.

An earlier mistake which may have cost the cloister some membership was Beissel's refusal to be concerned with any worldly things, including the title to the cloister land. Five members of the cloister, including Israel Eckerlin and his brother, Samuel, finally acquired the title to the land in 1739. When Prior Israel Eckerlin was deposed in 1745, his three brothers, including Samuel, left the cloister with him; but, nothing was done about changing the names on the land title. In 1764, Samuel, as the only one of the original titleholders still living, went back to the cloister and demanded a share in the products of the cloister. Beissel refused Samuel's request on the grounds that only those who attended worship services were entitled to any share in the produce of the cloister. Several years of legal battles ensued, and

---

[155]Ibid., p. 298.

some of the cloister members, including the prioress, worked on Samuel Eckerlin's side in an effort to overthrow Beissel. After Beissel's death in 1768, a settlement was reached;[156] but the failure to follow the principle against the use of legal force, and the antogonisms generated within the community by the dispute damaged the reputation of the cloister and probably contributed to the lack of new members.

The last years of Beissel's life were unhappy ones. Declining in health and in spirit, Beissel became a frequent drinker of wine, and on one occasion, the wine led to a leg injury when Beissel fell on a flight of stairs.[157] Beissel no longer held the respect and blind obedience of the celibate orders which he had once had. He must have seen the decline of the cloister as old friends left and as death took its toll. Yet Beissel must have looked back on his life with a sense of accomplishment. When he died at the age of 78 on July 6, 1768, it was after a half a century of wooing the Virgin-Sophia, forty years after the founding of the Seventh-Day German Baptist Church, thirty-three years after the founding of the Order of Spiritual Virgins, and twenty-eight years after Ephrata Cloister had completely become a communal society.

Following Beissel's death, Peter Miller became the leader and he led Ephrata Cloister until his death in 1796. During Miller's tenure, the cloister served as a hospital following the battle of Brandywine in 1777; in 1786 private personal property was again allowed at Ephrata

---

[156]Ibid., pp. 325-328.
[157]Ibid., pp. 332-336.

(though real property continued to be communally owned);[158] and, also in 1786, Miller, whose monastic name was Agrippa, helped to write and publish Chronicon Ephratense. In 1790, Miller addressed himself to the question of the cloister's future and said, "Our president (Beissel) did once declare to his Intimates, that he hath received assurance from God, that the seed of his work shall remain until the second coming of Christ."[159]

Three institutions which directly succeeded Ephrata Cloister, and which may have carried its seed were the various congregations of Seventh-Day German Baptists, the cloister known as Snow Hill, and the schools maintained at Ephrata Cloister. Of the elementary, Sabbath, and secondary boarding schools, the boarding school appears to have survived the longest, and there was even a new building constructed for the boarding school in 1837.[160] During the 19th century there probably were more pupils at the boarding school than there were members in the celibate orders.

The Snow Hill cloister grew out of the Antietam, Pennsylvania, congregation of Seventh-Day German Baptists, many of whom had been part of the migration from Gimsheim. For a time, the group appeared to lose its faith, but, in the early 1760's, a preacher named George Adam Martin was sent from Ephrata, and he revived the congregation. After Martin's death, Peter Lehman was sent from Ephrata to Antietam. He led the congregation from 1788 until his own death in 1823. Under Lehman's

---

[158]Reichmann and Doll, op. cit., p. 156. In Ebeling, see footnote #147.

[159]Ibid., p. 200. From one of Peter Miller's letters to Christopher Marshall.

leadership, a church building was constructed in 1793, and the original cloister building was constructed in 1814. A generous gift of land from Andreas Schneeberger had made possible the establishment of a cloister, and it was named Snow Hill Institute, in his honor.[161] Of the twenty-three members whose deaths are recorded in the Snow Hill Register, at least six were relatives or descendents of Andreas Schneeberger. There were never more than 30 celibate members of the Snow Hill Institute during its high point from 1820-1840, and after 1850 its numbers declined rapidly until the last brother died in 1895.[162]

Early in the 19th century, the members of Ephrata Cloister gave their land-title to the congregation as a whole. Sometime during that century, membership in Ephrata Cloister ended with the deaths of the last sister and the last brother. The congregation at Ephrata of Seventh-Day German Baptists continued the spirit of Ephrata Cloister until 1934, when the church was dissolved by the last few members.[163]

Perhaps the Ancient and Mystical Order Rosae Crucis, headquartered at San Jose, California, which looks back to the "Woman in the Wilderness" and Ephrata Cloister as the earliest Rosicrucian groups in America, still carries on part of the spirit of Ephrata; but the Rosicrucians do not profess, as a group, to be Christian.[164] Whether or not the mystic

---

[160]Doll, op. cit., p. 6.

[161]Sachse, Sectarians II, pp. 360-371. Schneeberg translates as Snowhill.

[162]Ibid., pp. 521-522.

[163]Reichmann and Doll, op. cit., p. 29. None of the reliable sources give any date for the deaths of the last celibate members of Ephrata.

[164]Ancient and Mystical Order Rosae Crucis, The Mastery of Life, Official Publication No. 21 (San Jose, California: AMORC, no date given), p. 16.

devotion of the cloistered celibates of Ephrata continues to leaven any part of Christianity, the cloister still fascinates the thousands who each year walk the narrow hallways, stooping at each doorway, marveling at the wood-bench beds with wood block pillows, and who silently wonder if they could live as the Ephratans did.

Chapter 6

THE SHAKER SOCIETY

INTRODUCTION

"The Shaker Society is alive and well at Sabbathday Lake." As a bumper sticker the above statement might sell quite well because many people would find humorous, and somewhat unbelieveable, the idea that a celibate communal society might have existed in the United States for 185 years. The Shaker Society has done just that and still exists, not only at Sabbathday Lake, Poland Spring, Maine, but also near Canterbury, New Hampshire. A few Shakers were practicing communism before the signing of the United States Constitution in 1787. Celibacy had been part of the Shaker teachings and practice in America since the first Shakers arrived 198 years ago in 1774.

The Shaker Society has lasted longer than any other communal society originally founded in the United States. Over the years more than 16,800 people joined the Shakers, giving that society the largest membership of any communal society founded in the United States. The Shaker order was divided into "families" which averaged between 50 and 100 members. From their beginnings at Watervliet and New Lebanon, New York, the Shaker Society expanded into 58 separate "families" located in 29 communities in ten different states. One of the locations was abandoned as early as 1819 and others followed that example, especially in the late 19th and early 20th century.[1]

By the early 1950's only two "families" were left, one at Sabbathday Lake and the other at Canterbury. Today the combined membership of those two "families" is less than 20. According to the present director of the Shaker Museum at Sabbathday Lake, the policies of the order do not permit the release of detailed information concerning the members, such as their exact number, their ages, or when they joined the society.[2] However, it is known that all of the present members are women in either their middle-age or older.

The first developments of the Shaker faith had occurred among members of the Wardley society, a dissident branch of the Quaker faith in Manchester, England, in the mid-18th century. Only eight former members of the Wardley society began the Shaker movement in America in 1774. Most of the first American members are known to have come from revivalist groups such as the "New Light" Baptists at New Lebanon, New York in 1780. The aftermath of revival meetings continued to be an important source of members for the Shakers, especially the "Kentucky Revival" in the first years of the 19th century.[3]

---

[1] Edward Deming Andrews, The People Called Shakers: A Search for the Perfect Society (New York: Dover Publications, 1963), pp. 290-292. First published in 1953 by Oxford University Press, Inc.

[2] Based on personal correspondence between Theodore E. Johnson, Director of the Shaker Museum and Library at Sabbathday Lake, Poland Spring, Maine, and the writer.

[3] Calvin Green and Seth Y. Wells, A Summary View of the Millenial Church, or United Society of Believers, Commonly Called Shakers, Comprising the Rise, Progress and Practical Order of the Society, Together with the General Principles of Their Faith and Testimony (Second edition, revised and improved; Albany, New York: C. Van Benthuysen, 1848), pp. 23-24. First edition published in 1823.

DEVELOPMENT BEFORE FOUNDING

The Founder of the Shaker faith, Ann Lee, was born to the family of a poor blacksmith in Manchester, England on February 29, 1736. Because she did not attend school, Ann never learned to read or write. The poverty of her family forced Ann into work in a cotton factory at an early age. Ann's position as the second child in a family which had eight children contributed to the forces which made her income necessary for the family. The effects of seven brothers and sisters might also have contributed to Ann's aversion to sexual intercourse. At an early age Ann is supposed to have scolded her mother for indulging in sexual intercourse.[4]

In 1758 at the age of 22, Ann joined a group known as the Wardley society, headed by the former Quakers, Jane and James Wardley. The distinctive feature of the Wardley society was its emphasis on direct inspiration. Under the influence of direct inspiration, which frequently came to the Wardley meetings, the members would tremble and move in various ways, so much so that they were derisively called, "Shaking Quakers."[5] The Wardley's emphasis on direct inspiration had come from their contact in 1747 with remnants, or spiritual descendants,

---

[4]Henri Desroche, The American Shakers: From Neo-Christianity to Presocialism (Amherst, Massachusetts: The University of Massachusetts Press, 1971), pp. 42-44.

[5]Andrews, op. cit., p. 6.

of a group of prophets, variously known as the French Prophets,[6] Camisards,[7] or Cevenoles.[8]

The Cevenole prophets from the Cevennes Mountains of southern France were French Protestants, who "in the year 1688, . . . gave themselves out to be prophets, and inspired by the Holy Spirit."[9] The actions of the Cevenole prophets, under the inspiration of the Holy Spirit, were very much like those of the Shakers in similar circumstances. In 1689 the Cevenoles were even called "Trembleurs,"[10] a French equivalent of the English, "Shakers." The prophecies of the Cevenoles often warned of the approaching millennium and called for repentance, such as, "Amend your lives; repent ye; the end of all things draws nigh."[11] The Cevenoles took part in Protestant revolts against the 1685 revocation of the Edict of Nantes. The revolts were crushed, which caused some of the Cevenoles to flee to England in 1706.[12]

In England the Cevenoles continued their prophecies. Though the number of their listeners soon dwindled, partially because of unfulfilled prophecies, the Cevenole prophets retained a few followers and inspired a few English prophets. The English and Cevenole prophets became two

---

[6] Benjamin S. Youngs and Calvin Green, Testimony of Christ's Second Appearing: Exemplified by the Principles and Practice of the True Church of Christ (4th ed.; Albany, New York: C. Van Benthuysen, 1856), p. 354. First edition published in 1808 at New Lebanon; authors: David Darrow, John Meacham, and Benjamin S. Young.

[7] Andrews, op. cit., p. 5.   [8] Desroche, op. cit., p. 16.

[9] Youngs and Green, op. cit., p. 354.

[10] Desroche, op. cit., p. 23.

[11] Youngs and Green, op. cit., p. 355.

[12] Andrews, op. cit., p. 5.

separate groups. Unfortunately it is not known which group directly influenced the Wardley's in 1747.[13] Several of the Cevenole prophets traveled on the European continent from 1712-1714, during which time they are known to have inspired Johann Friedrick Rock and Eberhard Ludwig Gruber, the founders of a German Pietist sect, "The Community of True Inspiration."[14] Conrad Beissel, the founder of Ephrata Cloister, was later influenced by Rock and the Inspirationists.[15]

The Cevenoles and the later Shakers shared several characteristics; a belief in direct inspiration and its accompanying state of religious ecstasy, millennialism, the important role of women, a working class background, an anti-clerical attitude, and a belief in pacifism.[16] The Wardley society which Ann Lee had joined in 1758 also exemplified all of those characteristics.

During the first decade of her association with the Wardley society, Ann Lee was not a particularly active member, nor did she yet have the indomitable will which later gave her so much strength. She also did not yet have the strength of will to refuse to marry Abraham Standerin; a marriage which may have taken place at the insistence of her family. Within a few years of their marriage in 1762 the Standerin's

---

[13] Desroche, op. cit., p. 22.

[14] Donald F. Durnbaugh, "Work and Hope: The Spirituality of the Radical Pietist Communitarians," Church History, Vol. 39, No. 1, (March, 1970), p. 84.

[15] Lamech and Agrippa, Chronicon Ephratense: A History of the Community of Seventh Day Baptists at Ephrata, translated by J. Max Hark (Lancaster, Pennsylvania: S. H. Zahm & Co., 1889), pp. 9-11.

[16] Desroche, op. cit., pp. 23-27. Not all of the Cevenoles were pacifists.

had four children, three of whom died in infancy. The other child, a daughter, died before she reached the age of seven. Ann's previous views concerning sexual intercourse had not really changed before her marriage and the deaths of her children appear to have added to her convictions.[17]

By 1766, Ann began to be more active in the Wardley society. The Wardley society might have been practicing celibacy privately. With the more active presence of Ann Lee in the Wardley society there began a gradual change which led to the open condemnation of sexual intercourse and criticism of marriage.[18] Ann's personal conflict with her husband, who would not agree to be celibate, may have been a major reason why Ann led the Wardley to a public advocacy of continence.[19]

As the Wardley society turned toward a more public ministry, the society's meetings produced complaints and eventually the public demonstrations led to the arrests of some members of the Wardley society. During one of her stays in jail, Ann Lee received the vision which formed the central thesis of the Shaker faith. Though she had previously received visions which she communicated to the society, Ann Lee had been convinced "there was nothing in all their religious professions nor practices that could save them from sin."[20] In her jail cell in 1770, Ann Lee saw and felt the presence of Christ and was given a "clear view of the mystery of iniquity, of the root and foundation of human depravity . . . ."[21] Ann had previously condemned sexual intercourse as

---

[17]Andrews, op. cit., p. 8.   [18]Ibid., p. 9.
[19]Desroche, op. cit., pp. 47-49.
[20]Green and Wells, op. cit., pp. 14-15.
[21]Ibid., p. 15.

sinful; the vision confirmed that view and identified "the lustful gratifications of the flesh as the source and foundation of human corruption."[22] From that time on Ann testified to all who would hear "that no soul could follow Christ in the regeneration while living in the works of natural generation or in any gratifications of lust."[23]

Ann Lee also believed that God's plan for the redemption of mankind had been revealed to her by Christ. Before understanding the Shaker beliefs about that plan of redemption there must be a recognition of the Shaker belief that God and Christ were androgynous. The Shakers believed that Jesus was not the Christ, but was only a manifestation of the Father spirit in Christ. They also believed that no one could have been truly born-again until the spiritual parenthood of Christ had been completed with the manifestation of the Mother spirit in Christ. In her vision, the spirit of Christ was invested in Ann Lee and, thereafter, "she, being a female, revealed and manifested the <u>Mother Spirit</u> in Christ and in Deity."[24] After Ann's vision of 1770, because Christ had then been manifested in the female part as well as in the male part, the Shakers believed the Christ's second coming had occurred. As it had first begun individually in the heart and soul of Ann Lee, the Shakers believed the second appearing of Christ would continue to occur gradually in the heart of each individual believer.[25]

---

[22]Ibid., p. 16.   [23]Ibid.

[24]Frederick William Evans, <u>Shakers: Compendium of the Origin, History, Principles, Rules and Regulation, Government, and Doctrines of the United Society of Believers in Christ's Second Appearing</u> (New York: D. Appleton and Co., 1859), p. 109. Emphasis in the original.

[25]Desroche, op. cit., pp. 77-81.

Following Ann's testimony of her vision, she was acknowledged by the members of the Wardley society, "as their spiritual <u>Mother in Christ</u>."[26] The Wardley society's acceptance of the leadership of Ann Lee was not hindered by her femaleness; their previous leader had also been a woman, Jane Wardley. Shaker writers have considered Jane Wardley a female "John the Baptist" who had prepared the way for Christ's second appearing.[27]

During Ann's leadership, the Wardley society, which had already earned the epithet, "Shaking Quakers,"[28] carried on more public demonstrations of their faith. Sometimes aroused citizens subjected Ann Lee and her followers to violence. There were also more occasions of arrest, fines and jail for Ann Lee, but the society gained few new members. Failure to grow in England may have encouraged Ann's second most important vision which revealed to her that many people awaited her message in New England. Others in the group headed by Ann Lee also received such visions and the decision was made in 1774 to go to America.[29]

All of the members of the Wardley society were invited to go with Ann Lee to America, but only eight others joined her. Those who sailed to America with Ann Lee in May, 1774, included James Whittaker, who was to become Ann Lee's successor; John Hocknell, one of the two patrons of the Wardley society and the man whose money financed the trip to America; and Ann's husband, Abraham Standerin. The absence of the

---

[26]Green and Wells, op. cit., p. 13. Emphasis in the original.
[27]Ibid., p. 16.   [28]Andrews, op. cit., p. 6.
[29]Ibid., pp. 11-13.

Wardleys and other members of their society, including the parents of James Whittaker, from the group of Shakers that sailed to America might have been an indication of a doctrinal split between Ann Lee and the Wardleys.[30]

After landing in New York in August, 1774, the small band of Shakers went separate ways until some cheap land was purchased near Albany at which is now known as Watervliet. Ann and her husband remained in New York, while the others were building the small colony at Watervliet. In 1775, Abraham, no longer able to endure the strans of a celibate marriage, finally left Ann Lee. Ann joined the group at Watervliet the following spring in 1776. The land around the small Shaker settlement was desolate and relatively uninhabited, a circumstance which appeared to counter the predictions made in England that a large number of people were waiting for the Shakers in New England. Not until 1780, after several years of doubt intermixed with faithful waiting did the Shakers convert any significant number of people.[31]

During the summer of 1779 a "New Light" Baptist revival had swept the area around New Lebanon, New York, Hancok, Massachusetts, and other nearby towns. The summer of revival meetings was filled with religious ecstasy, visions, and prophecies of the impending millennium. However, the revival was followed by a period of disillusionment when the excitement was gone in the fall and when the long hard winter was endured without the expected appearance of Christ. In the spring of 1780, two men who had experienced the revival and disillusionment at

---

[30] Desroche, op. cit., pp. 29-30, 47-52.

[31] Andrews, op. cit., pp. 14-18.

New Lebanon were on their way west when they happened to find the small Shaker community. The Shaker doctrine of a second appearing of Christ which occurred not on a day of universal judgment, but in the heart of each believer accepting salvation, found ready listeners in the two men from New Lebanon. During the following summer, many of the "New Light" Baptists, including their leader at New Lebanon, Joseph Meacham, made their way to Watervliet where they were converted by the Shakers.[32]

The Shaker ministry to the "New Light" Baptists marked the public opening of the Shaker testimony in America. One unfortunate result was the imprisonment of all of the Shaker leaders because of their pacifist beliefs. The Revolutionary War had certainly made suspect the preaching of pacifism in America by former British inhabitants of England. Ann Lee was in jail from August to November of 1780 at Poughkeepsie, New York, until the Shakers finally came to be viewed as harmless to the Revolutionary cause. The imprisonment of the Shakers may have increased public knowledge of them and contributed to the many requests for preaching visits which the Shakers received from towns in Massachusetts and Connecticut.[33]

In response to the various requests for her appearance, Mother Ann, with several companions, including James Whittaker and William Lee (her brother), began a preaching tour in May, 1781, which did not end until September, 1783. During the preaching tour the Shaker missionaries often faced opposition from abusive mobs. James Whittaker was severely whipped by one mob and suffered fractured ribs after being pushed off his horse by another mob. Despite the abuse which was heaped on the Shaker

---

[32]Ibid., pp. 18-32.   [33]Ibid., pp. 32-34.

missionaries and their new converts, the preaching tour was very successful. The converts won on that tour became the foundations for all of the Shaker communities which developed in Massachusetts and Connecticut. Indirectly, that preaching tour was also responsible for the Shaker communities which developed in New Hampshire and Maine.[34]

Celibacy, millennialism, and separation from the world were very much a part of the Shaker message which had been carried throughout New England. The sharing of property was also a part of that message, though it was not as fully developed as were the other beliefs. James Whittaker appears to have been responsible for the first developments of property sharing as a doctrine among the Shakers. The first members at Watervliet had shared their property in common and Whittaker was active in urging other Shakers to do the same. Early in 1784, in a letter to England, Whittaker described the community at Watervliet as one which shared property and he said, they had "all things in common with others that have come in to us."[35] Though practiced by many of the members, communism was not yet a requirement for membership in the Shaker faith in 1784.

Ann Lee died in September, 1784, at the age of 48, contrary to the beliefs of some of her followers that Ann Lee would live for at least one thousand years. Ann, herself, had always rejected such beliefs. Following the funeral of their departed leader, the Shakers gave their allegiance to James Whittaker. As the leader of the Shakers Whittaker at first continued his missionary efforts, preaching the Shaker faith to the world. After about a year he decided to end the

---

[34]Ibid., pp. 35-44.   [35]Ibid., p. 49.

missionary efforts, withdraw the testimony from the world, and consolidate the Shaker faith among those who were already believers. A meeting house was built at New Lebanon which James Whittaker made the headquarters of the Shaker faith when he began serving there as the minister in January, 1786. During a trip to Shakers in Massachusetts in 1787, Whittaker fell ill from exhaustion and died in July of that year at the age of 33.[36]

Whittaker was succeeded by Joseph Meacham, the first non-English leader of the Shakers. Meacham appointed Lucy Wright to share the leadership position with him, thus reaffirming the Shaker beliefs in the importance of women and in the androgynous natures of God and Christ. Together, Joseph and Lucy issued a call in September, 1787, for all believers to separate themselves from the world and gather at New Lebanon. By Christmas of that year communism had become an official practice of the Shakers,[37] though it was not until 1792 that the whole church organization "was considered as established in the principles of her present order and spirit of government."[38]

BELIEFS AND PRACTICES

The Shaker belief in direct inspiration was fundamental to an acceptance of almost all of the Shaker beliefs which distinguished them from other Christian groups. Without an acceptance of direct inspiration, Ann Lee's vision of sexual intercourse as the cause of human depravity

---

[36] Ibid., pp. 49-53.
[37] Ibid., pp. 54-57.
[38] Green and Wells, op. cit., p. 59.

becomes only a hypothesis, and the belief that Ann Lee had manifested the "Mother Spirit in Christ . . . ,"[39] thus beginning the millennium, would become only a delusion.

Since man is of the natural world, not of the spiritual world, the Shakers believed "nothing can be known of the true God, nor of his Divine nature, . . . except by Divine Revelation."[40] The Shakers were aware that others pointed to the Bible as containing all of the revelations of God sufficient for the salvation of mankind. The Shakers considered the Bible alone to be woefully inadequate for salvation because:

> Our own enlightened country gives ample and sorrowful evidence that the word of the scriptures, is so far from administering the power of eternal life to those even who study it, that it is actually wrested by them to justify slavery, war and bloodshed, with all their attendant vices.[41]

The Shakers also gave an explanation for the inadequacy of the scriptures, saying, "the scriptures cannot be truly understood, except by inspiration of the Spirit that gave them."[42]

In defense of their position on direct inspiration, the Shakers pointed to the absence of any instructions from Christ that his teachings should be collected in a book which would be sufficient for the salvation

---

[39] Evans, op. cit., p. 109.

[40] Green and Wells, op. cit., p. 231.

[41] William Leonard, A Discourse on the Order and Propriety of Divine Inspiration and Revelation; A Discourse on the Second Appearing of Christ; A Discourse on the Propriety and Necessity of a United Inheritance (Harvard, Massachussetts: United Society, 1853), p. 35.

[42] Green and Wells, op. cit., p. 234.

of others. Neither did the Apostles leave such instructions regarding their writings, and they did not declare divine revelation was at an end. Shakers cited John 14:21 in which Jesus said, "he that loveth me shall be loved of my Father, and I will love him and will manifest myself to him;" and also, in John 14:23, Jesus said, "my Father will love him, and we will come to him, and make our abode with him." From those lines the Shakers reasoned that the promised manifestation meant divine revelation and that each believer would be divinely inspired if the Father and Christ would abide in him.[43]

From the evidence given in John Chapter 14, the Shakers believed it was clear that those who professed to be Christian and yet denied any direct inspiration or revelation in their lives thereby declared they were not of Christ. The Shakers also believed Christ "would manifest himself to them . . ." who were true believers in Christ because "he has given a sure promise."[44] Thus, the Shakers moved beyond simply believing that direct inspiration still occurred to a position, like that of the Labadists, that made the receipt of direct inspiration almost a requirement for membership in the Shaker faith. The belief that true believers could be identified by knowing whether they received direct inspiration is evident in the following passage from A Summary View of the Millennial Church:

> Thus all who sincerely desire it, and are willing to sacrifice all to do the will of God, may obtain the revelation of the Divine Spirit. But those who cannot open the door into the kingdom of Heaven for the true seeker, are not the true ministers of Christ, and by their want of this divine power, they are known to every true believer.[45]

---

[43]Leonard, op. cit., pp. 29-32. [44]Ibid., pp. 30-31.

[45]Green and Wells, op. cit., p. 237.

One example of the Shaker belief in living by the inspiration of the Spirit was their attitude toward the rules which governed their lives. The rules or "orders" began as verbal pronouncements from Joseph Meacham and Lucy Wright. During their lifetimes, the orders were not distributed in a written form. After the death of Lucy Wright, a few copies of the orders were distributed and are now known as "The Millennial Laws of 1821."[46] Only the Elders and Elderesses of each family had copies. So that the members would know the spirit of the law, the Elders occasionally read from their copies of the orders in the meetings of each family. Written copies were not given to each member because it was believed written orders would encourage the members to live by the letter of the law rather than by the spirit of the law.[47]

Divine inspiration, through the vision Ann Lee received in 1770 was believed by the Shakers to have been the basis of their beliefs about the nature of God and man, the millennium, and celibacy. Along with their common origin in the vision given to Ann Lee, all Shaker beliefs about all three of those issues were inter-connected.

The Shaker belief about the nature of God was expressed in the following statement: "an all important, sublime and foundational doctrine of the Shakers is the existence of an Eternal Father and an Eternal Mother in Deity . . . ."[48] God was androgynous and the created universe of male and female, positive and negative, the kingdoms animal

---

[46]Andrews, op. cit., p. 244.

[47]Ibid., pp. 243-248.

[48]Evans, op. cit., p. 103.

and vegetable, and things natural and spiritual all clearly manifested "the two incomprehensible beings of one spirit and one substance . . . ."[49] As evidence that God was both male and female in one, the Shakers cited Genesis 2:27 which said, "So God created man in his own image, in the image of God created he him; male and female created he them."

Created male and female in the image of God, Adam and Eve were set over the natural world to govern that world. Within the natural world, according to the Shakers, generation or procreation occurred only as it fit the laws and seasons of nature; man was also to "propagate his species according to the law of nature."[50] Since they were to govern the natural world, Adam and Eve were given a higher law than that of nature as a test of their ability to govern themselves. Adam and Eve were given control of their animal propensities along with a higher, stricter law than the law of nature. They were to propagate only "under the sanction of Divine Authority, according to the times and season's of God's appointment, as well as in strict conformity to the law of nature."[51]

The Shakers believed the fall of man into sinfulness occurred when Adam and Eve, after listening to the insinuations of the serpent, violated the special law given to them as well as the law of nature. As a result, man lost his special position of dominance over nature and was even set below nature. To the Shakers, the fact that man was the only creature which propagates at any time without regard for the seasons

---

[49] Leonard, op. cit., p. 53.

[50] Green and Wells, op. cit., p. 155.

[51] Ibid., p. 134.

was clear evidence that man had fallen so far as to be no longer "governed by the law of God, nor regulated by the law of nature . . . ."[52]

The Shakers did not believe that the descendants of Adam and Eve were born with sin. Each individual was believed to be born not with the sin of mankind's first parents but with their propensities and inclinations which lead to sin. Had Adam and Eve not sinned, that would not have saved mankind from sin forever; because, according to the Shakers, each of their offspring would also have been tested and might have sinned.[53]

The remedy for the fall of man has been revealed in stages. Just as the natural world was not made all at once, so the spiritual world has progressed through various dispensations in which God has slowly revealed Himself to man. The Shakers also believed that as God has revealed more of himself and brought man closer to spiritual union with him, the requirements made of man have correspondingly increased.[54]

The Shakers believed there had been four major periods covered by individual dispensations: (1) the Antediluvian period with mankind under the law of nature; (2) the Hebrew period with mankind under revealed law such as the Ten Commandments; (3) the first Christian period with the manifestation of Christ in the male line and the presence of the Spirit by which man is to live by direct revelation; (4) the second Christian period with the manifestation of Christ in the female line and the beginning of spiritual rebirth and the millennium.[55]

The first two periods or dispensations had been concerned with raising mankind up within his state of nature. The third period marked

---

[52] Ibid., pp. 155-156.
[53] Ibid., pp. 139-140.
[54] Ibid., p. 185.
[55] Ibid., pp. 223-230.

the dividing line between the works of nature (works of the flesh) and the works of grace (works of the Spirit).[56] The Shakers believed the third and fourth dispensations made possible the redemption of mankind, through Christ, out of the natural order into the spiritual order.[57]

Before continuing with the Shaker beliefs about the way the redemption of mankind took place, the Shaker view of Christ should be considered. "Christ was a created Being, who was commissioned from a world nearer to God than is this world, and more spiritual . . . to effect the redemption and resurrection of the human race."[58] Christ, like God, was an androgynous being; therefore, Jesus was not the Christ, but only the manifestation of Christ in the male line. The Shakers believed Christ's second coming had manifested the female line through the person of Ann Lee in her vision in 1770.[59]

In Jesus the death and resurrection of the male manifestation of Christ signified the triumph of the spiritual world over the natural world and the beginning of the rebirth of man into the spiritual world. However, that rebirth of man into the spiritual world could not take place until the second coming of Christ. Man could not be reborn until Christ also had been manifested in the female line. As man's first natural parents were created male and female in the image of God, so also man's first spiritual parents, the Shakers believed, must be male and female in the image of God.

---

[56]Ibid., p. 225.

[57]Leonard, op. cit., pp. 58-59.

[58]Ibid.

[59]Green and Wells, op. cit., pp. 15-16; see also Evans, op. cit., p. 109.

The spiritual state of man, which is substantial and eternal, cannot be less perfect in its order, than his natural state, which is but temporal, and figurative of the spiritual.[60]

Therefore, Christ, who had come the first time in the male line, had to come the second time in the female line. Jesus and Ann Lee were regarded as the first man and woman "redeemed from the earth."[61] As manifestations of the male and female elements in Christ, Jesus and Ann became the Spiritual parents of those who would be redeemed and reborn into the spiritual world.[62] Ann Lee did not believe herself to be the Christ, but only the first person in whom Christ dwelt in his second coming.[63] Her spiritual parenthood was not such that others were reborn through her but rather by her example.

The second coming of Christ on earth had been fulfilled in Ann Lee and continued to be fulfilled throughout the world as others were reborn and infused with the spirit of Christ. With Ann Lee's vision in 1770, the views of the Wardley society that the second coming would soon occur were changed into a realization that the second coming had already happened.[64] The Shakers did not believe that Christ had appeared throughout the whole world at once, but that Christ appeared

---

[60] Green and Wells, op. cit., p. 261.

[61] Leonard, op. cit., p. 59.

[62] Ibid., p. 62.

[63] Theodore E. Johnson, Life in the Christ Spirit: Observations on Shaker Theology (Sabbathday Lake, Maine: United Society, 1969), p. 7.

[64] Evans, op. cit., p. 109.

throughout the world gradually as each true believer accepted the Spirit of Christ.[65]

Part of the importance to the Shakers of their millennial views was demonstrated in the two names by which the Shakers were known to themselves. Their official name was "The United Society of Believers in Christ's Second Appearing."[66] They also called themselves "The Millennial Church."[67]

The Shaker belief that the millennium had already begun was an important aspect of their way of life. The presence of the redemptive Spirit of Christ in each true believer was believed to have made possible a way of life which was free from sin. "Wherever the Spirit of holiness operates, it must effectually exclude sin . . . , for they cannot dwell together."[68] Writing about the workings of Christ in his life, James Whittaker declared, "A death to the man of sin have I found."[69] It was not a belief that ordinary human beings could live without sin. Nor was it a belief that extraordinary human beings could live without sin in ordinary times. Rather, the Shakers believed that

---

[65] Joseph Meacham, <u>A Concise Statement of the Principles of the Only True Church According to the Gospel of the Present Appearance of Christ: As Held to and Practiced Upon by the True Followers of the Living Saviour, at New Lebanon. Together With a Letter From James Whittaker, Minister of the Gospel in this day of Christ's Second Appearing--to his Natural Relations in England</u> (Sabbathday Lake, Maine: The United Society, 1963), pp. 10-11. Reprinted from the 1790 edition.

[66] Evans, op. cit., frontspiece, from the title.

[67] Green and Wells, op. cit., frontspiece, from the title.

[68] Ibid., p. 109.

[69] Meacham, op. cit., p. 12.

those who were saved according to the requirements of the fourth dispensation, the second appearing of Christ, could live free of sin.[70]

To have a life free from sin the true believer, though many other practices were also required, had to live a life without sexual intercourse. The gratification of lust and sexual intercourse were believed to be "the source and foundation of human corruption."[71] After her vision in 1770, Ann Lee had pointedly testified "that no soul could follow Christ in the regeneration while living in the works of natural generation or in any of the gratifications of lust."[72] Ann Lee's testimony formed the basis for the Shaker practice of celibacy as a membership requirement in their church.

According to the rules by which Shakers lived, "the gospel of Christ's second appearing strictly forbids all private union between the two sexes;" and, "One Brother and one Sister must not be together alone."[73] Shaker brothers and sisters worshipped together at the same meetings and met together in conversational groups, but most of their way of life exemplified monastic separation of the sexes. The brothers and sisters ate at separate tables, were seated on separate sides of the worship hall, worked in separate areas, and slept in separate rooms, often at opposite ends of the same building. Within the structure of the Shaker family, each sex functioned as a separate order. As much as possible those orders, though separate, were equal.[74]

---

[70] Nordhoff, op. cit., p. 134.

[71] Green and Wells, op. cit., p. 16.   [72] Ibid.

[73] Theodore E. Johnson (ed.), "The Millenial Laws of 1821," *The Shaker Quarterly*, VII, No. 2 (Summer, 1967), p. 49.

[74] Andrews, op. cit., pp. 177-178.

Celibacy, or the "virgin life," was one of the seven moral principles which contained "the practical and external law of life for the direction and government of Christ's followers . . . ."[75] The seven principles were duty to God, duty to man, separation from the world, practical peace, simplicity of language, right use of property, and a virgin life. Those principles were believed to be the same as the ones followed by the first Christian church.[76]

The Shaker attitude toward the practice of communism which they considered the only right use of property, was influenced by the example of the first Christian church. Yet, that practice was not a firmly established policy of the Shakers until 1787; therefore, its adoption as a membership requirement may have been the result of practical needs rather than the result of apostolic influence. An oral covenant pledging each member to share all property in "joint-interest" was agreed to in 1788, then written and signed in 1795. Within the preface to the written covenant of 1795 was a statement which gave the purpose for sharing all property in common:

> It then was, and still is our faith, being confirmed by our experience, that there can be no Church in complete order according to the law of Christ, without a joint-interest and union, in which all members have an equal right and privilege according to their calling and needs, in things spiritual and temporal.[77]

Another of the Shaker beliefs which separated them from much of Christianity was their attitude toward sacraments. True to the Quaker

---

[75] Green and Wells, op. cit., p. 307.

[76] Ibid., p. 307-333.

[77] Desroche, op. cit., p. 201. The 1795 covenant is reprinted in full, pp. 201-202.

heritage which Ann Lee had learned in the Wardley society, the Shakers did not practice special sacramental ceremonies. Yet, they did not consider themselves antisacramental, but rather suprasacramental. Shakers very definitely believed in the baptism of the Spirit. For them, baptism by water held no meaning, but the baptism of the Spirit was considered absolutely necessary for the true believer. The eucharist was also considered a sacrament by the Shakers, though they had no special ceremonies for its celebration. The Shakers believed that each meal they ate in common as a community of true believers marked an observance of the eucharist.[78]

As part of one of the seven moral principles, the simplicity of language, the Shakers prohibited oaths, titles, and anything which was done simply for ceremony.[79] On those issues, the Shakers were again following, or in line with, Ann Lee's Quaker background. One important Shaker practice that may have degenerated into meaningless ceremony was the Shaker dance. The dances were first begun as the involuntary actions of someone under the direct influence of the Spirit. As early as 1785 there was some ritualized dancing, and in later years, as dances were constantly practiced before being performed, they lost almost all spontaneity. The performance of the dances in the Sunday worship services, usually before an audience of outsiders, presented a spectacle much more like that of a well ordered drill team than that of believers operating under the influence of the Spirit.[80]

---

[78]Johnson, Life., pp. 7-8.

[79]Green and Wells, op. cit., pp. 320-325.

[80]Andrews, op. cit., pp. 140-141, 149.

Even in the beginning when faith in the operations of the Spirit may have been higher, the Shakers did not expect that everyone who tried to would really be able to continually live under the influence of the Spirit. Though the Shakers sincerely believed that "wherever the Spirit of holiness operates, it must effectually exclude sin . . . ,"[81] they apparently were not sure the Spirit would always be present because the required confession of sin was one of the early Shaker practices. The practice of confessing sins appears to have begun as part of the conversion process because prospective members in 1780 were asked to confess their sins to God before joining the Shakers.[82] The confession of sins continued to be such an important requirement among the Shakers that orders regarding that practice formed the first chapter in the 1821 "Millennial Laws." Not only was each member required to confess his sins to his superior, but also anyone who discovered the sin of another and had reason to believe that sin would not be confessed was required "to reveal it to the Elders so that sin may be put away."[83]

The second chapter of the 1821 "Millennial Laws" concerned worship services and orders regarding the Sabbath. Worship in some way was made a part of each believer's life every day, and on Sunday the whole day was devoted to worship among the Shakers. Certain kinds of activities were forbidden for the Shakers on Sunday. Shakers were not allowed to cut hair, read newspapers, polish shoes, or gather fruit and vegetables on the Sabbath.[84] In each case, the purpose of the regulation

---

[81] Green and Wells, op. cit., p. 109.

[82] Andrews, op. cit., p. 25.

[83] Johnson, Laws, op. cit., p. 47.

[84] Ibid., pp. 47-48.

was to avoid profaning the Sabbath and to maintain due respect. The Shaker's reverence for worship and their sense of order was illustrated in the "Millennial Laws" by the following rule: "No one is allowed to wear ragged or very dirty clothes into worship of God at any time."[85]

The principle of pacifism was not a part of the "Millennial Laws," but the Shakers were definitely pacifists like their Quaker and Cevenole predecessors. Shakers believed pacifisim had been one of the principles of the first Christian church,[86] and they have adhered to the principle of pacifism throughout their entire existence. During the War of 1812, the Shakers were required by the State of New York to pay an annual fine or to face conscription. The fines were paid until early in 1815 when it was decided that payment of the fines constituted indirect support of the war. In 1816 the Shakers of New York were exempted from military service by the legislature. As the events of history changed the military situations of various states the legislatures continued to legally change the status of the Shakers, but the Shakers themselves held on to the principles of peace and avoided military service. The Shakers also contributed pamphlets and some other support to peace movements. Those pamphlets were an indication of the importance to the Shakers of their pacifist principles, because the pamphlets represented the first Shaker involvement in the affairs of the world.[87]

---

[85] Ibid., p. 48.

[86] Charles Nordhoff, The Communistic Societies of the United States (2d ed.; New York: Dover Publications, Inc., 1966), p. 133. First published in New York: Harper and Brothers, 1875.

[87] Andrews, op. cit., pp. 214-217.

The separation of believers from the world of nonbelievers was one of the most important principles of the Shakers. They believed it had been a principle in the first Christian church,[88] and they identified it as one of their own seven moral principles. The Shakers believed they were separating themselves from a sinful world and joining the true church of Christ. The principle of separation from the world took place not only in regard to the believer's relations with the outside physical world, but also in regard to the natural world inside the believer. The self-denial of celibacy and of sharing all property in common was as much a part of separation from the world as were the rules against going out into the world. The acceptance of salvation and the influence of the Spirit in the life of each Shaker required a rejection and separation from the natural world.[89]

Total separation of Shakers from the world would not have been an economical policy, nor did the Shakers follow such a policy. Like most of the other celibate communal societies, the Shakers affected a compromise. Wherever possible, they maintained the separation of each believer from the world, but the society as a whole participated in the outside economic world.

As a young and vigorous society still gaining in membership, the Shakers were economically quite successful. Their products were widely sold because of their reputation for honesty, very high standards of workmanship, and quality goods. The Shakers made many inventions and improvements which helped to sell their products and to make the

---

[88] Nordhoff, op. cit., p. 133.

[89] Green and Wells, op. cit., pp. 58, 109, 307, 315-320.

production of those products more economical.[90] During the society's later years, the competition from more modern manufacturing concerns in the outside world created important problems which the Shakers did not have the resources to solve.[91]

The principle of separation from the world served to keep the Shaker society from involvement in reform movements as a general practice. Had they been involved in the world, the Shakers might have been in the forefront of the abolitionist movement because opposition to slavery had been part of the Shaker movement from the beginning. Negroes were welcomed as members of the society. There were two Shaker families whose members were all Negro; but in most cases, Negroes became members of existing families without regard for their race.[92]

In the world outside the Shaker Society, there were other similar Pietist societies that had beliefs and practices similar to the Shakers. In 1850, a plan for uniting the Shakers with the Harmony Society and with the Separatists of Zoar was briefly considered in all three societies.[93] Religious differences stood in the way of any mergers, but the proposal and its consideration in each of the three societies was a strong indication that each society had a great deal of respect for the pious life of the other two communities.

---

[90] John S. Williams, *Consecrated Ingenuity: The Shakers and Their Inventions* (Old Chatham, New York: The Chatham Courier Co., 1957), pp. 1-10.

[91] Andrews, op. cit., p. 228.

[92] Ibid., p. 21.

[93] Desroche, op. cit., p. 261.

Another celibate communal society for which the Shakers apparently had a large amount of respect was that of Ephrata Cloister. The Shakers believed that there had been many manifestations of the Holy Spirit before the second appearing of Christ. The following description of such manifestations among the "Dunkers" actually refers to Ephrata Cloister:

> But the purest descendants, and present remains of the ancient witnesses, are the people called Dunkers; some among this people, in a great degree, retain the uprightness, and simplicity of their predecessors.[94]

The Dunkers had originally practiced celibacy and the communal ownership of property; therefore, mention of those people that retained the qualities of their predecessors must have referred to the only Dunker group which still retained celibacy and communism when those lines were written in 1808. The only group with a Dunker heritage which fit that description was Conrad Beissel's Ephrata Cloister.[95]

As mentioned before, the Cevenole prophets to which the Shakers trace the foundation of their belief in direct inspiration were indirectly the source of a similar belief in direct inspiration in Ephrata Cloister. The Cevenole prophets had influenced the "Community of True Inspiration,"[96] which had in turn influenced the founder of Ephrata Cloister, Conrad Beissel.[97] Though the Shakers were not directly connected to Ephrata Cloister, it is significant that the belief in direct inspiration in both societies can be traced to the same source.

---

[94] Youngs and Green, op. cit., p. 355.

[95] Desroche, op. cit., p. 258.

[96] Durnbaugh, op. cit., p. 84.

[97] Lamech and Agrippa, op. cit., pp. 10-11.

Sometime in the 1790's or just after the turn of the century, one of the Shaker Elders visited in Philadelphia the descendants of the "Woman in the Wilderness." Later, the Elder described favorably the celibate and communal life of that mystic community. The "Woman in the Wilderness" was considered part of the "cloud of witnesses" which had preceded the Shakers and which had all testified that the second appearing of Christ would soon occur.[98]

The Shakers were not influenced in their development by the celibate communal societies mentioned above. Yet, the high regard which the Shakers had for those societies, particularly when compared with the Shaker view of the world at large, was evidence of some unity of belief which the Shakers shared with those societies.

GENERAL HISTORY AND DECLINE

The Shaker Society reached its largest growth shortly before the Civil War. Since that time the society has been in decline; though it still has a few members, the eventual demise of the society may come soon.

In his chapter on the decline of the Shakers, Edward Deming Andrews first discussed the reasons for the success of the Shakers. As factors which enabled the Shakers to be so successful, Andrews included inspiring religious principles, revivalism in the society and in the world, the binding nature of a communal organization, sexual controls, economic success, and the society's function as a sanctuary. Andrews regarded economic factors as very important in the decline of the society,

---

[98]Desroche, op. cit., pp. 64-66.

although he also blamed part of the failure of the society on the retention of beliefs which hindered the acquisition of new members.[99]

In many ways, as Andrews indicated, the Shakers declined because they had been suited for a different age;[100] success in any age is dependent upon adaptation to that age. As a certain religious, social, and economic level of society had provided the Shakers with members and with markets, so the emergence of a different religious, social, and economic level of society put the Shakers in a situation where they had to change or decline. Some changes occurred, but the Shakers held on to their faith, their requirements for membership, and their beliefs that had been so inspiring and fulfilling. It should be noted that for those who retained their Shaker faith, there was no failure of Shakerism. If Shakerism has failed, the failure has not come in the lives of the members, but in the inability of Shakerism to gain more members.

---

[99] Andrews, op. cit., pp. 224-238.
[100] Ibid., p. 228.

Chapter 7

THE SOCIETY OF UNIVERSAL FRIENDS

INTRODUCTION

Several important similarities between the Shaker Society and the Society of Universal Friends have led some historians to believe one of the societies influenced the development of the other. In 1951, Mark Holloway suggested that the Shaker Society had been consciously imitated by the founder of the Universal Friends.[1] Nearly 100 years earlier in 1853, A. J. MacDonald had suggested just the reverse, that former members of the Universal Friends had influenced the Shakers.[2] As the previous chapter has demonstrated that MacDonald's hypothesis was wrong, this chapter will demonstrate that Holloway's hypothesis was also wrong.

The founder of the Society of Universal Friends was Jemima Wilkinson, a former Quaker who began calling herself the "Public Universal Friend," following a mystical experience in 1776. The Universal Friend became an itinerant preacheress; preaching repentance and the immanence of the millennium. She traveled in Rhode Island, Massachusetts,

---

[1] Mark Holloway, Heavens on Earth (New York: Dover Publications, Inc., 1951), p. 59.

[2] Desroche, Henri, The American Shakers: From Neo-Christianity to Presocialism (Amherst, Massachusetts: University of Massachusetts Press, 1971), p. 69. Desroche cites A. J. MacDonald's manuscript which is in the Yale University Library.

Connecticut, and Pennsylvania, acquiring followers wherever she went. In an attempt to bring her scattered followers together and fulfill her belief in separation from the world, the Universal Friend decided to begin a new community where only her followers would live. The first settlement of the Society of Universal Friends was begun in 1788 near Seneca Lake in western New York, but internal dissension in the society caused the disintegration of that community in 1794. The Universal Friend and her loyal followers then moved about a dozen miles west to Keuka Lake where they established their second and final community, Jerusalem. After leading her community for more than 30 years, the Universal Friend died in 1819, leaving behind a religious society which continued to exist until 1863.[3]

Unlike each of the other societies in this study, immigrants to America did not play an important role in the founding or the development of the Society of Universal Friends. The movement began in Rhode Island where Jemima Wilkinson had been raised as a Quaker before she joined a group of "New Light" Baptists. Though many of her followers were from other states, most of them had also been members of either the Quakers or the "New Light" Baptists.[4]

Unfortunately, the number of people in various states who regarded themselves as members of the Society of Universal Friends before the move was made to western New York is not known. Some of the previous members were not willing to face the hardships of pioneer life. However,

---

[3] Herbert A. Wisbey Jr., *Pioneer Prophetess: Jemima Wilkinson, The Public Universal Friend* (Ithaca, New York: Cornell University Press, 1964), pp. 1-20, 163, 168.

[4] Ibid., pp. 8, 77-96.

according to census figures, there were 260 people at the settlement of the Universal Friends in 1790. Apparently, most of the people who had followed the Universal Friend to Seneca Lake also followed her to the new settlement of Jerusalem in 1794. The Society of Universal Friends was slowly declining even before the death of the Universal Friend and none of the new leaders were able to change that trend. The last known member of the society died in 1874.[5]

DEVELOPMENT BEFORE FOUNDING

The Wilkinson family had been in America for three generations before the birth of Jemima Wilkinson on November 29, 1752. Born near Cumberland in northeastern Rhode Island, Jemima was the eighth child of a Quaker family which included twelve children before her mother died when Jemima was 13. Along with the *Bible*, Jemima read works by Quaker authors such as George Fox, William Penn, and Roger Barclay. Early in 1776, Jemima became interested in and joined a group of "New Light" Baptists; as a result, she was disowned by the Quaker meeting to which she and her family had belonged. During the same year, one of Jemima's sisters and two of her brothers were also disowned by the Quaker meeting. The brothers were disowned for their participation in military training, which they undertook on the American side in the Revolutionary War.[6]

In October, 1776, Jemima Wilkinson fell ill, with what might have been typhus. After passing the most critical period of the illness, Jemima awoke with a proclamation that the person known as Jemima Wilkinson

---

[5]Ibid., pp. 111, 168.

[6]Ibid., pp. 8-9.

had died, that a Spirit sent from God had entered her body for the purpose of preaching repentance and to warn people of the coming of God's Kingdom. The supposed Spirit was called the, "Public Universal Friend." From that time on the person calling herself the "Universal Friend," considered Jemima Wilkinson to be dead. Soon after Jemima's supposed death and transformation into a Spirit sent from God, she began public preaching near her home.[7]

For the first two years of her ministry, the parental home of the Universal Friend remained her headquarters. In the fall of 1778, a plan was made to go to England to preach there. The Universal Friend received permission to pass through the American lines in British-held Newport, Rhode Island, but the British would not allow her to go to England. After preaching for a while in Newport, the Universal Friend went to the South Kingstown area where she met and converted Judge William Potter and his family. From the fall of 1779 until the fall of 1787, the home of Judge Potter was the headquarters for the activities of the Universal Friend. During those years, the preaching tours of the Universal Friend extended into southern Connecticut, Rhode Island, southeastern Massachusetts, and eastern Pennsylvania.[8]

While attracting followers, the preaching of the Universal Friend, which emphasized repentance and the approach of the millennium, also aroused opposition. The Universal Friend's claim to be the embodiment of a divine Spirit and her accusations that most people were leading sin-filled lives aroused against her the same kind of jeering

---

[7]Holloway, op. cit., pp. 59-60.

[8]Wisbey, op. cit., pp. 39-53.

laughter, angry shouts, and violence which had also been experienced by Ann Lee, the Shaker counterpart of the Universal Friend. In 1784, during her second visit to Philadelphia, the Universal Friend encountered her strongest opposition,[9] a factor which may have contributed to her decision in 1785 to separate her followers from the world by founding a new community.

In the fall of 1785, the Universal Friend sent her brother, Jeptha, to explore what is now Yates County, New York. After Jeptha's return in the spring of 1786, the decision was made to establish a community for the Society of Universal Friends in the Yates area. The exploring party, which was sent out in 1787 to pick the exact site, was followed in 1788 by the first of the Universal Friends who settled there. The leader of the society began her journey to the new community in the spring of 1789, but she almost drowned in a carriage accident while crossing a swollen creek. Although the Universal Friend had not been injured, she did not attempt the journey again until 1790 when she was successful in reaching her followers on the banks of Seneca Lake.[10]

BELIEFS AND PRACTICES

The only published material written by the Universal Friend was a small pamphlet which was printed in Philadelphia in 1784. The pamphlet was entitled, The Universal Friend's Advice, To Those of the Same Religious Society, and was intended for the use of her scattered followers when the

---

[9] Everett Webber, Escape to Utopia (New York: Corinth Books, 1959), pp. 80-81.

[10] Wisbey, op. cit., pp. 106-109.

150

Universal Friend was not present. The pamphlet was also advertised and sold to the public in Philadelphia in November, 1784. Unfortunately, the pamphlet was only eight pages in length and did not contain all of the society's beliefs.[11]

The most glaring omission from the Advice was the lack of any statements or claims regarding the special mission or person of the Universal Friend. Though some of her followers claimed the Universal Friend was the embodiment of the second coming of Christ, she never actually supported those claims or disowned them. Jemima Wilkinson had claimed that a Spirit sent from God had entered her body to preach repentance and to declare that the millennium was at hand. Whatever the Universal Friend said was, therefore, to be considered as direct revelation. The Universal Friend did not limit the principle of direct inspiration to herself. In the Advice she cautioned:

> Those whose mouths have been opened to speak, or to pray in public, are to wait for the movings of the HOLY SPIRIT, and then, speak or pray as the SPIRIT giveth utterance.[12]

Other sections of the Advice clearly express the principle that the Holy Spirit would abide in and inspire each true believer.

One of the messages with which the Universal Friend had supposedly been sent to inspire the world was an announcement that the millennium was about to begin. At the end of the Advice were the statements: "THE time is fulfilled--the kingdom of GOD is at hand.

---

[11] Ibid., pp. 87-88, 197-204. The entire contents of the pamphlet were reprinted on pages 197-204. The printer and other publishing data is not known.

[12] Ibid., p. 201. Emphasis in the original.

Repent ye, and believe the Gospel, that the kingdom of GOD may begin within you."[13] It is understandable that the statement of the Universal Friend claiming the time was fulfilled might have induced some people to believe she had claimed to be Christ. What the Universal Friend actually meant by that statement is not known. The second statement of the above quote indicates the Universal Friend may have believed the second coming of Christ gradually occurred as each individual accepted the Holy Spirit into his life.

In order that the kingdom of God might begin within her followers, the Universal Friend instructed them to take up their daily cross "against all ungodliness and worldly lusts."[14] She also admonished her followers to turn their attention not to the flesh but to the Spirit. Quoting from Romans 8:6, the Advice stated: "For to be carnally minded is death, but to be spiritually minded is life and peace."[15] That quote is the strongest statement in the Advice which might be interpreted as advocating celibacy. Marriage was not condemned by the Universal Friend, though she is known to have practiced and advocated celibacy.[16]

How many or what percentage of the Universal Friends practiced celibacy is not known. It is believed there were about 16 women living in the household of the Universal Friend at Jerusalem who practiced celibacy, though not all of the celibate women in the society resided in the house of the Universal Friend. There were also single men in the

---

[13]Ibid., p. 204. Emphasis in the original.

[14]Ibid., p. 198.

[15]Ibid., p. 200.

[16]Ibid., p. 66-67; see also Holloway, op. cit., p. 61.

society who practiced celibacy. Although it is believed that most of the society's members were married couples who did not practice celibacy there may have been some married couples who were celibate.[17]

    Communism was also not practiced by most of the society's members, nor is it clear whether the Universal Friend actually advocated communism for all of her followers. For the members who did practice communism the communal aspects of the Society of Universal Friends were not organized like those of any of the other societies in this study. In five of the other societies, communism was practiced by all church members; therefore, the name of those societies refers both to the church and to the communal organization. Only a portion of the church members associated with Ephrata Cloister or with the Universal Friends practiced communism. The name, "Ephrata Cloister," referred to a communal organization which was part of the church of the Seventh-Day German Baptists. The name, "Society of Universal Friends," referred to the whole church organization. Because of their particular practice of communism the Universal Friends did not have a separate communal organization and, therefore, did not have a name for such an organization.

    The communism practiced by the Universal Friends might be better described as the communal *use* of property rather than the communal *ownership* of property. There were three types of land use among the Universal Friends: some of the society's members owned and farmed their own land; some of the members farmed private portions of the land of the Universal Friend without paying rent, though they were farming for themselves; the third group consisted of members of the Universal Friend's

---

[17] Wisbey, op. cit., p. 68; see also Webber, op. cit., pp. 82-83.

household who farmed part of the land of the Universal Friend for the benefit of her household. Whenever extra help was needed for farming the land for the benefit of the household, those who helped were paid. The Universal Friend did not sell all and give to the poor, but she did give the use of what she had to the poor. Perhaps it should be noted that the property, which the Universal Friend freely allowed others to use, had been purchased by money which had been given to her by members of her society. The *Advice* of the Universal Friend did not contain any advocacy of communism, which may be explained by the fact that the first known mention of the Universal Friend's desire to gather her followers and build a new community occurred in 1785, a few months after the publication of the *Advice*.[18]

The *Advice*, also, did not mention the attitude of the Universal Friend toward the sacraments, which may have been because she and her followers did not observe any sacraments. The attitude of the Universal Friend toward the sacraments was part of an anti-ceremonial attitude and probably was the result of her early Quaker training. In her *Advice*, the Universal Friend had instructed her followers to "use plainness of speech and apparel, and let your adoring, not be outward, but inward . . . ."[19] Observance of the sacraments would probably have been regarded as showing a concern for outward adornments. The aversion to ceremony also kept the Universal Friends from giving oaths or vows. Confession was not mentioned in any of the sources and, presumably, was not practiced by the Universal Friends.

---

[18] Webber, op. cit., p. 82; see also Wisbey, op. cit., pp. 120-126.
[19] Wisbey, op. cit., p. 199.

One of the practices which set the Universal Friends apart from the Quakers was the observance of the Sabbath on the seventh-day. Since there are no accounts of the members of the society being arrested for violating the normal Sunday Sabbath, it can be assumed that the society observed Sunday as a day of rest, even though their main worship service was on Saturday. The change to the seventh-day Sabbath did not occur among the Universal Friends until after their leader had visited Philadelphia in 1782.[20] The exact reasons for the change are not known, though the Universal Friend may have come in contact with advocates of the seventh-day Sabbath during her visit in Philadelphia.

Following her Quaker heritage, the Universal Friend had been an advocate of pacifism and an opponent of war since the beginning of her ministry. In contrast to the treatment given the Shakers, the advocacy of pacifism did not cause any legal problems for the Universal Friends. The American background of the Universal Friends may have safeguarded them from the suspicions which surrounded the formerly English Shakers. There were also many supporters of the Universal Friend who were known as supporters of the American rebellion, including the two oldest brothers of the Universal Friend.[21]

The pacifism of the Universal Friends may have been a part of their principle of separation from the world. When the Universal Friend first began her ministry the principle of separation from the world was an inherent part of her message of repentance and preparation for the millennium. In her *Advice*, after an introductory section on holding worship services, the first substantial comments of the Universal Friend

---

[20] Ibid., p. 95.   [21] Ibid., pp. 35-36.

strongly advocate separation from the world. The members of her society are told to "shun, at all times, the company and conversation of the wicked world, as much as possible."[22] Later the Advice also urges the followers of the Universal Friend, "labor to keep yourselves unspotted from the world, . . ."[23] The desire to avoid the contaminating influences of a sinful world were at least partially, if not primarily responsible for the decision to build a new community in the wilderness. The proposition which the Universal Friend encountered in various localities was probably also a factor encouraging the Universal Friend's move to western New York.[24]

The area in which the Universal Friends settled in 1788 had just been opened up for settlement and was on the edge of the frontier. In picking the attractive land on which they settled, the Universal Friends may have made a mistake. The area was also attractive to other settlers, so much so that within a few years separation from the world was not as much of a reality as the Universal Friend had wanted. The rise in land values caused by the influx of settlers led to dissension within the society as the potential profits from the sale of land aroused the greed of some of the society's members.[25]

Though the Universal Friend was not able to save all of her members from the enticements of the commercial world, she was successful in keeping that world outside her settlement. The Society of Universal Friends, at least while their founder was alive, did not participate in

---

[22] Ibid., p. 198.   [23] Ibid., p. 199.
[24] Webber, op. cit., pp. 80-81.
[25] Wisbey, op. cit., pp. 114-118.

156

government affairs. Nor did they then engage in lawsuits, although there were quite a few lawsuits over the property of the Universal Friend after her death. The separation from the world did not stop visitors from going to the settlement of the Universal Friends. All who wished to leave the world, even temporarily, were made welcome, including Negroes.[26]

Though there were many visitors to the Society of Universal Friends, the society is not known to have had any direct contact with other communal societies. Yet, the Universal Friend has been accused of directly imitating Ann Lee and the Shakers.[27] There were some similarities between the visions of Ann Lee and the supposed death and resurrection of Jemima Wilkinson. Still, it hardly seems likely that Jemima was even aware of the existence of Ann Lee in 1776, when Jemima had her mystical experience. At that time Ann Lee had been in America only two years and had not begun any public preaching.[28] The plan of the Universal Friend to travel to England in 1778 should also be considered. If Jemima had known enough about Ann Lee to imitate her story of divine revelation in 1776, she would also have known that England would not have been a favorable place for her.

There were also similarities between the preaching tours of the Universal Friend and those of Ann Lee. In regard to the preaching tours of the Universal Friend and those of Ann Lee the theory that the Universal

---

[26]Ibid., pp. 35, 146-147.

[27]Holloway, op. cit., p. 59.

[28]Edward Deming Andrews, *The People Called Shakers* (New York: Dover Publications, Inc., 1963), pp. 14-18. First published in 1953 by Oxford University Press, Inc.

Friend had imitated Ann Lee breaks down entirely. Ann Lee had not started her famous preaching tour until 1781,[29] but the Universal Friend had been touring Rhode Island since 1778 and had established three churches by 1782.[30] Both the Shakers and the Universal Friends became aware of the existence of each other in 1781. Both societies were mentioned in Valentine Rathbun's book, <u>Some Brief Hints of a Religious Scheme</u> which supposedly exposed the deceit of the Shakers.[31]

    The Universal Friends did not imitate the Shaker communal society because plans for a community settlement apart from the world were made by the Universal Friend as early as 1785, two years before the Shakers were called together at New Lebanon by Joseph Meacham. However, the idea for such a settlement might have come to the Universal Friend through a friend of the Ephrata Cloister. During the Universal Friend's visits to Philadelphia in 1782 and 1784 she had many conversations with Christopher Marshall, a long-time friend of Ephrata Cloister. Though no record was kept of their conversations the close involvement of Marshall with Ephrata Cloister indicates that communal society may have been the subject of some of their conversations about religion. An important indication of the influence which Ephrata Cloister may have exercised on the Society of Universal Friends was the adoption by the Universal Friends of the seventh-day Sabbath. Ephrata Cloister was the only other celibate communal society which regarded the seventh-day as the Sabbath. The Society of Universal Friends did not adopt the seventh

---

[29]Ibid., pp. 35.

[30]Holloway, op. cit., p. 60.

[31]Wisbey, op. cit., p. 71.

day Sabbath until after the Universal Friend had visited Philadelphia and talked with Christopher Marshall in 1782. When the Universal Friend visited Philadelphia in 1784 she stayed at the home of Christopher Marshall's son. The plans of the Universal Friend to establish a new community of her own followers are not known to have existed until 1785, after her second visit to Philadelphia.[32]

The evidence is not unequivocal, but there was a strong likelihood that the example of Ephrata Cloister as explained by Christopher Marshall influenced the development of the Universal Friends. Apparently, none of the other celibate communal societies influenced the Universal Friends, nor were the Universal Friends known to have influenced the development of any other society.

GENERAL HISTORY AND DECLINE

The Society of Universal Friends might have been more successful had their luck been better when they chose the first site for their communal settlement. The land which they desired had been owned by the Iroquois Indians and closed to settlement until a treaty was signed with the State of New York. Before the signing of that treaty a company of land speculators had negotiated a 999 year lease with the Iroquois for some of their land. The Society of Universal Friends purchased their land from the lease-holders because of the low price which was offered by that company. Unfortunately for the Universal Friends, the state, after signing its treaty with the Iroquois declared the lease to be invalid. A large section of the former Iroquois land was then purchased

---

[32]Ibid., pp. 82-84, 94-96.

from the state by a group of British speculators and resold to other people. Because the lease had been declared invalid the title of the Society of Universal Friends to their land was also invalid. Before the Universal Friends could purchase their land from the state a large portion of the former Iroquois land was sold by the state to a group of British speculators who then resold it to other people. When the original survey was made for the British purchase the homes of the Universal Friends were declared to be within that purchase. However, the survey had been fraudulently made; eventually the Universal Friends were informed their land was still owned by the state.[33]

The state was willing to recognize the hardship which had been visited on the Universal Friends; for a low price the Universal Friends were able to purchase their land from the state, in October 1792, four years after their original purchase. When the Universal Friends had first moved to New York they had hoped to be able to purchase a section of land large enough to adequately provide land for those whose money had been used in the purchase, while also giving land to the poor members of the society. By 1792 when the society had legally purchased the land from the government, the general rise in land prices, plus the improvements made by the society, aroused the greed of some of the wealthier members of the society. In 1793 the members who had actually paid for the land demanded a division of the land among the contributors without regard for the homes or improvements made by the other members. The demand was fulfilled;

> Only seventeen persons shared in the actual division and several who had come with the pioneer party in 1788

---

[33]Ibid., pp. 103-117.

>received no land at all and even lost the value of their improvements. Greed for land, and the wealth it represented shattered the unity of the society of Universal Friends . . . .[34]

Those who still followed the Universal Friend moved with her about a dozen miles west to the shores of Keuka Lake to a township which they named Jerusalem. The move was completed in 1794. Jerusalem was the home of the Universal Friend until her death in 1819. Although the mantle of leadership was passed on to others no one else had the powers of Jemima Wilkinson and new members were not forthcoming. From her will it is clear that the Universal Friend expected her society to continue, and money was paid out from her estate to help the poor for 43 years after her death; although much of the estate was soon given to the relatives of Rachel Malin, the longest surviving executor of the estate.[35] Jemima's last home still stands, but the society she founded ceased to exist before the end of the Civil War.

---

[34] Wisbey, op. cit., p. 118.

[35] Ibid., pp. 168-170.

Chapter 8

THE HARMONY SOCIETY

INTRODUCTION

If the subject of a study of religious communism was to be picked from among the celibate communal societies, the best choice would be the Harmony Society. On a per capita basis the Harmony Society was the most economically successful, it had the largest number of members operating as one economic unity, and the Harmony Society gave communism a higher place among its religious beliefs than was given to communism by the other celibate communal societies.

Formed by Separatist immigrants from Wurttemburg, Germany, under the leadership of George Rapp, the Harmony Society was formally established at their first settlement in Harmony, Pennsylvania, on February 15, 1805, by the signing of articles of association. Harmony, which was in Butler Co. north of Pittsburgh, proved to be an unsatisfactory location, because the tract of land was too small to accommodate the expected numbers and it was not suitable for viniculture, which had been an important occupation among the Harmonists in Germany. In 1814 and 1815 the Harmonists moved to a large site in southwestern Indiana on the Wabash River a few miles upstream from the Ohio River; but New Harmony proved to be continually infected with malaria and as the Harmonists turned more and more to manufacturing it became apparent that the Indiana site was too far from the markets for their goods. The Harmonists next bought a site on the Ohio River northwest of Pittsburgh, a short distance from their first American home, to which they moved in 1824 and 1825. This third, and final home of the Harmony Society was named Economy, and is now part of the town of Ambridge. Before 1905, when the last three members dissolved the Harmony Society, much of the land had been sold to the American Bridge Co. and today only a few blocks containing some of the Harmonists' most important buildings comprise the historical site of "Old Economy," which is maintained by the Pennsylvania Historical and Museum Commission.

The largest number of the members of the Harmony Society had migrated to the United States from small villages near Stuttgart in Wurttemburg, Germany, where they had been members of the established Lutheran Church before joining groups of Separatists. By 1786, George Rapp was a leader of the Separatists in his home village of Iptingen, and in 1803, he described himself as the leader of most of the Separatists of Lower Wurttemburg.[1] There were many Separatists who did not leave Wurttemburg, or who went to Russia, and even of those who migrated to the United States there were many who did not join the Harmony Society; yet the Harmony Society continued to acquire new members directly from Wurttemburg until 1819. Throughout the society's history, only a few outsiders, who had already been living in the United States, were admitted to the community as prospective members; and all of them were of German descent, an admittance restriction which may have been imposed because German was the Harmony Society's everyday language. The only

---

[1] Karl J. Arndt, George Rapp's Harmony Society 1785-1847 (Philadelphia, Pennsylvania: University of Pennsylvania Press, 1965), p. 47.

other significant source of new members were the children who grew up in the society; however, after the adoption of celibacy in 1807, that source of new members also had a limited future.[2]

Counting the children and the adult members, the society had its largest number of people when there were approximately 750 people living in the community around 1820, of whom there were about 440 adult members. The society had its largest number of adult members in 1827 when there were 522, but the increase in the number of adult members came from the maturing of children already in the community rather than from an increase in the community's size. Due to death and defection the total population of the community had dropped to 706 by 1830. In 1832 there was a large defection of members which reduced the society's adult membership to 357. That defection will be discussed in the section on the general history and decline of the society. With the maturing of children within the society the adult membership rose again to 403 by 1834, but it steadily declined thereafter until the last three members dissolved the society on December 5, 1905.[3]

DEVELOPMENT BEFORE FOUNDING

The development as Separatists of George Rapp and his followers was clearly recorded in the declarations of faith signed by those Separatists and by the various investigations by authorities in

---

[2] Ibid., pp. 9, 78. Also John Archibald Bole, The Harmony Society (Philadelphia, Pennsylvania: Americana Germanica Press, 1905), pp. 33-34.

[3] Bole, op. cit., pp. 33-34. Also John S. Duss, The Harmonists: A Personal History (Harrisburg, Pennsylvania: Pennsylvania Book Service, 1943), p. 387.

Wurttemburg. Unfortunately, the development of the particular beliefs which characterized the Harmony Society as a distinct part of Separatism was not clearly recorded. Though some of the distinctive beliefs of the Harmonists can be identified as part of George Rapp's beliefs by certain dates, there are no indications as to whether or not those beliefs were accepted by other future Harmonists at those times. The Harmonists and Separatists were not clearly divided into separate groups until after the migration to the United States. In the first boatload which brought those who founded the Harmony Society, there were many Separatists who went their own way and did not join the society. Therefore, the terms refering to "Separatists" in the following section include many people who did not become Harmonists.

The leadership of George Rapp was unique among the celibate communal societies in this study, for he was the only leader who led his people through all of the developmental stages, including breaking away from a regular, non-Pietist church, as members of a Pietist group, and through the founding and development of a celibate communal society. All of the other societies either had more than one important religious leader during their founding and development as celibate communal societies or developed from groups that were already Pietist.[4]

The founder of the Harmony Society, Johann George Rapp,[5] was born in Iptingen, about 12 miles northwest of Stuttgart, Germany, on November 1, 1757, and lived to the age of 90 before he died in Economy,

---

[4]Such differences will be explored more fully in the chapters on comparisons and conclusions.

[5]By 1805, and perhaps before, Rapp dropped his first name and used only "George Rapp" as his name.

Pennsylvania, on August 7, 1847. When Rapp was 14, his father died; shortly thereafter Rapp learned the trade of a weaver. He left Iptingen to travel as a journeyman weaver; but, when he began those travels, where he traveled, or when he returned to Iptingen is not known. From what is known about his life in Germany, it appears that, although Rapp might have been strongly influenced religiously during those travels, most of the development of his religious thinking occurred after his return to Iptingen.[6]

Rapp was married to Christine Benzinger in February, 1783, in Iptingen, and they had two children, a son, Johannes, born in December, 1783, and a daughter, Rosina, born in February, 1786. Very little is known about Christine Rapp and even the date of her death was not reported in the sources, although she apparently died sometime in the late 1830's. Johannes came with his father to America in 1803, but later had a falling out with his father and he is not known to have ever joined the society. Johannes' daughter, Gertrude, did join the society. After the death of Christine Rapp, Gertrude became the first lady of the society. Rosina Rapp came to America with the Harmonists in 1804, lived as a member of the society, and did not marry.[7]

According to a statement he made in 1785, George Rapp was living in personal religious turmoil from 1780 until 1782 when he changed his way of life and began to attempt living like a Christian. Some time later, probably in 1784, he joined a devotional group which had been

---

[6]Arndt, op. cit., p. 17. See also the following paragraphs.

[7]Ibid., pp. 17, 99, 585-586. New research by Karl Arndt has proven the Johannes Rapp who brought suit against the society in 1806 was not George Rapp's son. From personal correspondence between Karl Arndt and the writer.

started by the local minister and which was meeting in private homes. Rapp did not find the group pious enough for him; after accusing the lay leader of greed, he stopped attending the group's meetings. At the same time, early in 1785, Rapp also stopped attending church and told his close friends of his religious feelings. Some of those friends began to join Rapp in private religious gatherings and also in avoiding attendance at church, a development which aroused the attention of the local minister and the local church council. Rapp was called before the church council of Iptingen in April, 1785 and was asked to present his objections to the church in writing, which he did on April 17, 1785.[8]

In the document which George Rapp submitted to the Iptingen church council he described part of his conversion experience, his efforts to completely surrender his will to God, and his personal relationship with Jesus. He believed that relationship eliminated any need he might have had for the church, and he said, "I have not come to church again, . . . because I needed nothing else since I had found Jesus."[9] Rapp also said his own Christianity was weakened by the different interpretations of the word of God which he was exposed to in church. He had stayed away from church for that reason rather than out of pride or stubborness. He did not deny the usefulness of the church or its role for others as a storehouse of grace, but said, "I used the means of grace until I found Jesus, the fountain himself."[10]

When F. Ernest Stoeffler's definition of Pietism[11] is compared with Rapp's declaration of faith, several points stand out: In Rapp's

---

[8]Ibid., pp. 17-18.   [9]Ibid., p. 18.

[10]Ibid., p. 19.

[11]Ernest F. Stoeffler, The Rise of Evangelical Pietism (Leiden, The Netherlands: E. J. Brill, 1965), pp. 13-23. The four characteristics are: experiential, perfectionist, Biblical, and oppositive.

statement there is only a hint of opposition to the established church; Rapp's position is not buttressed by an appeal to the authority of particular passages in the Bible; and he does not call for any particular way of life or anything that could be regarded as an appeal to perfectionism. What is emphasized in Rapp's declaration is his personal relationship with God, with the Holy Spirit, and especially with Jesus. In Stoeffler's terms, Rapp's confession of faith emphasizes the experiential; it speaks again and again of a personal relationship which can only be called mystical, as can be seen from the following example, "the love of Jesus became so precious to me because for the third time he had shown me his mercy and had sought me . . . ."[12]

Rapp's early mysticism was never lost, although in the development of his religious beliefs the other elements of Pietism also played important roles. The other elements appear to have been added very rapidly, for when Rapp and other Separatists were investigated by church authorities in 1787, examples of perfectionism, Biblicism, and opposition to the church were clearly part of his beliefs. Although Rapp might not have declared everything he could have in 1785, it is more likely that the changes were brought on by the influence of other Separatists, for Rapp was by no means the only leader of the group at Iptingen. Another leader, Christian Hornle, was the first to refuse to baptize his child in church and another of Hornle's children was the first to stop attending school. Rapp did not mention baptism in 1785 and since his daughter Rosina was baptized in 1786, Rapp's declaration in 1787 that baptism was useless

---

[12] Arndt, op. cit., p. 18. Arndt translated and reproduced the entire document.

unless it represented an internal change in the recipient must have come from a change in his beliefs.[13]

Except for several more investigations, fines for not sending their children to school, a brief imprisonment for Rapp and Hornle, and orders to stop their private religious gatherings, the civil government and the church government generally did not bother the Separatists. Even the orders to stop the private religious gatherings were not enforced. The lenient attitude of the governments probably came from a recognition that except in matters of religion the Separatists were quiet, law-abiding citizens who paid their taxes; even in matters of religion the Separatists were quiet, for they did not attempt to convert others through evangelism, but waited for others to come to them. As the Separatists grew in numbers and became more capable of threatening the government, attitudes changed; when the Separatists left in 1804 and 1805 they did so partially because of the worsening situation.[14]

In 1798 the Separatists petitioned the legislature for permission to organize a new community made up entirely of Separatists, which would live according to the precepts of the Separatists. Part of the legislature's response was a request for a statement of the Separatists' beliefs. The 1798 Articles of Faith which George Rapp and other Separatist leaders signed was divided into seven parts preceded by a preamble; its major headings were on the subjects of the church, baptism, communion, school, confirmation, government and oaths, and military service in that order.[15] In the areas it covered, the 1798 statement expressed beliefs later held by the Harmony Society as well as those of the Separatists in

---

[13]Ibid., pp. 19-25. [14]Ibid., pp. 25-58.

[15]Ibid., pp. 35-40. Arndt includes his own translation of the whole document.

1798, and therefore it will be discussed more fully in the section on the "Beliefs and Practices of the Harmony Society."

While Rapp's beliefs were developing along normal Separatist lines he was also developing beliefs which later distinguished the Harmonists from other Separatists. During the investigation at Iptingen in 1787 Rapp spoke in terms which indicated that he felt himself to be directly inspired and guided by God. When a guard chided him for making a prediction about the future of Separatism, as he was being imprisoned in 1791, Rapp is said to have replied, "I am a prophet and am called to be one."[16] Rapp advocated celibacy for the elect in 1791 and might have practiced celibacy since 1786 after the birth of his second child. By 1794 Rapp is also known to have believed in the androgynous nature of perfected man, incorporating both the masculine and feminine in one, in the image of God.[17]

In 1799 Rapp is known to have expressed a belief in the imminent approach of the millennium. From remarks made by Frederick Rapp[18] in 1824, it appears that George Rapp had carefully studied history in reference to the Book of Revelation and the millennium at least since 1794. The beliefs which the Harmonists held about the millennium's nearness were also held by many other Separatists and were important factors in the migration of many Separatists to Russia and the United States in the early 19th century. Two other important factors which influenced the Harmonists and other Separatists to leave Wurttemburg

---

[16]Ibid., pp. 26, 30.   [17]Ibid., p. 40, and Duss, op. cit., p. 11.

[18]Frederick Rapp's name had been Johann Friedrich Reichert and was changed when he was adopted by George Rapp sometime after the Harmonists arrived in the United States. Frederick had organized the Harmonists for their move from Germany to the United States and throughout the rest of his life he was second only to George Rapp and was in charge of the society's business affairs.

were the government's refusal to allow them to set up their own semi-autonomous area and the increasing pressure which the government used to try to limit the growth of the Separatists.[19]

George Rapp contacted the French government for the purpose of buying land in the Louisiana Territory, but the area was sold to the United States before a purchase could be made and land in the Pyrennes was offered instead. In 1803, following another investigation by the Wurttemburg government, George Rapp and several others went to the United States to look for land; they were followed in 1804 and 1805 by most of those who became Harmonists.[20]

BELIEFS AND PRACTICES

The beliefs of the Harmonists regarding the nature of God and man, celibacy, the millennium, and communism, although they were accepted at different times, had by the 1830's developed into an interdependent system. The most important outside sources for the Harmonists' beliefs were the works of Jacob Boehme, Jung-Stilling, Herder, their Lutheran heritage, and the commentary contained in the Berleburger Bibel. Within the society, the religious leadership of George Rapp was supreme and was followed throughout most of the society's 100 year history.[21]

_____

[19]Arndt, op. cit., p. 49.   [20]Ibid., pp. 458, 50-90.

[21]Ibid., pp. 97-98, 256, 416; see also Bole, op. cit., p. 126. The Berleburger Bibel was published in Berleburg, Wittgenstein, Germany, in 8 volumes from 1726-1742 by members of the Philadelphian Society, mystics who studied the works of Jacob Boehme. The translation was a new one and was accompanied by a mystical and symbolic commentary. The commentary was important to the Harmonists, especially in their interpretation of Revelation, which will be discussed later.

The influence of Jacob Boehme was most important in regard to the Harmonists' views of the nature of God and man, and in regard to celibacy. The Harmonists believed, as did Boehme, that God was both masculine and feminine in one being and that the first man, Adam, was also masculine and feminine in one being.[22] They also believed that the first fall of mankind came not from the eating of the fruit of the tree of knowledge, but from Adam's desire for an external mate as the animals had, "which . . . violated his own inward Sanctuary and his own female function . . . ."[23] The fall of man, then, to the Harmonists, occurred when Adam, "was deprived of his feminine half and lost the true image of God, two in one." They believed that in the ultimate rebirth and regeneration of man the true image of God would be restored as it had been in Adam and was in Christ.[24]

Like many other Pietists the Harmonists believed that only someone who is truly reborn could be considered a follower of Christ. With their belief that ultimately, the reborn, regenerated man would be androgynous, like Adam was in the beginning, it is not surprising that they also believed those reborn in Christ should renounce their animal-like sexual nature and become spiritual virgins. Exactly why or under what conditions the Harmonists adopted celibacy in 1807 can only be surmised for the Harmonists never produced any official statements of their beliefs about celibacy, nor did they sign any community agreement concerning celibacy.

---

[22]Arndt, op. cit., p. 98.

[23]Bole, op. cit., p. 53. Quoting a letter by Jacob Henrici, 1853. He was the Society's leader from 1868 to December, 1892.

[24]Arndt, op. cit., p. 583. Quoting R. L. Baker, 1857.

In a letter to a newspaper editor in 1819, written partially to defend celibacy, Frederick Rapp described the Harmonists as people "who practice the religion of Jesus in daily life and who strive with all their heart for sanctification." He also said some of the Harmonists (meaning those who were celibate) had, by the power of Christ and his sacrifice, " . . . been so enobled in their virtue that they have voluntarily renounced fleshly intercourse and are preparing themselves solely for Christ and his kingdom."[25] R. L. Baker, who had been 14 years old at the time when celibacy was adopted, described the adoption of celibacy as resulting from a realization that leading a Christian life demanded more than the Harmonists had previously realized, and they became convinced that they, "should live a life of self-denial and discipline, as is written; those who have women as if they had none."[26]

Although there was a considerable amount of social pressure which strongly encouraged celibacy and discouraged any lapses from celibacy, each member who adopted the practice of celibacy did so on his own for it was never made a membership requirement. Frederick Rapp's previously cited letter to a newspaper in 1819 indicated there were more than 80 children in the society who had been born since 1807. Although there were no marriages performed from 1807 to 1817, George Rapp performed at least five marriages during and after 1817. Some of the young people who grew up in the society left to become married, and then after several years, rejoined the society with their family. Yet, the exceptions to

---

[25]Ibid., p. 210.

[26]Ibid., p. 97. Baker's statement was made in 1860. He was the Society's leader following the death of George Rapp until his own death in 1968. He was quoting from I Corinthians 7:29.

the practice of celibacy must not be over-emphasized. The spiritual development of the community was viewed as a long-term process; those who could not finally adapt to the practice of celibacy left the society. Another important consideration is the almost total lack of any means for enforcing celibacy, except social pressure. The only special ways in which men and women were separated was in sleeping arrangements in which the men and women slept on different floors in the houses and in the practice of having several generations or members from several families living in the same house. Generally in the Harmony Society celibacy was enforced by the personal conviction of each member.[27]

Along with the previously mentioned beliefs about the nature of man, another Harmonist belief which probably encouraged the practice of celibacy was their belief that Christ's second coming would soon occur, within their lifetime. The Harmonists hoped and believed they would be among the 144,000 virgins spoken of in Revelation Chapter 14, who will be redeemed from the earth before the house of judgment, which would not have been possible if they had not become spiritual virgins. George Rapp had been carefully watching for signs of the millennium since the early 1790's, and in 1807 the year celibacy was adopted, Frederick Rapp wrote to a prospective member, "Our hope in the imminent appearance of Jesus and in the Revelation of his Kingdom is becoming firmer and firmer. No time is left."[28]

---

[27]Ibid., pp. 97-98, 210, 418. See also Duss, op. cit., pp. 26-27. The information about sleeping arrangements came from a guide at "Old Economy." The other sources are silent on that point.

[28]Arndt, op. cit., p. 100.

In their interpretation of the book of Revelation, the Harmonists believed they had a special role to play in the events leading to Christ's second coming and his thousand year reign on earth. In one of his sermons George Rapp said, "the Revelation of St. John was not given for the world but for the Congregation, and therein you are called the Philadelphian pillar . . . ."[29] Rapp was referring to one of the seven churches for which St. John was given letters in the first three chapters of Revelation. The church at Philadelphia was the only one that was praised for keeping the word of God, for which it has often been considered a symbol of the "true church," which is the way George Rapp interpreted it. The "Woman in the Wilderness," described in Revelations Chapter 12, has also often been considered a symbol of the "true church;" of her George Rapp once wrote: "The woman clothed with the sun is the center. All events actually course about her, and she is the Philadelphian Congregation."[30] Rapp believed the moves made by his society paralleled the moved made by the "Woman in the Wilderness." Harmonie, the German name for the society and the first two settlements, and the German name for the last settlement, Oekonomie, were taken from the commentary in the Berleburger Bibel. The name Oekonomie reflected Rapp's belief that his society was or would soon be ready for the second coming of Christ.[31]

---

[29]Ibid., p. 566, from an 1838 sermon.

[30]Ibid., p. 569, from a letter dated 1842.

[31]Ibid., pp. 353, 417-419.

As described in Revelation 12:5, the "Woman in the Wilderness" was to bear a child; and in 1844 George Rapp wrote, "The woman clothed with the sun and with the moon at her feet has given birth, her son lives in the community spirit."[32] In 1842 Rapp had written, "The son whom the congregation has born has the iron rod,"[33] which corresponded with Revelation 12:5 which says in part, "And she brought forth a man child, who was to rule all nations with a rod of iron . . . ." That child, described by Rapp as the community spirit, was to be part of the new order of reborn man, and Rapp's description shows that the Harmonists believed the establishment of communal property and the replacement of selfish interest with communal interest was to be an important part of the regeneration of mankind in conjunction with the renouncement of man's sexual nature.

The Harmonist Book, Thoughts on the Destiny of Man, which was either written by or under the supervision of George Rapp in 1824,[34] shows clearly that the Harmonists believed communism was God's plan for the establishment of his kingdom on earth. For the destiny of man the Harmonists believed it was "decreed, that the whole Human Race shall become united, by the sacred bond of mutual interest, and brother affection: but few indeed, have yet attained their destiny."[35] For the

---

[32] Ibid., p. 572. [33] Ibid., p. 569. [34] Bole, op. cit., pp. 46-51.

[35] Harmony Society, Thoughts on the Destiny of Man, Particularly with Reference to the Present Times (Harmony, Indiana: Harmony Society, 1824), p. 89. The book was printed in both German and English versions but only the German version was sold to the public. Rapp was not satisfied with the English version and it was to be revised before being offered to the public. Partially because of the move to Pennsylvania in 1824-1825 the revision never took place and the English version was not published. The book was influenced very much by J. G. Herder's Outlines of a Philosophy of the History of Man (1800). See Arndt, op. cit., pp. 255-257. A microfilm copy of the English version of Thoughts on the Destiny of Man is in the writer's possession.

purposes of achieving that union the Harmonists believed Christ had "laid the foundation in the Christian Religion (Acts Chapter 4 v. 34) & the Apostles of the Lord accordingly, held everything in common."[36] The Harmonists also claimed that if such a brotherly union were to exist, "the true principles of religion, and the prudent regulations of industry and economy . . ." would, "by their united influence, produce <u>a heaven upon earth--a true HARMONY</u>."[37] Under the leadership of George Rapp, the Harmonists believed themselves to be such a brotherly union, a heaven on earth. In <u>Thoughts on the Destiny of Man</u> it was suggested for anyone who thought such a heaven on earth could not exist, "Let him inquire, if something of the kind be not already in existence."[38]

Though their views on communism were highly developed by 1824 whether the Harmonists had originally intended to adopt communism after their emigration from Germany was not known. Some of the original Separatists who landed with Rapp's followers in 1804 did not join the Harmony, but their reasons for refusal to join were also unclear. They may have refused to join because of the adoption of communism or because of a misunderstanding concerning the site where the society would be located. Some of those who did not join the society, including Rapp's son, Johannes, bought land in Ohio early in the fall of 1804 in an area George Rapp had investigated. However, the land on which Harmony was later located was not purchased until December, 1804. Although there had been no formal agreement, the land which George Rapp bought was signed for in the name of "George Rapp with Society." Two months later

---

[36]Ibid., p. 73.

[37]Ibid., pp. 65-66. Emphasis in the original.   [38]Ibid., p. 66.

on February 15, 1805 the Articles of Association were signed, and the Harmony Society came into existence.[39]

The first articles of association signed by the Harmonists cover only what the members are to do for the group and what the group is to do for the members. The society is referred to only as "George Rapp and his Associates;" there is no statement of purpose or principle or any indication of why the members joined the community. In 1821, new articles of association apparently intended for new members were drawn up and said in part that the people joining the society were doing so, "by virtue of their religious principles . . . ."[40] Frederick Rapp in 1822 described the Harmony Society as follows:

> our Society is entirely founded upon religious principles, and in every respect totally instituted after the pattern of the first Church laid down in the New Testament, see the Acts, Chapter 2 and 4.[41]

A similar statement is made in the preamble to the revised Articles of Association which were signed on March 9, 1827. There was a statement of purpose which said, "the single object sought is to approximate, so far as human imperfection may allow, to the fulfillment of the will of God . . . ."[42] Years later a jury would declare that the Harmony Society

---

[39] Arndt, op. cit., p. 67-68, 70.

[40] Bole, op. cit., p. 11. With the exception of by-laws adopted in 1832 all of the articles of association and similar agreements signed by the Harmonists are printed in English translation in Bole, op. cit., pp. 7-33. The 1832 by-laws are printed in Arndt, op. cit., pp. 482-483. The agreement to dissolve the society in 1905 was not printed in any of the sources.

[41] Arndt, op. cit., p. 235.

[42] Bole, op. cit., p. 12; also Arndt, op. cit., p. 355, and Nordhoff, Charles, The Communistic Societies of the United States, Dover Publications, Inc., New York (1966) (reprint of 1875 edition by Harper & Brothers, New York), p. 81. In Nordhoff the 1827 articles are erroneously identified as those of 1805.

had not been founded for religious purposes,[43] but for the early Harmonists the foundations of their communism were unquestionably religious. Part of the circumstances which led to that later judicial decision came from the society's legal status. The society was not chartered by the state as a corporation; therefore, there was no need for the society to declare themselves to be or to not be a religious organization. The articles of association were contracts which, in effect, created an unusual family, and in fact, the name by which that family was known, the Harmony Society, was not even mentioned in those contracts until 1836.[44]

So far the discussion of the Harmonists' beliefs has been concerned with those ideas which set the Harmonists apart from most other Pietists. The following discussion about other Harmonist beliefs generally deals with ideas which are more acceptable to other Pietists and to other celibate communal societies. For the following topics the most important primary sources on the Harmonist beliefs come from the period before the migration to the United States, a time when the future members of the Harmony Society were associated with other people as Separatists. The most important document from that period is the Articles of Faith which the Separatists sent to the Wurttemburg Legislature in 1798.[45]

The Articles of Faith were written in a positive manner and, when possible, presented the beliefs of the Separatists without attacking those of the Lutheran Church which were different. The primary emphasis

---

[43]Duss, op. cit., p. 398.   [44]Bole, op. cit., p. 7-15.
[45]Arndt, op. cit., pp. 35-40.

which permeated most of the articles was a concern that man's internal feelings and beliefs must coincide with his external expressions of Christianity. The Separatists felt too much attention was paid to external things, such as receiving the sacraments, and not enough attention was given to man's internal condition.

In the Articles of Faith baptism was described "as being the seal of Christianity, but as useful only to him who has first been moved by God . . . ." and usefully only as such a person is able "to rise from the old and to walk in a new and better life . . . ." The article goes on developing the idea that since baptism is the mark of a Christian, and becoming a Christian is a matter of free choice, such an institution is not suited for children, "until they themselves want to become Christians in true form . . . ." Yet, according to the example of Jesus, who blessed the children brought to him, Mark 10:13-16, the Separatists also believed their children ought to be blessed. As a means of blessing the children, they baptized the children in a manner which was intended not as a sacrament or as a mark of Christianity, but simply as a blessing.[46]

Communion was described as being held several times a year, as part of a love-feast to which each member brought a gift, out of which a common meal was prepared. Before the meal, as a means of insuring the internal nature of the sacrament, public and private confession was held, and all disagreements hampering the unity of the group were settled. There were short sermons before and after the meal, then bread and wine

---

[46]Arndt, op. cit., pp. 36-37. The entire document is reprinted by Arndt on pages 35-40.

were blessed and distributed to each member. In the 1798 statement, the group's feeling of harmonious unity and their spiritual status as one body were emphasized as important parts of communion; I Corinthians 12:13 was quoted,[47] which says:

> For by one Spirit are we all baptized into one body whether we be Jews or Greeks, whether we be bond or free; and have all been made into one Spirit, for even the body is not one member, but many.

In the 1798 Articles of Faith, there was no direct mention of the Separatists' aversion to ceremonies, but there were several other topics which brought out some of the Separatist feelings about ceremonies. In the article about the church in general, they discussed, as one reason for leaving the established church, the lack of opportunity to speak out in church when moved by the Spirit. They believed the first Christian church of the Apostles had not had such restrictions and that they, the Separatists, were returning to the manner of worship conducted by the first Christians.[48] In that instance, they believed that static forms and ceremonies suppressed the Spirit; while in regard to infant baptism or to the partaking of communion by those who did not live a Christian life, the Separatists believed the spirit was being ignored. In the Iptingen investigation of 1787, George Rapp had been carefully questioned about such matters and he had then expressed his disapproval of the ceremonies of the established church, especially those of baptism and communion. He had said that too much attention was given to the external partaking of the sacraments, while the lives of the participants did not reflect the inner regeneration which baptism was supposed to

---

[47]Ibid., p. 37.

[48]Ibid., p. 36.

symbolize or the inner communion with the Holy Spirit which communion was supposed to symbolize.[49]

The same kind of reasoning is expressed in the 1798 article concerning confirmation. The Separatists believed that most often the children were interested in the customary new clothes rather than in their confirmation vows; since the external vow was useless without the internal conviction, the Separatists and later the Harmonists did not practice the custom of confirmation. Similar reasons might have been advanced for the Separatist refusal to swear oaths, but in the case of oaths they had the clear language of James 5:12 which says,

> But above all things, my brethren, swear not, neither by heaven, neither by the earth, neither by any other oath: but let your yea be yea; and your nay, nay; lest ye fall into condemnation.

They also cited Matthew 5:33-34 which says essentially the same thing.[50]

Confession has already been mentioned as part of the Separatists' observance of communion. That practice was followed among the Harmonists and members of the society were encouraged to confess their sins to the society's religious leader at any time.[51] All new members were required to completely confess their sins to one of the elders before they could be admitted to the society.[52]

The last article of the 1798 Articles of Faith dealt with military service and the Separatists' refusal to take part in the military. They described "true Christianity" as "useless for such an occupation . . .," and said, "those who possess the inner peace of God do not like to hurt

---

[49] Ibid., p. 25.   [50] Ibid., p. 38-39.

[51] Bole, op. cit., p. 54.   [52] Nordhoff, op. cit., p. 87.

creatures, and accordingly they may bear no weapons of war . . . ."
But they were not opposed to paying taxes rather than serving in the
military, and they were not opposed to the military service of their
sons who did not object to the military.[53] During the Civil War in the
United States, the Harmonists supported the Union cause with money,
manufactured goods, and food.[54] Perhaps by that time their pacifism
had weakened, or perhaps they were never as pacifist as some of the
other celibate communal societies.

    The Harmonists observed the Sabbath on Sunday like most other
Christian groups, yet George Rapp was once fined in Wurttemburg for
working on Sunday. At that time in 1799, he declared that every man
could do as he pleased in his own home and that the Separatists observed
Sunday only for the sake of others.[55] As the religious leader of the
Harmonists, Rapp often preached twice on Sunday and once on Wednesday
evening;[56] perhaps the practical aspects of set days and set times for
worship and for a day of rest brought the Harmonists to observe Sundays
for their own sake, as they once had for the sake of others.

    Even in their days as Separatists, the followers of George Rapp
had never attempted to go out and seek new members; the same policy was
followed by the Harmonists throughout their history. Those who did join
the society from the outside often had problems, for the close communal
spirit of the society had been developed through years of pioneering
hardships in which the newcomers had not shared. Even when their former
neighbors and fellow Separatists came from Wurttemburg to join the

---

[53] Arndt, op. cit., pp. 40-41.   [54] Duss, op. cit., p. 124.
[55] Arndt, op. cit., p. 44.   [56] Bole, op. cit., p. 71.

Harmonists, the society and the newcomers often found it difficult to adjust to each other. After 1819 there were no more large groups of new members from Germany. After the large secession of members in 1832, no new members were accepted from the outside, except close relatives of members, until 1890. The policy was changed in 1890 only to admit new members who would help to keep the society functioning.[57]

While the relationship between the Harmony Society and the outside world was very extensive in many ways, the individual members, during the days of George Rapp at least, were not allowed to communicate with the outside world unless they were given permission. Why the Harmonists were not allowed to communicate with the outside world is not known, but it may have been part of an attempt to keep the personal relationships of the Harmonists centered on the community and away from any ties to the outside world. When the society was split apart in its move, from Indiana back to Pennsylvania, even communication with distant members of the society was not allowed except by permission.[58]

The ban on communication with the outside world was mostly a one way ban, for the society received newspapers and books and generally kept up with the history of the world around them. Such communications could be controlled and probably were allowed because they tended to emphasize the separation of the members of the community from the world. Private letters from the outside to a member or from a member to the outside were not allowed.[59]

---

[57]Arndt, op. cit., pp. 546-548 and Duss, op. cit., pp. 223-227.
[58]Arndt, op. cit., p. 189.   [59]Ibid., p. 432.

The Harmonists certainly did not ignore the workings of the outside world. They paid taxes, voted in elections on all levels, and Frederick Rapp even served as a delegate to the convention which wrote the first constitution of the state of Indiana. The society's position on slavery can be seen in Frederick's vote at the convention against slavery and for making Indiana a free state.[60] Perhaps the major reason for the society's participation in elections was their economic interest in tariff protection for their manufactures, especially woolen goods. By the time of George Rapp's death in 1847, the Harmonists were wealthy. Before the end of the Civil War they had invested in railroads, coal mining, lumbering, oil wells, and land development. Later, they also invested heavily in nearby manufacturing concerns and organized a bank, known as the Economy Savings Institution.[61]

The moves made by the society, the reputation of its manufactures, its financial success, and its location on the Ohio River in Pennsylvania made the society well-known in the early 19th century. They received many letters from people interested in starting communal societies, and their example certainly helped to start some of the socialist communal societies founded in the first half of the 19th century. Their example also had some affect on the founding by Separatists from Wurttemburg of the Zoar community in Ohio. Zoar was founded in 1817 on a site which George Rapp had once considered as a home for the Harmonists, and the man from whom the Zoarites bought the land on favorable terms, Godfrey Haga, was a good friend of the Harmonists. The Zoarites did not begin

---

[60] Ibid., pp. 165-169, 409-414.

[61] Bole, op. cit., pp. 132-135.

to practice communism until early in 1819[62] and must have heard of the Harmonists by then, even if they had not heard of the Harmonists in Germany.

During the 1850's serious consideration was given by the leaders of the Harmony Society to a possible union of the Harmonists with the Shakers or with the Zoarites. Some of the western Shakers in Indiana had first proposed a union with the Harmonists in 1816. Gertrude Rapp lived with the Indiana Shakers for a while to learn English, but little came of the talk about union then.[63] In 1856, Economy was visited by a Shaker delegation from New Lebanon, New York; a correspondence between Jacob Henrici, then a trustee of the Harmonists, and the Shakers was carried on until 1858, when the Harmonists broke off the correspondence with a firm rejection of the Shaker beliefs. Shortly thereafter, religious differences also kept the Harmonists from uniting with the Zoarites; correspondence concerning a possible union with the Zoarites was brought to an end in 1859.[64] In 1892 when the Harmonist's financial picture was near collapse, John S. Duss turned to the New Lebanon Shakers as a possible source of a large loan. At that time the Shakers were also having financial difficulties and were unable to loan the large sum required by the Harmonists.[65]

One communal society which may have influenced the Harmonists, either in their religious development or in their decision to migrate to the United States, was the community at Ephrata. The Harmonists were

---

[62] Nordhoff, op. cit., p. 101; also Arndt, op. cit., 76-77.
[63] Arndt, op. cit., p. 251.   [64] Bole, op. cit., pp. 126-127.
[65] Duss, op. cit., p. 286.

aware of Ephrata at least by 1820, for in that year the Harmonists included 60 hymns from a 1766 Ephrata hymnal in their own Harmonische Gesangbuch which contained 518 hymns.[66] It is even possible that the Harmonists were aware of Ephrata Cloister before the Harmonists' emigration from Germany. A list of books owned by the Harmonists in 1830[67] included two books which contained relatively accurate accounts of Ephrata Cloister.[68] Both books were about life in the United States, and both were published in Germany before 1800. It seems very likely that the Harmonists had purchased those two books as means of learning more about the United States before they came to this country in 1804. If the Harmonists had owned those two books in 1804 they might have been influenced in their decision to adopt communism and later, celibacy, by the successful example of Ephrata Cloister whose beliefs were similar to those of the Harmonists.

The Harmonists might also have come in contact with Ephrata Cloister during the journey of the Harmonists from Philadelphia to their first settlement near Pittsburgh. Ephrata Cloister was on a route which

---

[66] Arndt., op. cit., p. 253.   [67] Bole, op. cit., p. 148.

[68] Felix Reichmann and Eugene E. Doll, Ephrata as Seen by Contemporaries, Seventeenth Yearbook of the Pennsylvania German Folklore Society (Allentown, Pennsylvania: Schlechter's, 1952), pp. 135-138. A reprint of the section on Ephrata from Johann David Schopf, Reise durch enige der Verienigten Staaten, Erlange, Germany, 1788. It was translated by Alfred J. Morrison and published in 1911 by William J. Campbell, Philadelphia, Pennsylvania as Travels in the Confederation. Volume II, pp. 15-19 has the section on Ephrata; see also in Reichmann and Doll, op. cit., pp. 155-156. A reprint of the section on Ephrata from Christoph Daniel Ebeling, Erdbeschreibung und Geschichte von America, Carl Bohn, Hamburg, Germany, 1797, IV, pp. 331-334. The section on Ephrata was translated by Reichmann and Doll. Both the work by Schopf and the work by Ebeling appear on the list of books owned in 1830 by the Harmonists. See footnote #67.

the Harmonists might have taken. The contact which might have occurred between the two societies in such circumstances would explain how and when the Harmonists acquired one of the hymnals from Ephrata Cloister. When and how the two societies became aware of each other remains a mystery, but the publication by the Harmonists of hymns written at Ephrata Cloister is strong evidence that the Harmonists approved of some, if not all, of the beliefs exemplified by Ephrata Cloister.

GENERAL HISTORY AND DECLINE

The Harmonists believed their community was the embodiment of the "Woman in the Wilderness" mentioned in Revelation 12:4-6. As part of that belief the Harmonists interpreted the relocations of their own community as a fulfillment of the moves prophesied for the "Woman in the Wilderness" in Revelation. Therefore, the Harmonists expected the millennium to begin sometime in the fall of 1829. In answer to their expectations the Harmonists received a letter on September 24, 1829 which supposedly came from the Lion of Judah. In Revelation 5:5 the Lion of Judah was identified as the one who would loose the book with seven seals and begin the fulfillment of the prophesies in Revelation. The letter which the Harmonists received demonstrated enough knowledge of the Harmonists' beliefs about their role in the millennium that it appeared to have been written by one privy to their secrets. It was very convincing. About the role in God's plan which the Harmony Society was to fulfill, the letter said, "Through the inner organization and the external constitution of your congregation God has expressed himself for the preparation of the future . . ." and, "so the Lord will also reveal himself to you . . . and according to his divine law will settle in your communion . . . in which he has laid the first foundation stone for the City of God in truth."[69] The letter also said the Lion of Judah would with his followers come to the Harmony Society from which the divine truth would be spread over America and Europe. An example of the impression made upon the Harmonists by that letter can be seen in the following passage, from the reply which the Harmonists sent a month later: "Everyone here is taking new courage and inspiration in expectation of the opening of the Kingdom of Jesus Christ."[70]

The man who believed himself to be the Lion of Judah arrived in the United States in September, 1831, traveled under the name of Count Leon, and with his entourage of about fifty people entered Economy on October 18, 1831. Prior to Count Leon's arrival, even from the time of the 1829 letter, George Rapp had spoken of this man as the next leader of the congregation and as the one who would lead the Harmonists to fulfill their great purpose. After many religious discussions, Rapp realized that Count Leon was not the man to fulfill the prophecies of Revelation. The Count and his party would have been asked to leave if winter had not begun. Discontent with celibacy and with the leadership of George Rapp had been growing for some time. Count Leon, during his stay in Economy, became a rallying point for that discontent. By the beginning of February, 1832, there was an open revolt among the Harmonists which resulted in the secession from the society of approximately 250 people, who, under the leadership of Count Leon, founded the New Philadelphia Congregation at Phillipsburgh, Pennsylvania, about ten miles northwest of Economy. As part of the settlement with the Harmony Society,

---

[69] Ibid., pp. 433-442. Quote from p. 440.

[70] Ibid., p. 443.

the seceders received $105,000, which enabled them to establish their new community.[71]

Although the loss of so many members was a blow to the Harmony Society, George Rapp had always regarded the withdrawal of members as part of the refining process his society went through to become more pure and more a community of the elect. Another of the positive effects of the seceders revolt was a change in the society's government, which added a twelve-man Council of Elders. The Elders were to be elected by all male members over 21 and given the duties of examining prospective members, expelling members when necessary, deciding disputes within the society, and overseeing the business affairs of the society. The Council of Elders actually wielded little power while both Frederick and George Rapp were alive, but it provided valuable experience for future leaders of the Harmonists and served as part of the foundation for governing the community after the Rapps had died. The adoption of the by-laws which instituted the Council of Elders occurred on February 19, 1832, during the secession and may have helped to keep some of the members in the society.[72]

Frederick Rapp died in June, 1834, at the age of 60 after many months of illness. From that time on, George Rapp became the society's financial leader as well as spiritual leader. Frederick's death was an important loss to the society as well as to his adopted father, although in financial matters the two assistants appointed by George Rapp, Romelius Baker and Jacob Henrici, carried on the society's business quite well.[73]

---

[71]Ibid., pp. 469-498.   [72]Ibid., pp. 482-483.
[73]Ibid., pp. 531-534.

The society became closed to new members after Frederick's death. On October 31, 1836 a change was made in the articles of Association. The 6th article of those signed in 1827 was declared void. That article had stipulated that members who wished to leave the society would be given whatever property they had contributed on joining, or if none, then they would be given money according to the length of their stay and their conduct. The new article declared that any contribution made to the society was irrevocable, and if anyone withdrew "it shall be left altogether to the discretion of the superintendent to decide whether any, and if any, what allowance, shall be made to such member."[74] The new article was adopted primarily to avoid lawsuits from former members or their heirs; the society had fought one such lawsuit in 1834 and one in 1835 which was not finally decided until it reached the State Supreme Court in October, 1836.[75]

Although the society prospered materially, death continued to decrease the number of members, and in 1847, the membership had dropped to 288. George Rapp died on August 7, 1847, at the age of 90. He had led the Harmony Society for 42 years after its founding. He is reported to have believed to the end that he would not die before the second coming of Christ.[76] It is unfortunate for his memory that the material prosperity he helped to develop lasted longer than the religious beliefs which he preached.

After George Rapp's death, new articles of association were signed which reduced the Council of Elders to nine members and created

---

[74]Bole, op. cit., p. 17.   [75]Arndt, op. cit., pp. 538-548.
[76]Ibid., p. 577.

a two-man Board of Trustees. The Board of Trustees was to carry on all of the business of the society and to be under the direct supervision of the Council of Elders. The first two trustees were Romelius Baker and Jacob Henrici. Baker, as senior trustee, also became the religious leader of the society.[77] The two trustees were completely honest and were never supervised closely by the Council of Elders, but that lack of supervision led to considerable problems as will be discussed later.

Because the Harmonists continued their policy of not admitting new members, their declining numbers forced the society to change its economic policies. Unable to adequately staff its factories, the society closed some factories and began to invest its money outside the community. By 1855 the largest part of the society's assets were in external investments.[78] The society did hire outsiders to work in Economy, but not in large enough numbers to run whole factories. Even the woolen mill was closed in the 1860's.[79]

Romelius Baker died in 1868, at the age of 75; his place as senior trustee was taken by Jacob Henrici, who led the society until his death on Christmas Day, 1892. The number of members steadily diminished over the years. Although several members were admitted in 1887, in 1889 there were only 25 members and new members had to be taken in or there would not have been enough men to fill the Council of Elders. One of the stipulations in the 1832 by-laws was that the Council of Elders would be elected by all of the male members over 21, and only men had served as Elders or Trustees. Early in 1890, 19 new members

---

[77]Duss, op. cit., pp. 94-95.   [78]Ibid., pp. 114-115.

[79]Arndt, op. cit., p. 547.

were admitted, among them John S. Duss, who became a trustee a few months later. In 1892, after the death of Henrici, Duss became the senior trustee and leader of the Harmony Society.[80]

Duss described the religious views of the 1890 Harmonists by dividing them into three groups: those who had been members before the death of George Rapp, those admitted in 1887, and those admitted in 1890. Those who had been admitted before the death of Rapp had still followed, somewhat, the teachings of Rapp through the preaching of Henrici, but most of them were not as devoted to that faith as was Henrici. The group of seven which had joined in 1887 were strong Pietists, but without the mystical theology of George Rapp; and the 19 admitted in 1890 comprised no particular religious group except a diversified one. Duss spoke of his own religious faith as Lutheran and said,

> when it became my duty to preach to the congregation, the members of which had various faiths and some no faith whatever, I adopted the theory of the Apostle Paul and by "Becoming all things to all men" I managed to keep our religious barque on an even keel.[81]

Although the religious differences were a problem for the society, the most important problems were in the area of finances. After becoming trustee of the society in 1890, John S. Duss discovered many laboring practices among the society's members and its hired workers which were losing money for the society, and an attitude that the society was rich and could afford waste. The more Duss looked into the finances of the society, the more he was shocked and apalled. No accurate system of accounts was kept; many of the society's investments

---

[80] Ibid., pp. 223-227, 232, 294.   [81] Ibid., pp. 234-238, 241-243, 262.

had turned out to be bad ones resulting in large losses to the society; and Henrici, rather than foreclosing on loans made to nearby factories which were losing money, had been loaning more and more money and piling up a large indebtedness against the society.[82] Since Henrici had no consistent method of keeping accounts and generally tried to keep track of everything in his head, it seems likely that even he was not completely aware of the society's actual financial situation. The Harmonists would probably have been better off if they had required complete statements of the society's accounts at least once a year, and then, at least the man who made up the statements would know what the society's financial position actually was.

By the middle of 1891, Duss had discovered the society was near financial collapse; even though according to newspaper accounts, which most of the Harmonists believed, the society was worth millions. With secrecy on his side, with several years hard work by himself and some able assistants, and with the help of a large loan gained by a secret mortgage of the home property at Economy, Duss was able, by the end of 1896, to extricate Economy from most of its financial difficulties without any loss to its creditors or to the depositers of the Economy Savings Institution.[83]

Death continued to take its toll of the Harmonists; even more effective in reducing their number were the many lawsuits filed by ex-members, heirs of ex-members, and even spurious heirs of George Rapp, all of which made life at Economy seem precarious and many members left to seek peace elsewhere. Of the members left in December, 1892, after

---

[82]Ibid., pp. 234-238, 241-243, 262.   [83]Ibid., pp. 336-338.

the death of Henrici more than half did not live out their days in the society, but withdrew from membership before the society was dissolved in 1905. Although the lawsuits cost the society much in peace, lawyers fees, and money, in a few out of court settlements, the society never lost any of the lawsuits.[84]

During the last few years when there were not enough men to fill the Board of Elders, women were elected to the vacancies. Finally, even with the service of women, the number of Elders had to be reduced; after 1897, John S. Duss was the sole trustee. In May, 1903, John Duss resigned his office and withdrew from the society to follow a career as a concert band conductor, and his wife, Susie C. Duss, was elected trustee; there were four members in the society at that time. In 1905, the last three members of the Harmonists dissolved the society and divided what was left of the assets among themselves; the agreement was signed on December 5, 1905.[85]

In 1907, Duss' musical career was cut short by yet another lawsuit from the heirs of George Rapp. Before that suit was settled in 1910, the state of Pennsylvania filed suit to escheat the society's assets as of its dissolution in 1905 on the grounds of an 1855 law covering religious institutions. In 1916, a settlement was made between the ex-Harmonists and the state's attorneys, a resolution was passed by the legislature authorizing the settlement, and a trial by jury recognized and accepted the agreement. The state acquired $15,000 and part of two of Economy's most important blocks,[86] while the ex-Harmonists and those

---

[84]Ibid., pp. 294-361.

[85]Reibel, Daniel B., A Guide to Old Economy, Harmony Associates, Old Economy, Ambridge, Pennsylvania (1969), p. 12.

[86]Duss, op. cit., pp. 397-398.

to whom they had sold land acquired a statement from the jury which said in part,

> none of the said property ever was or is held by any religious society or for any religious or charitable uses, and that the defendants, their heirs, grantees, successors and assigns have a good and indefeasible title thereto.[87]

While it was a travesty against the memory of George Rapp and his loyal followers to have the last two trustees of the Harmony Society declare that it was not a religious society, the findings of the jury, though overstated, were on firm legal ground. The Harmony Society did not meet the definition of a religious society which was in the 1855 law. Although they followed one system of belief in their early years, the membership was never required to formally declare their beliefs or to sign any statements attesting to those beliefs. It should also be noted that the Harmony Society did not apply to the state for any recognition as a religious society, and the Harmonists always paid their taxes as though they were simply an economic association. Probably the most important evidence used in determining their legal status was the 1805 Articles of Association, as translated into English by Jacob Henrici in 1835. Within Henrici's translation, the total membership is always referred to either as "George Rapp and his Associates" or simply as the "community," and there was only one relatively unimportant reference to the church. According to Henrici's translation, which the jury used in 1916, whatever George Rapp and his Associates may have thought of themselves, the Harmonists were not

---

[87]Arndt, op. cit., p. 581.

legally organized as anything other than a unique economic association.[88]

A new translation of the 1805 Articles of Association was published in 1965 by Karl J. R. Arndt, in which the term Henrici had translated as "community" is translated as "congregation."[89] There is a German term, "Geminde" which means either "community" and, or "congregation."[90] Considering the small villages of Wurttemburg from which the Harmonists came, where everyone had belonged to the one established church, it seems likely that the economic versus religious distinctions which Americans make in using the terms "community" and "congregation" did not exist for the Harmonists in 1805. Certainly considering the religious views of the Harmonists regarding communism and the destiny of mankind it appears that Henrici's translation of the term as "community" may have indicated a higher religious meaning for the Harmonists than would have been the case with the more ordinary term "congregation."

While the jury's decision that the Harmony Society was not legally a religious society as a fair one, their statement went much too far when it said none of the property of the Harmonists had ever been used for religious or charitable uses. The Harmonists had contributed to many charitable causes, including the constant feeding of many tramps

---

[88] Duss, op. cit., pp. 393-394, translation on pp. 419-420.

[89] Arndt, op. cit., pp. 72-74. He is the head of the German Department at Clark University, Worcester, Massachusetts.

[90] Klatt, E. and Golze, G, Langenscheidt's German-English, English-German Dictionary, Washington Square Press, Inc., New York (1952), pp. 101, 311, 313.

for whose lodging a house had been set aside.[91] Each time they built a community the Harmonists had also built and maintained a church in which they regularly attended worship services. The original leaders of the society had stated unequivocally that the Harmony Society was founded on religious principles for religious reasons. The Articles of Association of 1827 were very clear in their statement of the religious principles on which the society was founded[92] as was Frederick Rapp when he said in part, "our Society is entirely founded upon religious principles . . . ."[93]

Although financial gain may have been part of the reasons for dissolving the Harmony Society, the last Harmonists may well have been sincere in their belief that the Harmony Society was not a religious society. What they believed about the society came from living within the society, not from reading George Rapp's sermons or from reading the statements of previous members, but from living with each other. That the religious beliefs of the last members were so different from the beliefs of the founders of the Harmony Society should not be, in this country of religious freedom, a matter of discredit for either group.

---

[91]Nordhoff, op. cit., pp. 66-67.

[92]Bole, op. cit., p. 12.   [93]Arndt, op. cit., p. 235.

Chapter 9

THE SEPARATIST SOCIETY OF ZOAR

INTRODUCTION

When Lot fled from the destruction of Sodom and Gomorrah, he first went to the small city of Zoar. In 1817 a group of Separatists, fleeing from religious persecution in Germany, used the name "Zoar" for their new home in America. The Separatists' choice of the name "Zoar" may have reflected a belief that the worldliness of most professed Christians was comparable to the sinfulness of Sodom and Gomorrah, or they may have chosen the name "Zoar" from Lot's description of that city in Genesis 19:24:

> Behold now, this city is near to flee unto, and it is a little one: Oh, let me escape thither, (is it not a little one?) and my soul shall live.

The Separatists of Zoar had originally come from Wurttemburg, Baden, and Bavaria, Germany. After their arrival in 1817, the Separatists purchased land in eastern Ohio, where they adopted communism in 1819. Under the leadership of Joseph Bimeler, the society became successful, declined after the death of Bimeler, and was finally dissolved in 1898 after 79 years of communism.

There were about 225 Separatists in the original migration from Germany to Zoar. Later, more members came from Germany, with the largest influx of new members occurring in the years 1830-1834 when 170 new members joined the society.[1] The society's membership never exceeded 500 members.[2] "No native American (from outside the society) is known to have entered the society . . . ,"[3] although one New Englander, who had been a Shaker, is known to have lived with the society for quite a while without actually joining the society.[4] The Separatists did not attempt to recruit American members, though friends and relatives from Germany were encouraged to join the society.

For unknown reasons, the society had more female than male members throughout its history. The ratio of male to female members may be seen from the 53 men and 104 women who signed the Articles of Association in 1819 and from the 60 men and 104 women who signed amendments to those articles in 1824. The same membership rights given to men, including the right to vote, were given to women in the Zoar society. According to the constitution adopted by the society in 1832, there were two classes of members, novices and full members. Anyone wishing to join the society, including the children of members, had to serve as a novice for at least one year before being admitted to full membership. Full members had to give all of their property to the society; no one was accepted as a full member if he had any debts.[5]

---

[1] Francis P. Weisenburger, The Passing of the Frontier: The History of the State of Ohio, II, ed. Carl Wittke (Columbus, Ohio: Archaeological and Historical Society, 1941), p. 160.

[2] William Alfred Hinds, American Communities (New York: Corinth Books, 1961), p. 26. First published in 1878.

[3] E. O. Randall, History of the Zoar Society (3rd ed.; Columbus, Ohio: Fred J. Heer, 1904), p. 11.

[4] Charles Nordhoff, The Communistic Societies of the United States (New York: Dover Publications, Inc., 1966), p. 112. First published in (New York: Harper & Brothers, 1875).

[5] Randall, op. cit., pp. 7-8, 19-11.

DEVELOPMENT BEFORE FOUNDING

The history of the Separatists of Zoar before they arrived in the United States has remained virtually unknown. Even most of the towns in which they began their Separatism in southern Germany are unknown.[6] The Separatists suffered religious persecutions in those towns and villages because they would not send their children to the schools controlled by the orthodox clergy and because they were pacifists. As a result, some of the Separatists from Baden, Bavaria, and Wurttemburg, gathered near Stuttgart, Wurttemburg, where they hoped to be protected by a friend at court. After living there a few years, the Separatists again faced persecution and decided to migrate to America in 1817.[7]

The first known leader of the Zoar Separatists, before their emigration from Germany, was Barbara Grubermann. A native of Switzerland, Barbara Grubermann had been driven from her home because of her religious views, including her belief that she was divinely inspired. Barbara Grubermann would go into a trance, then, after her return to consciousness, she related to her audience the visions she had seen in the trance. Exactly what Barbara Grubermann saw in her visions was not reported in the sources. Nor was any indication given of her age, when she was driven from Switzerland, whether the Separatists existed before she arrived in Germany, or the year of her death. Apparently, the Barbara Grubermann's

---

[6] Based on personal correspondence between Howard Palmer, Manager, Zoar State Memorial, Ohio Historical Society, Zoar, Ohio, and the writer.

[7] Nordhoff, op. cit., p. 100.

leadership of the Separatists occurred near the end of the 18th century.[8]

There may have been other leaders, but the next known leader of the Separatists was Joseph Bimeler. Bimeler was born in 1778 as Joseph Baumeler and changed his name upon his arrival in the United States. Bimeler's leadership of the Separatists began in 1807, when he was 29, and continued until his death in 1853. Much of the success of the Zoar community was the result of his leadership, even though he opposed the idea of communism when it was first proposed in 1819.[9]

Most of the Separatists under the leadership of Joseph Bimeler in Germany were not wealthy people. When the decision was made to migrate to America, the more prosperous Separatists helped those who were poor, but even then many would not have been able to migrate without the financial aid given by English Quakers. The English Quakers had known of the religious persecution which the Separatists had suffered and were also aware of the financial plight of the Separatists. After aiding the migration of the Separatists, the English Quakers also sent about $4,000 to Philadelphia for the Separatists when they arrived in America.[10]

In August, 1817, the Separatists purchased a tract in Ohio of 5,600 acres from Godrey Haga, a Philadelphia Quaker and friend of the Harmony Society. The land was purchased under favorable terms for the Separatists: $3.00 an acre, a low down payment, fifteen years to pay

---

[8] Hinds, op. cit., p. 35; see also Catherine R. Dobbs, *Freedom's Will: The Society of the Separatists of Zoar* (New York: William Frederick Press, 1947), pp. 20-25.

[9] Dobbs, op. cit., pp. 26-30; see also Randall, op. cit., p. 79.

[10] Randall, op. cit., pp. 5-6.

the balance, and the first three years were to be without interest. Yet, even with favorable terms, the Separatists later found many of their members would be unable to pay for their share of the land.[11]

Out of the land purchased by the Separatists, each family was given land proportionate to the amount of money they had provided for its purchase. Though all of the Separatists at Zoar helped each other, the hard pioneering life was frequently too much for the older members. Some of the Separatists, even with the help of the Quakers, had been too poor to journey directly to Zoar and establish their farms. The poor members hired themselves to American families in other communities in exchange for boarding, a few wages, and training in farming or other skills. By 1819, it had become clear that both the older and the poorer members would not be able to pay for their share of the land. The result would have been the scattering of the religious community whose members had gone through so much together. After a thorough discussion of the problems, an agreement was reached in April, 1819, which established the communal ownership of property and united all members in the "Separatist Society of Zoar."[12]

BELIEFS AND PRACTICES

Among the beliefs which were important to the development of the Separatists of Zoar was a belief in direct inspiration. Apparently,

---

[11] Ibid.; see also Karl J. R. Arndt, George Rapp's Harmony Society, 1785-1847 (Philadelphia, Pennsylvania: University of Pennsylvania Press, 1965), p. 76.

[12] Nordhoff, op. cit., pp. 100-101; see also Randall op. cit., pp. 6-8.

the individual members of the Separatists were not expected to receive direct inspiration. However, the two most important leaders of the Separatists, Barbara Grubermann and Joseph Bimeler, were believed to have frequently received direct inspiration. Speaking of his preparations for the worship services, Bimeler said, "When I come here, I generally come empty, without knowing whereof I am going to Speak."[13] Bimeler did not prepare sermons because he expected to receive direct inspiration. The Zoarites considered Bimeler's speeches to be "direct manifestations of the Holy Ghost . . ."[14] and called his speeches "discourses," not sermons.

It is not known whether the millennial beliefs of the Separatists of Zoar were influenced by their beliefs in direct inspiration. Hopes and expectations that the millennium would soon occur were part of the beliefs of the Zoarites during their early years. As the years wore on, the beliefs of the Zoarites changed until they no longer believed the millennium would begin instantaneously throughout the whole world. They had come to believe the millennium would occur gradually, within the souls of individuals, rather than outwardly where all could see it.[15]

The millennial beliefs of the Zoarites might have influenced their beliefs about celibacy, as was the case in several of the other societies. Both millennialism and the advocacy of celibacy were part of the Separatists' beliefs in Germany, but whether both beliefs were changed at the same time or whether there was any connection between the two beliefs was not presented in the sources.

---

[13] Randall, op. cit., pp. 17-18.
[14] Ibid., p. 16.   [15] Ibid., p. 19.

Celibacy was not generally practiced by the Separatists in Germany, though its practice was considered better than marriage. Exactly when celibacy was adopted as a practice by the Zoarites in the United States is not known. Celibacy probably became an established practice among the Zoarites about the same time as the establishment of communism. Sometime between 1828-1830, celibacy was abandoned as a required practice by the Zoarites. In 1878, the Zoar school teacher said, "It was never intended that celibacy should be a permanent principle of the community."[16] Celibacy might have been adopted by the community to stop any growth in the number of people to be fed before the community was financially secure. However, it is most likely that celibacy was adopted primarily for religious reasons.

While still in Germany, the Zoarites had included a statement advocating celibacy in the "Principles of the Separatists," which they presented to government of Wurttemburg as a statement of their faith. That statement was:

> All intercourse of the sexes, except what is necessary to the perpetuation of the species, we hold to be sinful and contrary to the order and command of God. Complete virginity or entire cessation of sexual commerce is more commendable than marriage.[17]

A religious foundation for celibacy clearly existed among the Zoarites. Bimeler is known to have always considered celibacy a higher state than

---

[16] Hinds, op. cit., p. 32.

[17] Randall, op. cit., p. 14. The "Principles of the Separatists" are reprinted in full by Randall; see also Nordhoff, op. cit., pp. 103-104, and George B. Landis, "The Society of Separatists of Zoar, Ohio," *American Historical Association Annual Report* (1898), p. 188.

marriage. Even in 1875, the older Zoarites still believed that celibacy was more commendable than marriage.[18]

According to Randall's History of the Zoar Society, celibacy had been adopted for religious reasons and was abandoned because Bimeler fell in love and married.[19] Randall's book was prefaced by a letter from the secretary of the Zoar Society in 1899 endorsing the book as "fair and impartial . . ." and, "entirely worthy of credence . . . ¡"[20] therefore, the Zoarites must have adopted and abandoned celibacy for the reasons given by Randall. None of the other sources disagreed with Randall's account of the abandonment of celibacy. Bimeler's success in changing the society's practices from expecting all members to be celibate to the practice of marriage illustrated the importance of his leadership within the society.

Bimeler's position among the Zoarites was not that of a dictator, nor was his opinion always followed. When communism was being considered in 1819, Bimeler had been opposed to its adoption; the Separatists voted to adopt communism over Bimeler's objections. Though he had been opposed to communism Bimeler accepted the wishes of his fellow Separatists and wholeheartedly supported the society as its financial and religious leader.[21] The financial problems of the poor and elderly members had been the prime factor in the adoption of communism by the Zoarites, but that does not mean the intended purpose was financial gain. The preamble to the 1819 Articles of Association stated:

---

[18]Nordhoff, op. cit., pp. 107-108

[19]Randall, op. cit., p. 20.   [20]Ibid., p. i.

[21]Ibid., pp. 7-8, 79.

> The undersigned, members of the Society of Separatists of Zoar, have, from a true Christian love towards God and their fellow men, found themselves convinced and induced to unite themselves according to the Christian Apostolic sense, under the following rules through a communion of property.[22]

The Separatists of Zoar united themselves through communism not because of hope for financial gain, but because of love for their fellow man. Their statement quoted above also indicates the example of the first Christian church had influenced the decision of the Zoarites to adopt communism. Yet, without the special circumstances which existed early in 1819, the Zoarites would not have adopted communism.

The special circumstances had been the result of the Separatists' adherence to the beliefs from which they had earned the name, "Separatists." One of the most fundamental of those beliefs was the Separatists' rejection of ceremonies of which they said, "All ceremonies are banished from among us, and we declare them useless and injurious; and this is the chief cause of our Separation."[23] A rejection of any sacraments, including the sacraments of baptism and the eucharist, was part of the Separatists' rejection of ceremonies. The Separatists also declared themselves to be free from all "ecclesiastical connections and constitutions, because true Christian life requires no sectarianism, while set forms and ceremonies cause sectarian division."[24] Oaths, vows, required confession, and other forms were not practiced by the Separatists. Even the ceremony of marriage was changed, of which the Separatists said, "Our marriages are

---

[22]Ibid., pp. 7-8.

[23]Ibid., p. 13. Article V. of the "Principles of the Separatists."

[24]Ibid., p. 14. Article VII.

contracted by mutual consent, and before witnesses. They are then notified to the political authority; and we reject all intervention of priests or preachers."[25]

One set form which the Separatists did not abolish was observance of the Sabbath on the first day. According to a description of a Sunday service in the late 1890's, the Zoarite men and women sat on opposite sides of the church, sang an opening and closing hymn, and listened for about an hour to a reading from Bimeler's Discourses.[26] While Bimeler was alive, the observance of the Sabbath was not always held. When seeds needed planting or when crops needed harvesting, the necessary work was done whether it was Sunday or not. Bimeler noted that crops planted on Sundays were treated as well by nature as crops planted on other days. Bimeler also believed that each day was as sacred as any other.[27]

Failing to observe the Sabbath in Germany would have produced legal difficulties for the Separatists. The Separatists had antagonized the government of Wurttemburg in a more direct way by their advocacy and practice of pacifism. The Separatists declared, "We can not serve the State as soldiers because a Christian can not murder his enemy, much less his friend."[28] Realizing their pacifism aroused the displeasure and perhaps the suspicions of the government, the Separatists also declared their allegiance to the government. After emphasizing their belief that a government was necessary to protect good citizens and punish others,

---

[25] Ibid. Article VIII.
[26] Landis, op. cit., p. 189.
[27] Randall, op. cit., p. 18.
[28] Ibid., p. 14. Article XI.

the Separatists said, "no one can prove us to be untrue to the constituted authorities."[29]

During the Civil War, about twenty of the youths of Zoar withdrew from the society, forsook the principle of pacifism and joined the Union Army. Most of them died in the war; none of them ever returned to the society.[30] Though they had abandoned one of the society's principles, the actions of those young men also indicated the society was opposed to slavery.

Separation from the world was not a clearly stated principle of the Separatists, yet, like each of the other societies, that principle was included in their practices. The "separatism" of their name which directly referred to separation from the established church might have also included separation from the sinful world. Unless the choice of the name for their community was accidental, the Biblical description of "Zoar" as a place to which one might flee and escape from the sinful world must have been an indication that separation from the world was part of the Zoarites' beliefs. The years which the Separatists spent in America free from religious persecution apparently mellowed their principle of separation from the world. Outsiders began to be hired by the society in 1834,[31] a hotel was constructed which served visitors to Zoar,[32] and the economy of the Zoarites gradually changed from one of subsistence to one of commercial trade. Democracy was practiced within the Zoar society, and the members voted in the presidential election of 1896, if not before then.[33]

---

[29]Ibid. Article XII.

[30]Dobbs, op. cit., p. 75.

[31]Hinds, op. cit., p. 28.

[32]Nordhoff, op. cit., p. 103.

[33]Randall, op. cit., p. 41.

If any of the other celibate communal societies influenced the Zoarites, it must have been the Harmonists. The two societies had both been Separatist groups in Wurttemburg, Germany at the same time and may have been aware of each other's existence before either society migrated to America. The Zoarites purchased their land from Godfrey Haga, a friend of the Harmony Society who had offered to sell the same land to George Rapp in 1804.[34] The first and third settlements of the Harmonists were within 80 miles of where the Zoarites established their community in 1817. The Zoarites certainly had opportunities to learn about the Harmony Society and follow their example in the adoption of communism and celibacy. Unfortunately, no records exist of any actual contacts between the two societies during the early years of the Zoar Society. The Zoarites probably became aware of the Shaker Society sometime in the 1820's; there were several Shaker communities in western Ohio when the Zoarites arrived in America. In 1825, a Shaker community was begun at North Union, Ohio, now part of Cleveland, about 75 miles from Zoar. In the 1850's, consideration was given by the Zoarites, the Harmonists and the Shakers to the proposal for a union of all three societies.[35] Religious differences between the three societies could not be overcome, therefore, all merger considerations among the three societies or any combination of them were rejected by 1859.[36] No other connections were known to have existed between the Separatists of Zoar and other celibate communal societies.

---

[34]Arndt., op. cit., p. 76.

[35]Henri Desroche, *The American Shakers: From Neo-Christianity to Presocialism* (Amherst, Massachusetts: University of Massachusetts Press, 1971), p. 261.

[36]John Archibald Bole, *The Harmony Society* (Philadelphia, Pennsylvania: American Germanica Press, 1905), pp. 126-127.

GENERAL HISTORY AND DECLINE

During their first years as a communal society, the Zoarites were quite poor and their struggle was difficult. In 1827, the Zoarites received a contract to build that part of the Ohio and Erie Canal which was to cross their land. By that time, the Zoarites were well organized and conditions in Zoar had considerably improved. The building of the canal was a great success for the Zoarites: they earned a considerable amount from their own construction of one canal section; they sold large quantities of produce to workers constructing other nearby sections of the canal; and the finished results of the canal furnished the Zoarites with cheap and easy transportation for selling their products.[37]

The continued success of the Zoar Society was threatened in 1834 by a cholera epidemic which cost many Zoarites their lives. After the epidemic, a major change in policy was instituted with the hiring of laborers from outside the society to work in the shops and on the land.[38] The society continued to hire outsiders for the rest of its history, a policy which became a major factor in the decline of the Zoarite's faith in communism.

Another major factor in the decline of the Separatist Society of Zoar was the lack of effective religious leadership, following the death of Joseph Bimeler in 1853. No one else in Zoar was a good speaker or felt directly inspired to speak. After Bimeler's death, the first worship services were conducted by reading from devotional books. When that proved to be unsatisfactory, the society began to conduct services

---

[37] Randall, op. cit., p. 52.   [38] Hinds, op. cit., p. 28.

by reading from Bimeler's discourses, a practice which continued for the rest of the society's life.[39]

Written copies of Bimeler's discourses were available to the society only because a young man had begun in 1822 to write them out for the benefit of his deaf father. Between 1856 and 1861, the Zoarites worked at publishing three volumes in German which contained all of Bimeler's *Discourses*. About one hundred copies were made and then distributed to each family in Zoar. The *Discourses* have never been translated into English, except for a few parts such as the "Principles of the Separatists."[40] Though Bimeler's *Discourses* may have contained very worthy and inspiring thoughts, the repeated readings of those *Discourses* over a period of 45 years seriously weakened the religious feeling of the community. Shortly before the decision was made to abandon communism in 1898, attendance at the Sunday worship services had dwindled to only one-third of the members.[41] By the summer of 1898, after the decision to return to private property had been made, but before the distribution had actually occurred, the religious services were discontinued.[42]

Zoar had also been declining economically because it did not keep up with the changes that were occurring in the outside world. More and more the Zoarites found the cost of producing goods was higher than the cost of purchasing similar goods, such as tanned leather and beer, in the outside world. Many of Zoar's customers, such as local farmers who had previously purchased shoes in Zoar, also found prices cheaper

---

[39] Randall, op. cit., p. 17.   [40] Ibid., pp. 13-17.
[41] Dobbs., op. cit., p. 77.   [42] Randall, op. cit., p. 45.

elsewhere. The principle of communism was also threatened by the Zoarites who managed to acquire personal income that did not belong to the society. Working on their own time, some families raised chickens and sold eggs to the hired people of Zoar; others washed clothes and performed similar services for the hirelings.[43]

The actual decision to abandon communism was given impetus by a newspaper called Nugitna, which was produced by Levi Bimeler, Joseph Bimeler's son. Levi published Nugitna every four weeks from December 1895 to March 1896 until he was ordered by the leaders of the society to either stop publishing the paper or leave the society. The Nugitna had been primarily concerned with convincing the Zoarites that communism ought to be abandoned. Two years after the last issue of the Nugitna the Zoarites did decide to abandon communism and after several months of deciding how the property should be divided the actual distribution took place in the fall in 1898.[44]

Though its principles were finally abandoned, the Separatist Society of Zoar had provided a fulfilling life for its German-American members for 79 years. Few other American towns which lasted as long could boast that none of its citizens had ever spent a night in jail.[45] The love of their fellow man which had induced the Separatists to adopt communism in 1819 was unfortunately directed almost exclusively toward

---

[43] Ibid., pp. 36, 50.

[44] Ibid., pp. 53-68. Randall reprinted all four issues of Nugitna. None of the sources explained the meaning of the name, Nugitna.

[45] Henry Howe, Historical Collections of Ohio, Vol. III, An Encyclopedia of the State (Columbus, Ohio: Henry Howe & Son, 1891), p. 389.

their own members, but within the limitations they set for themselves the Zoarites were both successful and somewhat admirable.

Chapter 10

COMPARISON AND CONCLUSIONS

INTRODUCTION

The purpose of this study has been to investigate the background, development, beliefs, practices, and general history of seven celibate communal societies in order to prove whether their similarities justify the classification of those societies as similar examples of a particular type of religious phenomenon. Those societies have often been considered as isolated groups coming out of several religious movements. However, in emerging from several religious movements the similarities of those societies may have delineated a new movement made up of those seven societies and others like them.

A series of charts and tables have been constructed which compare some details of each society's history, origins, and beliefs and practices. Those tables will be used to gauge the accuracy of the belief that the seven celibate communal societies should be considered as related examples of a particular movement rather than as isolated groups.

A comparison of the backgrounds of the members of the seven societies shows that the societies did not come from the same religious denominations or from the same countries. Tables 1, 2, and 3, respectively, compare the religious background and the main geographic source of each society's original members plus the area from which each society solicited members after being established in America. The comparisons presented in those tables clearly show that similarities among the seven societies were not based on collectively homogeneous members within the societies as a whole. Having come from three separate countries and six religious traditions, the societies were no more collectively homogeneous in their cultural and religious backgrounds than they had been in their temporal origins.

Table 1. Religious Background of Original Members

German Lutheran	German Baptist & German Reformed	Dutch Reformed	Quaker & New Light Baptist
Woman in W. Ephrata C. Harmony S. S. of Zoar	Ephrata C.	Bohemia M.	Shaker S. Universal F.

Table 2. Main Geographic Source of Members

Germany	Germany + America	Holland	America
Woman in W. Harmony S. S. of Zoar	Ephrata C.	Bohemia M.	Shaker S. Universal F.

Table 3. Solicitation of Members After Establishment in America

In Germany	None Known	In America
Woman in W. Harmony S.	S. of Zoar	Bohemia M. Ephrata C. Shaker S. Universal F.

Though most of the societies received new members from the outside after their establishment, the societies as a whole did not become much more collectively homogeneous than they had been when each was founded. In only two societies was there a possibility that the solicitation of new members from the outside could have significantly changed the religious background of the society. Those two societies were Ephrata Cloister in which the new members were usually of the German Baptist or Dunker faith, as the original members had been, and the Shaker Society, whose religious background soon encompassed many faiths, overwhelming the numerical strength of its former Quakers and New Light Baptists, but only gradually changing the Shaker beliefs and way of life. In the other five societies, only two had major influxes of new members from the outside, "Woman in the Wilderness" and the Harmony Society. Most of the new members in both of those groups migrated directly to the society from the same German backgrounds which had produced the original members.

Whatever changes did occur in the membership of each society as the society developed, most of the beliefs and practices of each sect were fairly well developed before the establishment of each celibate communal society. The members of the seven societies did not come from the same religious or cultural backgrounds and did not share the same experiences, before or after the establishment of the celibate communal societies. Therefore, if those societies were related examples of one particular religious movement, the similarities which demonstrated their essential unity would have been present in their beliefs and practices.

If a comparison of beliefs and practices among the seven celibate communal societies would determine their essential unity or disunity, such a comparison must be based on those beliefs and practices related to issues which tend to separate the celibate communal societies from other Christian groups. In the study of each society particular attention was given to beliefs and practices which might have fulfilled the above criterion and to any beliefs and practices found to have been particularly important for any of the societies. From those beliefs and practices a list of issues was compiled. Each society's position on those issues was presented and discussed in the "Beliefs and Practices" section of the previous chapters. In regard to most of those issues the beliefs and practices of the seven societies were fundamentally different, while in regard to some of those issues the beliefs and practices of the seven societies were fundamentally in agreement. Direct comparisons between the societies will be presented in the following section. The first section, containing Tables 4-12 will compare the societies' positions on issues about which they fundamentally disagreed and the second part, containing Tables 13-26 will compare the societies' positions on issues about which they fundamentally agreed.

COMPARISON OF BELIEFS AND PRACTICES

Table 4 compares the day of Sabbath observance by each society. Ordinarily when the Sabbath practices of a Christian sect are unknown, the sect might be assumed to have observed the Sabbath on the first day of the week. In the case of the "Woman in the Wilderness" there is evidence for believing that society observed the Sabbath on Sundays and there is also evidence for believing that society observed the Sabbath on Saturdays.

Table 4. Sabbath Observance

Seventh-Day	Day Unknown	First-Day
Ephrata C. Universal F.	Woman in W.	Bohemia M. Shaker S. Harmony S. S. of Zoar

Although three of the societies required their celibate communal members to confess their sins, the practices of those three societies varied considerably. At Ephrata Cloister each member was required to write out his confession each week, and those confessions were publicly read within the cloister on each Sabbath. Among the Shakers there was no set time for confession but each member was required to confess his sins to the elder or eldress and to bring to the elder or eldress knowledge of the sins of any other member which the informant had reason to believe would not be confessed by the sinner. Confession was encouraged among members of the Harmony Society and was required from all who wished to become members. Of Bohemia Manor and the "Woman in the Wilderness," whose positions on confession were not reported in the sources, Bohemia Manor is the one most likely to have required or practiced confession. The spiritual founder of Bohemia Manor, Jean de Labadie, had once been a priest within the Roman Catholic Church; and his experiences in that church might have led to the practice of confession in the sect which he founded.

Table 5. Confession

Required At Some Time	Unknown	None Required
Ephrata C. Shaker S. Harmony S.	Bohemia M. Woman in W.	S. of Zoar Universal F.

None of the sources state unequivocally that confession was not required or practiced by the Society of Universal Friends or by the Separatists of Zoar, but their very strong stands against ceremonies and the lack of any mention by the sources of any practice of confession indicate that confession was at least not required in either society. The strong stand against ceremonialism by the Zoarites and the Universal Friends which is presented in Table 6 on "Ceremonialism," also shows up in their positions against sacraments as presented in Table 7 and in their position against vows or oaths presented in Table 8. Classifying the positions of the other societies on ceremonialism was more difficult.

Table 6. Ceremonialism

Mystical Ritual	Normal Ritual	No Ceremonies
Woman in W. Ephrata C. Shaker S.	Bohemia M. Harmony S.	Universal F. S. of Zoar

The occult elements present in the ceremonial practices of "Woman in the Wilderness" and Ephrata Cloister mark those societies as definitely belonging under the heading of "Mystical Ritual," but the type of mysticism exemplified by those societies was different from that of the Shaker Society which is also included under the same heading. The prime source of Shaker mysticism was a belief in direct inspiration, and the actions of Shakers believed to be under the influence of direct inspiration led to the development of dances and their use in worship services. As the Shakers developed the dances were transformed from highly individual responses to inspiration into group efforts whose intricate choreography was practiced daily before actually being performed in a worship service. The categorization of Shaker dances as "mystical ritual" is open to debate for as they became more ritualized the dances appear to have become less mystical, but in comparison with the ceremonies or lack of ceremonies in some of the other celibate communal societies, "mystical ritual" is a fitting term for the Shaker dances.

The characterization of the ceremonial practices of Bohemia Manor and the Harmony Society as "Normal Ritual" was based on the observance by both societies of the sacraments of eucharist and baptism and their lack of mystical ceremonies. The ritual of those societies was not so much normal in comparison with church-type organizations as it was in comparison with the ritual or lack of ritual in the other societies.

Table 7. Sacraments

Adult Believers Only	No Observance of Sacraments
Bohemia M.	Shaker S.
Woman in W.	Universal F.
Ephrata C.	S. of Zoar
Harmony S.	

In those societies which observed sacraments, the only ceremonies which are known to have had sacramental status were baptism and the eucharist.

Table 8. Vows

Vows Pledging Celibacy	Unknown	No Vows or Oaths
Woman in W. Ephrata C.	Bohemia M.	Shaker S. Universal F. Harmony S. S. of Zoar

Table 9. Signed Covenants

None	Unknown	Legal Covenant
Ephrata C. Universal F.	Bohemia M. Woman in W.	Shaker S. Harmony S. S. of Zoar

Tables 8 and 9 provide an interesting comparison between societies that required their members to give vows of celibacy and those that required their members to sign communal property agreements. With the exception of Bohemia Manor, whose policies on either issue are unknown, only one society, the Universal Friends, did not require its members to either give a vow of celibacy or sign a communal agreement. Of those five societies known to have required one act or the other, none of the societies required both a vow of celibacy and a signed communal agreement.

Table 10 compares the position of women in each society. In "Woman in the Wilderness" there were no female members; that appears to have been the result of a definite policy of exclusion. In all of the other societies, women either began on an equal voting basis with men or, as in the case of the Harmony Society, were given voting power much later when there were too few male members to fulfill the society's legal covenant. The Shaker Society and the Society of Universal Friends were each founded by a woman. Women always held important leadership positions within those societies, and within Ephrata Cloister. Only at the end of its existence did women hold positions of power in the Harmony Society.

Table 10. Position of Women

Held Power From The Beginning	Changed To Power	Women Excluded
Bohemia M. Ephrata C. Shaker S. Universal F. S. of Zoar	Harmony S.	Woman in W.

In Table 11 on slavery, Bohemia Manor appears with those societies which were against slavery and as the only society known to have held slaves. In its beginning, the society's principles denounced slavery, but following the modification of the society's communism in 1698, some of the community's members acquired slaves for the purpose of raising tobacco. It is likely that the three society's whose positions on slavery are unknown were against slavery, for none of them were known to have even owned any slaves.

Table 11. Slavery

Against Slavery	Unknown	Held Slaves
Bohemia M. Shaker S. Universal F. Harmony S.	Woman in W. Ephrata C. S. of Zoar	Bohemia M.

All of the societies which were classified as pacifist either made statements declaring their pacifism or some of their members were involved in incidents during which the members' behavior proclaimed pacifism as part of their society's principles. Bohemia Manor was classified as nonpacifist because the society's leader when threatened with danger had helped to load a cannon.

Table 12. Pacifism

Pacifist	Nonpacifist
Woman in W. Ephrata C. Shaker S. Universal F. Harmony S. S. of Zoar	Bohemia M.

Unfortunately, as noted several times above, there were issues presented in Tables 4-12 about which the position of one or more of the societies was not given in the sources. Yet, even with the available information, there are some important statements which can be made from all of the information in Tables 4-12 which would not be changed by filling in each society's now unknown positions. The societies did not fundamentally agree on any of the issues in Tables 4-12, but their disagreement was qualified, to some extent, by the fact that the positions of each society fit at least once with those of each other society. No two societies disagreed with each other on every issue, and it is also noteworthy that no two societies agreed with each other on every issue in Tables 4-12.

If the seven celibate communal societies or any number of them fit together as a group which can be called "Radical Pietists," that group will not be defined by the issues presented in Tables 4-12. There are six issues about which all of the societies fundamentally agreed and which might define such a group. Those issues are direct inspiration, millennialism, separation from the world, asceticism, celibacy, and communism. The positions of each society on those issues will be compared in Tables 13-26.

If Tables 13-26 were to simply follow the format of Tables 4-12, all of the societies would be lined up under one heading on each table because each of the societies believed in and practiced direct inspiration, millennialism, separation from the world, asceticism, celibacy, and communism. Beyond that essential unity, there were differences among the societies on those issues. Tables 13-26 will present and compare those differences and as a result, Tables 13-26 will inadvertently emphasize those differences. The reader should keep in mind the underlying fundamental unity which the societies shared in regard to those six issues.

For some of the six issues about which the societies fundamentally agreed, more than one table was necessary to explore and relate the positions of each of the societies. Therefore, the comparisons on some of the issues, such as separation from the world, which is presented in Tables 15 and 16 will be presented in a series of tables.

The first table comparing the position of each society on an issue of fundamental agreement among the celibate communal societies is about "Direct Inspiration." All of the societies believed that one or more of their members received, at one time or another, from God, Jesus Christ, or the Holy Spirit some direct guidance, inspiration, or revelation. In the table, the societies are divided into categories representing an estimation of how important the belief in direct inspiration was for each society.

Table 13. Direct Inspiration

Very Important	Not as Important	Important to Celibacy
Bohemia M.	Woman in W.	Shaker S.
Ephrata C.	Harmony S.	Universal F.
Shaker S.		
Universal F.		
S. of Zoar		

Those who led the societies were most often the ones who claimed to receive direct inspiration, but in the Shaker Society, members at all levels claimed to have experienced direct inspiration which ranged from involuntary "jerks" to the grand vision given to Ann Lee which became the foundation of several Shaker beliefs, including their avowal of celibacy. Claims for acting under the influence of direct inspiration appear to have been less frequent for both the leaders and the members in the "Woman in the Wilderness" and the Harmony Society than among the other societies.

Only among the Shakers is there any known connection between direct inspiration and celibacy. Yet, Jemima Wilkinson's ideas about herself as the incarnation of a messenger from God and her espousal of celibacy certainly point to a connection between the two principles in her Society of Universal Friends.

The reliance of all of the societies upon untrained spiritual leaders appears to have been a result of the idea that some people would be directly inspired to spiritually lead the others. Ordained ministers were important leaders at one time or another in the "Woman in the Wilderness" and among the Shakers, but both societies, like all the others, primarily relied on untrained ministers whose personal sense of being called was one of their chief qualifications for positions of spiritual leadership.

Members of each of the celibate communal societies at one time hoped and believed the millennium would come within their lifetime. Such hopes and expectations were weakest in the communities of Bohemia Manor and Zoar. In the other societies those hopes and expectations formed an important part of each society's beliefs, especially during the early years of each society's history. Except for Bohemia Manor, about which the relevant data is unknown, all of the societies held their beliefs concerning the millennium before they adopted celibacy or communism. The reasons for the adoption of celibacy, in the cases of Bohemia Manor and the Separatists of Zoar, were probably not connected to millennialism, but in all of the other societies beliefs about the immanence of the millennium were important factors leading to the adoption of celibacy.

Table 14. Millennialism

Very Important	Not as Important	Important To Celibacy	Important To Communism
Woman in W.	Bohemia M.	Woman in W.	Shaker S.
Ephrata C.	S. of Zoar	Ephrata C.	Harmony S.
Shaker S.		Shaker S.	
Universal F.		Universal F.	
Harmony S.		Harmony S.	

Among the Harmonists and the Shakers millennial beliefs were also important for the adoption of communism. According to Harmonist conceptions, communism was going to be the future condition of mankind during the millennium. Their practice of communism was adopted partially to prepare themselves to be among the "elect" when Christ's second coming occurred. The Shakers believed Christ's second coming would not be an instantaneous event which would occur throughout the world; they believed the second coming was already occurring in the lives of "true believers" as each achieved salvation.

Expectations that Christ's second coming would soon occur or was already occurring and that the world was doomed were important factors in the strength of the separation from the world practiced by the celibate communal societies. In each of the societies some of the members, if not all of the members, were expected to be almost totally separated from the world outside the society or congregation. Yet, the separation from the world expected of individual members was not usually required for the society or congregation as a whole. Unless the society chose to be completely economically self-sufficient, the only way to maintain separation from the world for individual members was for the society as a whole to economically participate in the world. Table 15 compares the societies in regard to separation from the world for individual members; Table 16 compares the way each society handled the separation from the world on an economic level.

Table 15. Separation of Believers From the World

Individual Separation For All Church Members	Individual Participation For Some Church Members	Political Participation For Church As A Whole
Bohemia M. Woman in W. Shaker S. Harmony S. S. of Zoar	Ephrata C. Universal F.	Harmony S. S. of Zoar

Table 16. Economic Separation From the World

Economic Separation For All Members And For Whole Church	Economic Separation For All Members, But Participation For Whole Church	Economic Separation For Some Members And Participation For Some Members
Woman in W.	Bohemia M. Shaker S. Harmony S. S. of Zoar	Ephrata C. Universal F.

Five of the seven societies required individual separation from the world for all church members. However, in the congregations to which members of Ephrata Cloister and the Society of Universal Friends belonged there were more secular members than celibate communal members. The principle of separation from the world, though often observed, was not required for the secular members of those two congregations. Although the principle of individual separation from the world was followed in Harmony and Zoar, both societies voted in elections. With the exception of one Harmonist, Frederick Rapp, who participated as a delegate in the convention which created the constitution of the state of Indiana, none of the members of the celibate communal societies held elective office outside the societies.

"Woman in the Wilderness" was the only society whose policies maintained separation for the whole church in economic matters. Yet, the discussion of Daniel Falkner's activities in the history of that society has already demonstrated that economic separation from the world, while expected of all members, was not enforced as a membership requirement in the "Woman in the Wilderness."

With the possible exception of "Woman in the Wilderness" about which the relevant data is unknown, all of the celibate communal societies had adopted the principle of separation from the world before they adopted communism. The relative order of the adoption by each society of celibacy and separation from the world is harder to determine; while communism is necessarily a group activity, both celibacy and separation from the world could have been practiced by one individual, such as the founder of each society for years before the society was established. Although it usually appears in those seven societies as part of the principle of separation from the world, communism does not necessarily imply separation from the world as does celibacy which always signifies a rejection of part of the natural world. When the advocacy of celibacy appears in each of the societies, the presence of the principle of separation from the world can be assumed. In most of the societies, the adoption of celibacy and of separation from the world might have come at relatively the same time. Only in regard to Harmony and Zoar was there really definite evidence that the principle of separation from the world was advocated as part of the society's beliefs before the adoption of the advocacy of celibacy.

Like all of us born of the children of Adam, the members of the celibate communal societies were inherently part of the natural world. To be totally separate from the world, then, involved for them a denial of self, of which the most prominent example was the practice of celibacy. Celibacy was not the only type of asceticism practiced in each of the seven societies. Table 17 compares the general degree of asceticism practiced in each of the societies.

Table 17. Asceticism

Fasting And Mortification	Austere Life	Plain Life
Bohemia M.	Shaker S.	Universal F.
Woman in W.		Harmony S.
Ephrata C.		S. of Zoar

Of the societies under the heading, "Fasting and Mortification," the members of Ephrata Cloister appear to have been the most ardent practicioners of self-denial through mortification of the flesh. Fasting, including vegetarianism, was often part of the austere Shaker life, while the life of the last three societies, though plain and pious, was more comfortable than that of the Shakers. In their early existence, all of the societies lived the hard life of pioneers. In their later years, perhaps because of the advancing average age of their members, more attention was given to physical comfort.

The placement of societies in the three categories of ascetic practice reflecting decreasing degrees of ascetic severity corresponds with the chronological order in which the societies were originally established. In other ways, the chronological order of the societies does not seem to be significant. Dancing was banned in the three earliest societies, was practiced as an important part of worship services held by the Shakers, and was banned in the three latest societies. The highly decorative, ornamental writing produced at Ephrata, which was intended as a worshipful activity would have been regarded by the Shakers as sinfully superfluous, while it might have been artistically appreciated among the Harmonists.

In several of the celibate communal societies, the asceticism inherent in celibacy was not simply based on a personal denial of oneself as a sinner, but was also based on the idea that mankind's heterosexual nature was basically sinful. In four of the societies that idea was closely connected to beliefs regarding the androgynous nature of God. Three of the societies also believed that Adam had been androgynous. Table 18 shows the positions of the societies in regard to the androgynous nature of God and Adam.

Table 18. Androgynous God and Adam

God and Adam Androgynous	God Androgynous	Attitude on Androgynous God and Adam Unknown
Woman in W. Ephrata C. Harmony S.	Shaker S.	Bohemia M. Universal F. S. of Zoar

Those societies which believed God was androgynous also believed Christ was androgynous. Among the Shakers the belief that God was androgynous appears to have come from the vision which Ann Lee had in 1770. Whether the Wardleys who preceded Ann had believed God was androgynous is not known. Each of the three societies of German origin which believed God was androgynous also believed Adam had originally been androgynous. The mystical ideas of Jacob Boehme were an important influence on the beliefs of those societies about the androgynous nature of God, Adam, and Christ. The Separatists of Zoar might also have had contact with the ideas of Jacob Boehme but their beliefs on the issue presented in Table 18 are unknown. Those three societies which believed Adam had lost his androgynous nature through sinfulness believed that ultimately the redemption of mankind would restore that androgynous nature. The positions of the societies in regard to androgynous redemption are presented in Table 19.

Table 19. Androgynous Redemption

Redemption Androgynous	Attitude On Androgynous Redemption Unknown	Redemption Not Androgynous
Woman in W. Ephrata C. Harmony S.	S. of Zoar	Shaker S.

With the possible exception of the Zoarites, whose unknown position is noted above, the German celibate communal societies believed Jesus the Christ was androgynous and that, ultimately, those of mankind to be redeemed would become androgynous like Adam had been originally. The Shaker view of Christ and the ultimate redemption of mankind was quite different. They believed Jesus had manifested only the male Spirit of Christ and Ann Lee had manifested the female Spirit of Christ. The manifestation of Christ in two separate beings was connected to the Shaker belief that Adam had not been androgynous; that the androgynous nature of God had been reflected in Adam and Eve as male and female, not in Adam alone. Therefore, the Shakers did not believe mankind would become androgynous when redeemed. The different views of the ultimate effects of redemption were important barriers to the merger attempts between the Shakers and the Harmonists and Zoarites which had been proposed in the 1850's.

Since the views of the Separatists of Zoar and the other German societies on the androgynous nature of God and Adam had come from the same source in the works of Jacob Boehme, it is likely that the Zoarites had believed redemption would ultimately bring a restoration to mankind of the androgynous nature lost in Adam. However, the abandonment of celibacy after a period of about ten years indicates the Zoarites might have had different ideas about the future redemption of mankind.

The two previous tables on beliefs about the androgynous nature of God, Adam, and redemption presented the positions of each society on issues of belief which encouraged the practice of celibacy. The next two tables are concerned with some of the ways the celibate communal societies put their beliefs about celibacy into practice. In Table 20, the position of each society will be compared on the practice of requiring celibacy as a part of church membership. In Table 21 the societies will be compared according to the means which they used to enforce celibacy among their celibate members.

With the possible exception of "Woman in the Wilderness," which may have come directly from groups of church-pietists, all of the celibate communal societies developed from independent sects or churches which had broken off from larger denominations. When celibacy was adopted as a practice within each of those independent sects, each group had to face the question of whether celibacy was to be a membership requirement within that church. In regard to celibacy, the membership practices of the seven societies divided the societies into three groups: (1) those which required celibacy for membership in their church, (2) those which expected the practice of celibacy from each member but did not require it, and (3) those which did not require or expect all of their church members to be celibate.

Table 20. Relationship of Celibacy to Church Membership

Required For The Whole Church	Expected Of All But Not Required	Practiced By Part Of The Church Only
Bohemia M. Woman in W. Shaker S.	Harmony S. S. of Zoar	Ephrata C. Universal F.

Unlike the preceding tables, the organizations compared in Table 20 were the churches associated with the celibate communal societies rather than the societies themselves. Among the five societies which required or expected their church members to practice celibacy, the church members and the members of the celibate communal society were one and the same. In the churches associated with Ephrata Cloister and the Universal Friends, most of the members were not celibate and did not hold property in common. Even the name of the Society of Universal Friends refers not to the celibate communal members but to the church as a whole. The celibate communal members within that church did not have a separate name or a separate organization. The church organization to which the members of Ephrata Cloister belonged was the Seventh-Day

German Baptist Church. The celibate communal society of Ephrata Cloister was a separate organization within that church.

The five societies which required or expected each member to practice celibacy appear to have adopted such membership expectations because of the importance of celibacy to their churches. Another factor which might have been influenced or determined by the importance of celibacy to each society's church was the means or social structure used to enforce celibacy in each society. Both the comparisons presented in Table 20 of the relationship of celibacy to membership in each society and the comparisons which will be presented in Table 21 of the means used to enforce celibacy in each society have categories which indicate the societies were basically divided into two groups: one in which celibacy was very important to each society and one in which celibacy was of less importance to each society.

Table 21. Means of Enforcing Celibacy

Monastic Control	Social Pressure
Bohemia M.	Universal F.
Woman in W.	Harmony S.
Ephrata C.	S. of Zoar
Shaker S.	

In Table 21, the categories of "Monastic Control" and "Social Pressure" refer basically to the living arrangements used in each society. Those societies which required separation of the sexes in different living quarters and throughout most of their daily activities have been categorized as using monastic means to enforce celibacy. Although celibacy was not required for membership in the church with which Ephrata Cloister was associated, it was required for membership in Ephrata Cloister, and celibacy was also required in each of the other societies which used monastic means to enforce celibacy. There may be some significance in the chronological division between the societies which used monastic control and those which relied on social pressure to enforce celibacy. The earliest four societies used monastic control and the last three societies used social pressure.

Celibacy was not required for membership in any of the three societies which used social pressure to control celibacy, although celibacy was expected of members in the Harmony and Zoar societies. The use of social pressure, rather than strict monastic conditions, in those three societies may have been the result of the large number of married members in all three of the societies. There were unmarried members in each society, and apparently, unmarried women made up the largest group of celibate members among the Universal Friends. Also among the Universal Friends as well as in the Harmony and Zoar societies, there were married members who practiced celibacy while living in the same homes. In the Harmony Society married couples who practiced celibacy slept in rooms on separate floors of the same house. There were usually other adults, such as relatives, living in the same house. The Zoarites and the Universal Friends appear to have had similar practices. The use of social pressure was not neglected by the societies using monastic controls to enforce celibacy. Similarly, the societies relying on social pressure also practiced some voluntary separation of the sexes.

Presumably the practice of requiring or expecting all church members to be celibate and the use of monastic controls to enforce celibacy were each strong indications that celibacy was important to a particular society. Yet of the five societies which expected all of their church members to be celibate there were only three societies which used monastic controls. Monastic controls were also used by one society which did not expect all church members to be celibate. The societies which indicated a high importance or a low importance for celibacy on one issue of comparison might be expected to indicate the same degree of importance on other issues of comparison but the positions of several societies did not do so in Tables 20 and 21. Another comparison of the importance of celibacy to each society's church is presented in Table 22 which compares the longevity of the Church with the longevity of the practice of celibacy in the society, after celibacy was adopted by the society.

Table 22. The Church and the Longevity of Celibacy

Celibacy Lasted To Church's End	Celibacy Abandoned Before Church's End
Bohemia M. Woman in W. Shaker S.? Harmony S.	Ephrata C. Universal F.? S. of Zoar

The Shaker Society was listed with a questionmark in Table 22 because that society still exists, however, all present evidence strongly indicates celibacy will be practiced by the Shaker Society as long as there are any members. The Universal Friends were listed with a question mark because knowledge concerning the later years of that society's history is so scant that when the practice of celibacy ended or under what conditions is not known. It is believed celibacy gradually ceased to be practiced among the Universal Friends as the older members died. A similar situation occurred at Ephrata Cloister, where celibacy ceased to exist only because new celibate members were not forthcoming rather than because of any official abandonment of the practice. Among the Separatists of Zoar the expectation that all members would practice celibacy was abandoned because the leader had decided to marry. Celibacy still retained a higher status than marriage among the Zoarites, but that high status was not one which the Zoarites continued striving to achieve.

Celibacy was actually abandoned by only one society, the Zoar Society. In the Zoar Society the end of the practice of celibacy appears to have occurred as a result of the desire of the society's leader to be married. The Zoarites retained their principle that celibacy was better for those who could practice celibacy but when their leader ceased to practice celibacy the expectation of celibacy from all members also ended throughout the society. Celibacy was not abandoned by any group action in Ephrata Cloister or among the Universal Friends but slowly ceased to be practiced as those members which practiced celibacy died and no new members adopted the practice of celibacy.

In Tables 20, 21, and 22, the societies have been compared on issues which gave some indication of the importance of celibacy to the church of each society. For the individual members who actually practiced celibacy the degree of importance which his church attached to celibacy might not have been personally meaningful. With the exception of the different living conditions which arose out of each society's choice of means to control celibacy the sacrifices of each member and the expected rewards appear to have been basically the same in each of the seven societies. On a different level, the continued longevity of each celibate communal society may have been significantly affected by the choices each society's church made in regard to the relationship between celibacy and church membership and on the means of enforcing celibacy.

In Tables 20, 21, and 22, the categories which indicated celibacy was of a high degree of importance to a society's church were the requirement or expectation that celibacy would be practiced by all church members, the use of monastic controls to enforce celibacy, and the retention of the practice of celibacy until the end of the church's existence. The categories which indicated celibacy was of a lesser degree of importance to a society's church were allowing the practice of celibacy to be optional for church members, relying on social pressure to enforce celibacy, and the abandonment of celibacy before the end of the church's existence.

Four of the five churches which required or expected their members to practice celibacy managed to retain the practice of celibacy for as long as the church existed. In both of the churches for which celibacy was an optional practice, the practice of celibacy ceased to exist before the end of the churches. Therefore, the correlation between the importance given to celibacy as a membership practice and the longevity of celibacy in relation to the existence of the church was quite high. For six out of the seven societies the degree of importance given to celibacy as a membership practice was an accurate indicator of the longevity of celibacy in relation to the church's existence.

Three out of the four societies which enforced celibacy through monastic controls managed to retain the practice of celibacy for as long as the society's church existed. In two out of the three societies which enforced celibacy only through social pressure, celibacy did not last as long as did the society's church. The correlation between the means used to enforce celibacy and the longevity of celibacy in relation to the existence of the church was significant, but not as high the correlation between membership requirements and longevity. For five out of the seven societies the degree of importance given to the means for enforcing celibacy was an accurate indicator of the longevity of celibacy in relation to the church's existence.

Three of the five societies which required or expected celibacy for church membership used monastic controls to enforce celibacy. One of the two societies which had made celibacy an optional part of church membership used only social pressure to enforce celibacy. The correlation between the importance given celibacy as a part of church membership and the importance given celibacy in choosing the means to enforce celibacy was significant, but not as high as the correlation between the importance given to celibacy as a part of membership and the longevity of celibacy in relation to each church's existence, and not as high as the correlation between the importance given to celibacy in the choosing of the means to enforce celibacy and the longevity of celibacy in relation to each church's existence. In four out of seven societies the importance given celibacy as part of church membership was an accurate indicator of the type of controls which each society would choose for enforcing celibacy.

It should be noted that the relative importance of celibacy to each society was not dependent on when celibacy was adopted as a general practice in each society's history. Table 23 shows order in which celibacy and communism were first advocated within each society. The order in which those two principles were advocated is unknown for two of the societies, Bohemia Manor and the "Woman in the Wilderness." All of the other societies are known to have advocated the practice of celibacy before they advocated the practice of communism.

Table 23. Order of Advocacy of Celibacy and Communism

Celibacy Advocated Before Communism	Unknown	Communism Advocated Before Celibacy
Ephrata C.	Bohemia M.	None Known
Shaker S.	Woman in W.	
Universal F.		
Harmony S.		
S. of Zoar		

Because Jean de Labadie is known to have taken a personal vow of celibacy long before he founded the sect which led to the establishment of Bohemia Manor, it is probable that celibacy was also advocated before communism was advocated in Labadie's sect. Because of the influence attributable to the works of Jacob Boehme in Johann Zimmermann's life, the founder of the group which established the "Woman in the Wilderness," it is also probable that celibacy was advocated before communism was advocated in that mystic community.

Though celibacy may have been advocated in each of the societies before communism was advocated, communism was actually established in two of the societies before celibacy was established. Those two societies were the Harmony Society and the Separatist Society of Zoar. Which of the two principles was established first in Bohemia Manor and in the "Woman in the Wilderness" is not known. Celibacy was established before the establishment of communism in Ephrata Cloister, the Shaker Society, and the Society of Universal Friends. Even though communism was not advocated in most of the societies until after celibacy was advocated, communism was a requirement for membership in two more of the churches than was celibacy. The Harmonists and the Zoarites had expected celibacy from their members; they <u>required</u> communism from their members. Table 24 shows the relationship between communism and church membership in each of the societies.

Table 24. Relationship of Communism to Membership

Communism Required For Whole Church	Communism Practiced By Part Of Church Only
Bohemia M. Woman in W. Shaker S. Harmony S. S. of Zoar	Ephrata C. Universal F.

Comparing the longevity of communism in one society with the longevity of communism in another society is more complex than making similar comparisons about the longevity of celibacy. For individuals the practice of celibacy was relatively the same in one society as it might have been in another, particularly when compared to the differences which existed in the practice of communism in any two of the seven societies.

Some of the communal members of the Universal Friends shared the use of the land, but not much else. Within Ephrata Cloister the communal members shared nearly everything including personal items. In the Separatist Society of Zoar communism was supposed to extend to everything except personal property like shoes, but the members of Zoar could work on their own time and earn money which did not belong to the society. Among the members of Ephrata Cloister there were very few personal possessions and all of the working efforts of each member always belonged to the cloister. Table 25 which compares the longevity of communism with the existence of each society's church should be viewed with certain limitations in mind. Those societies which modified their communism before the society ceased to exist modified in different ways systems of communism that had already been different from each other. Those societies which did not modify their communism before the church and society ceased to exist also practiced different systems of communism.

Table 25. The Church and the Longevity of Communism

Communism Unchanged To Church's End	Modified Communism Practiced From The Beginning	Communism Modified Before Church's End
Shaker S.? Harmony S. S. of Zoar	Universal F.	Bohemia M. Woman in W. Ephrata C.

The communism of the Universal Friends was a communal use of property rather than communal ownership, therefore, when compared with the communism of the other societies it should be considered a modified form of communism from its beginning. After Bohemia Manor and the

"Woman in the Wilderness" had modified their communism it is believed their modified communism then lasted until their church and society no longer existed. The churches of both the Universal Friends and Ephrata Cloister existed for some time after the communal society of both groups had ceased to exist.

The longevity of communism is compared with the longevity celibacy in Table 26. There may be different forms of practicing celibacy, perhaps even varying degrees of celibacy just as there are varying degrees of communism, but none of the seven societies modified their celibacy as some had modified communism. When changes were made in the practice of celibacy the changes were complete and resulted in the abandonment of celibacy. Therefore, in Table 26 the comparison is based on whether celibacy or communism were first changed in a society in any way. Therefore, in Table 26, the modification of communism is compared with the abandonment of celibacy.

Table 26. Longevity of Celibacy Compared with Longevity of Communism

Communism Modified Before Celibacy Was Abandoned	Communism And Celibacy Ended At The Same Time	Celibacy Abandoned Before Communism Was Modified
Bohemia M. Woman in W. Ephrata C.	Shaker S.? Harmony S.	Universal F. S. of Zoar

The comparisons in Table 26 contrast not the importance of celibacy and communism but the strength of those principles, strengths which varied among the seven societies. Of the two societies which did not change either practice throughout their existence, the Shakers emphasized celibacy more than communism and the Harmonists emphasized communism more than celibacy. However, as a whole, the comparisons in Table 26 indicate the strengths of the two principles were approximately equal.

Within the Christian world the practice of celibacy and the practice of communism has been unusual enough that the term "celibate communal societies" readily identifies those few groups outside the Roman Catholic Church who have practiced celibacy and communism for religious reasons. Unfortunately, the term "celibate communal societies" is a somewhat misleading term for it focuses attention on part of the principles of those societies while overlooking the other beliefs which were important to their formation.

Along with the effects of celibacy and communism, the seven societies were also set apart from the world by their beliefs in direct inspiration, millennialism, separation from the world, and asceticism. Though expressed in different ways by each society, those beliefs were, nonetheless, shared beliefs whose importance and similarity in each society identify those societies as examples of a particular segment of Pietism. Considering the nature of their beliefs the seven societies and others like them might be appropriately called "Radical Pietists."

RELATIONSHIPS

The seven societies need not be classified as part of one group simply because their beliefs and practices were very similar. Other indications of their unity can be found in an examination of the influences and relationships known to have existed between those seven societies. Each of the societies appears to have had some kind of a relationship with at least one of the other societies. The relationships among the societies

246

included actions which expressed approval of other societies, consideration of possible mergers with other societies, direct influence affecting the development of other societies, and indications of unproven, but highly probable, indirect influences affecting the development of other societies.

There is no definite evidence that Bohemia Manor of the "Woman in the Wilderness" affected each other or even knew of each other's existence until 1721. However, Phillip Jacob Spener or Benjamin Furly may have had knowledge of both societies and communicated that knowledge to members of either society before or shortly after the founding of "Woman in the Wilderness."

Both Bohemia Manor and the "Woman in the Wilderness" directly influenced the founding of Ephrata Cloister. Conrad Beissel, the founder of Ephrata Cloister, had traveled to America for the purpose of joining the "Woman in the Wilderness" and he is known to have studied with the leader of that society during 1720-1722. Beissel visited Bohemia Manor in 1721. Though Beissel had studied with many other mystical and Pietist groups, Bohemia Manor was the only place where he found men and women living in a celibate communal society under monastic conditions.

Circumstantial evidence suggests that Ephrata Cloister was indirectly influential in the development of the Society of Universal Friends. Both societies observed the seventh-day Sabbath, an observance which may have occurred among the Universal Friends because of influence received from Ephrata Cloister through Christopher Marshall. Marshall was a good friend of Ephrata Cloister and was known to have had several religious discussions with the Universal Friend before her followers adopted the observance of the seventh-day Sabbath. The founding of a communal settlement by the Universal Friends might also have been influenced by the example of Ephrata Cloister through the conversations of the Universal Friend with Christopher Marshall.

Similarities between the Universal Friends and the Shaker Society have led to suggestions that they influenced each other but no known connections existed between the two societies. Although the Shakers became the largest of the seven societies there is no evidence that they influenced the early development of any of the other societies. However, the Shakers were connected to other societies in different ways. Shaker writers have approvingly described both the "Woman in the Wilderness" and Ephrata Cloister as examples of the witnesses who heralded the approach of Christ's second coming. The strongest relationships which the Shakers had with other societies were with the Harmonists and the Zoarites. During the 1850's a proposed merger was considered by all three societies. Though certain doctrinal differences eventually stopped the societies from merging, even the existence of such a proposal and its consideration is very strong evidence of a basic unity of belief shared by those three societies.

The Harmony Society might have been indirectly influenced in its development by Ephrata Cloister. The successful example of Ephrata Cloister might have been known to the Harmonists before they left Germany if they had purchased by that time certain books which they are known to have owned by 1830. Two of the books in the Harmonist library in 1830 contained accurate accounts of Ephrata and were published in Germany before 1800. Sometime after coming to America the Harmonists are known to have been aware of and somewhat approving of Ephrata Cloister because the Harmonists published a hymnal in 1820 which contained some hymns written at Ephrata.

The Harmony Society might have been influential in the development of the Separatist Society of Zoar. The Zoarites might have known about the Harmonists before the Zoarites migrated to America in 1817 because both had been Separatist groups in Germany. Even more likely, the Zoarites probably learned about the existence of the Harmonists when they purchased their land from a friend of the Harmonists, Godfrey Haga. Before establishing themselves as a communal society in 1819 the Zoarites probably heard about the Harmonists through other sources because they were only 80 miles from the original American home of the Harmonists.

One other connection between two societies should be considered, although neither society had any influence on the other. Ephrata Cloister and the Shaker Society did not influence each other but the importance which both of them attached to direct inspiration can be traced back to the same source. When Conrad Beissel, the founder of Ephrata Cloister, sojourned with the Community of True Inspiration he learned to put himself into a state of trance in which he was supposed to receive direct inspiration. The beliefs of the Community of True Inspiration regarding direct inspiration had developed from contacts which their founders had with a few of the French Prophets, Camisards, or Cevenoles. The Shaker Society traced its beliefs in certain forms of direct inspiration back to the Cevenoles who appeared in England in 1706. Thus, both the Shaker Society and Ephrata Cloister were indirectly heirs of the Cevenoles.

All of the societies had some kind of relationship with at least one other society which demonstrated some special unity with that particular society. Through those relationships, through direct and indirect influences, expressions of approval, and interconnections with other societies each society was connected to each other society. All of the societies were friends of mutual friends, an indication of their unity as a group within Pietism.

SUMMARY AND SUGGESTIONS FOR FURTHER STUDY

As a group, celibate communal societies have been the most successful communal societies in the United States. Unfortunately, though there have been many valuable studies of the celibate communal societies as individual societies, there have been no major studies investigating their unity as a religious group, as examples of a particular phenomenon within Pietism. This study, limited to the seven earliest, celibate communal societies, has attempted to prove that the beliefs and practices of those seven societies gave them a unity within Pietism which was similar to the unity of Pietist groups within Christianity.

Much of the development and history of the seven societies demonstrated the distinct individuality that was a part of each religious sect which founded a celibate communal society. Considering the historical background of each society the recognizable individuality of each society was to be expected; the founding of the first two and last two societies was separated by more than 100 years, the members of the societies came from several different countries, and the societies developed from different religious traditions. Outside of the expected differences, the striking features which stood out among the histories of the celibate communal societies were their unities of belief and similarities of practice.

The tables of comparison demonstrated the unity of the societies in six important beliefs: direct inspiration, millennialism, separation from the world, asceticism, celibacy, and communism. The celibate communal societies have long been considered as groups set apart from the rest of the world by their celibacy and communism. Each of the four other beliefs which also delineated those societies may have been as important to the existence of the societies as were celibacy and communism.

Not all of the seven societies were aware of each others existence, but those relationships which did occur among the societies indicated some recognition of their unity and frequently contributed to that unity. Some of the societies expressed approval of other societies, there were proposed mergers between three societies, and the development of one society was directly influenced by two earlier societies. There was some evidence that three other societies may have been influenced by their celibate communal predecessors.

Considering their beliefs and practices and their position within Pietism, the seven celibate communal societies should be called, "Radical Pietists." Those seven societies might not have been the only groups whose beliefs and practices fit the criteria for being included in the category or group known as Radical Pietists. In addition to Bohemia Manor, "Woman in the Wilderness," Ephrata Cloister, the Shaker Society, the Universal Friends, the Harmony Society, and the Separatist Society of Zoar, there were at least seven other communal societies which practiced celibacy in the United States before 1910. Those later seven societies included Bishop Hill in Illinois (1846-1862), the Brotherhood of the New Life in New York, Virginia, and California (1851-1900), St. Nazianz in

Wisconsin (1854-1896), the Woman's Commonwealth in Texas and the District of Columbia (1876-1906), the Lord's Farm in New Jersey (1889-1902), the Koreshans in Illinois and Florida (1894--believed to still be in existence in Florida), and the House of David in Michigan (1903-1928).[1] Perhaps the beliefs and practices of some or all of those later societies fit the criteria for "Radical Pietists." If so, a comparative study of those later celibate communal societies could be useful in refining the criteria for identifying "Radical Pietists" and could add to an understanding of the seven societies covered in this study.

---

[1] Ralph Albertson, "A survey of Mutualistic Communities in America," *Iowa Journal of History and Politics*, Vol. 34 (1936), pp. 375-440. Another communal society which might have fit the criteria for "Radical Pietists" was the Community of True Inspiration which migrated from Germany to New York in 1843. They later moved to Iowa where they became known as the Amana Society. Celibacy was never a common practice within the Amana Society, but they frowned on marriage and regarded it as a hindrance to spiritual life. See Charles Nordhoff, *The Communistic Societies of the United States* (New York: Dover Publications, 1966), pp. 35-36.

BIBLIOGRAPHY

BIBLIOGRAPHY

A. PRIMARY SOURCES

Beissel, Johann Conrad. *A Dissertation on Man's Fall*, trans. by Peter Miller. Ephrata, Pennsylvania: Ephrata Cloister, 1765, in American Antiquarian Society, *Early American Imprints, 1639-1900, Readex Microprint of the Works Listed in Evans American Bibliography*. Worcester, Massachusetts: American Antiquarian Society, 1955.

Bible, The Holy. King James Version. New York: World Publishing Company.

Danckaerts, Jasper. *Journal of Jasper Danckaerts, 1679-1680*, trans. by Henry C. Murphy. eds. Bartlett B. James, and J. Franklin Jameson. New York: Charles Scribner's Sons, 1913.

Duss, John S. *The Harmonists: A Personal History*. Harrisburg, Pennsylvania: Pennsylvania Book Service, 1943.

Evans, Frederick William. *Shakers: Compendium of the Origin, History, Principles, Rules and Regulation, Government, and Doctrines of the United Society of Believer's in Christ's Second Appearing*. New York: D. Appleton and Co., 1859.

Green, Calvin, and Seth Y. Wells. *A Summary View of the Millennial Church, or United Society of Believers, Commonly Called Shakers, Comprising the Rise, Progress and Practical Order of the Society, Together with the General Principles of Their Faith and Testimony*. 2d. ed. Albany, New York: C. Van Benthuysen, 1848.

Harmony Society. *Thoughts on the Destiny of Man, Particularly with Reference to the Present Times*. New Harmony, Indiana: Harmony Society, 1824.

Hinds, William Alfred. *American Communities*. New York: Corinth Books, 1961.

Hudson, David. *Memoir of Jemima Wilkinson*. 2d ed. Bath, New York: R. L. Underhill, 1844.

Johnson Theodore E. (ed.). "The Millenial Laws of 1821," *The Shaker Quarterly*, VII, No. 2 (Summer, 1967), 35-58.

Lamech and Agrippa. *Chronicon Ephratense: A History of the Community of Seventh-Day Baptists at Ephrata*, trans. by J. Max Hark. Lancaster, Pennsylvania: S. H. Zahm and Co., 1899.

Leonard, William. *A Discourse on the Order and Propriety of Divine Inspiration and Revelation; A Discourse on the Second Appearing of Christ; A Discourse on the Propriety and Necessity of a United Inheritance.* Harvard, Massachusetts: United Society, 1853.

Meacham, Joseph. *A Concise Statement of the Principles of the Only True Church According to The Gospel of the Present Appearance of Christ: As Held to and Practiced Upon by the True Followers of the Living Saviour, at New Lebanon.* Bennington, Vermont: Haswell and Russell, 1790.

Nordhoff, Charles. *The Communistic Societies of the United States.* 2d ed. New York: Dover Publications, Inc., 1966.

Reichmann, Felix, and Eugene Doll (ed.). *Ephrata as Seen by Contemporaries.* Seventeenth Yearbook of the German Folklore Society. Allentown, Pennsylvania: Schlechter's, 1952.

Spener, Philip Jacob. *Pia Desideria*, trans. Theodore G. Tappert. Philadelphia, Pennsylvania: Fortress Press, 1964.

Universal Friend. *The Universal Friend's Advice to Those of the Same Religious Society.* Philadelphia, Pennsylvania: Francis Bailey, 1784.

Youngs, Benjamin S., and Calvin Green. *Testimony of Christ's Second Appearing: Exemplified by the Principles and Practice of the True Church of Christ.* 4th ed. Albany, New York: C. Van Benthuysen, 1856.

B. PRIMARY SOURCES REPRINTED IN SECONDARY SOURCES

Beissel, Johann Conrad. "Instructions on the Voice," Ephrata, Cloister, *Turtel taube.* Ephrata, Pennsylvania: Ephrata Cloister, 1747, trans. in Sachse, Julius Friedrich, *The Music of Ephrata Cloister.* New York: AMS Press, 1970, pp. 66-69.

_____. "Letter to Elimelech," 1738, trans. in Sachse, Julius Friedrich, *The German Sectarians of Pennsylvania, 1708-1742; A Critical and Legendary History of the Ephrata Cloister and the Dunkers,* I. Philadelphia, Pennsylvania: printed for the author, 1899, pp. 370-373.

_____. "Preface," *Mysterion Anomias, The Mystery of Lawlessness: or Lawless Antichrist discovered and disclosed, Shewing that all those do belong to that Lawless Antichrist, who wilfully reject the Commandments of God, amongst which, is his holy, and by himself blessed Seventh-Day Sabbath, or his holy Rest, of which the same is a Type,* trans. by Michael Wohlfarth, Philadelphia, Pennsylvania: Andrew Bradford, 1729, in Sachse, Julius Freidrich *The German Sectarians of Pennsylvania, 1708-1742: A Critical and Legendary History of the Ephrata Cloister and the Dunkers,* I. Philadelphia, Pennsylvania: printed for the author, 1899, pp. 145-148.

Ephrata Cloister. "Foreword," Turtel taube. Ephrata, Pennsylvania: Ephrata Cloister, 1747, trans. in Sachse, Julius Friedrich, The Music of Ephrata Cloister. New York: AMS Press, 1970, pp. 53-58.

Fahnestock, William M. "A Historical Sketch of Ephrata: Together with a Concise Account of the Seventh-Day Baptist Society of Pennsylvania," Hazard's Register of Pennsylvania, XV (1835), 161-167, in Reichmann, Felix, and Doll, Eugene, Ephrata as Seen by Contemporaries, Seventeenth Yearbook of the German Folklore Society. Allentown, Pennsylvania: Schlechter's, 1952, pp. 165-184.

Harmony Society. "Articles of Association," 1805, trans. in Arndt, Karl J. R., George Rapp's Harmony Society, 1785-1847. Philadelphia, Pennsylvania: University of Pennsylvania Press, 1965, pp. 72-74.

_____. "Articles of Association," 1805, trans. by Jacob Henrici, in Duss, John S., The Harmonists: A Personal History. Harrisburg, Pennsylvania: Pennsylvania Book Service, 1943, pp. 419-420.

_____. "Articles of Faith of 1798," trans. in Arndt, Karl J. R., George Rapp's Harmony Society, 1785-1847. Philadelphia, Pennsylvania: University of Pennsylvania Press, 1965, pp. 35-40.

_____. "By-Laws of 1832," trans. in Arndt, Karl J. R., George Rapp's Harmony Society, 1785-1847. Philadelphia, Pennsylvania: University of Pennsylvania Press, 1965, pp. 482-483.

Kelpius, Johannes. "Declaration of Civil Death Refusing Power of Attorney," in Sachse, Julius Friedrich, The German Pietists of Provincial Pennsylvania, 1694-1708. Philadelphia, Pennsylvania: printed for the author, 1895, p. 170.

_____. "Letter to Hester Palmer," May 25, 1706, in Sachse, Julius, Friedrich. The German Pietists of Provincial Pennsylvania, 1694-1708. Philadelphia, Pennsylvania: printed for the author, 1895, pp. 180-191.

_____. "Letter to Johannes Fabricus," July 23, 1705, in Sachse, Julius Friedrich. The German Pietists of Provincial Pennsylvania, 1694-1708. Philadelphia, Pennsylvania: printed for the author, 1895, pp. 229-233.

_____. "Letter to Steven Momford," December 11, 1699, in Sachse, Julius Friedrich. The German Pietists of Provincial Pennsylvania, 1694-1708. Philadelphia, Pennsylvania: printed for the author, 1895, pp. 129-136.

Miller, Peter. "Letters to a Gentleman of Philadelphia," December 5, 1790, Hazard's Register of Pennsylvania, XV (1835), 253-256, in Reichmann, Felix and Doll, Eugene. Ephrata as Seen by Contemporaries, Seventeenth Yearbook of the German Folklore Society. Allentown, Pennsylvania: Schlechter's, 1952, pp. 196-200.

Rapp, George. "Letter to Church Authorities at Iptingen," April 17, 1785, trans. in Arndt, Karl J. R., <u>George Rapp's Harmony Society, 1785-1847</u>. Philadelphia, Pennsylvania: University of Pennsylvania Press, 1965, pp. 18-19.

Schmid Committee of Seceeders from the Harmony Society. "Petition to the Pennsylvania House of Representatives," February 25, 1832, in Arndt, Karl J. R., <u>George Rapp's Harmony Society, 1785-1847</u>, Philadelphia, Pennsylvania: University of Pennsylvania Press, 1965, pp. 485-489.

Separatist Society of Zoar. "Articles of Association," April 19, 1819, trans. in Randall, E. O., <u>History of the Zoar Society</u>, 3rd ed. Columbus, Ohio: Fred J. Heer, 1904, pp. 7-8.

_____. "Principles of the Separatists," trans. in Randall, E. O., <u>History of the Zoar Society</u>, 3rd ed. Columbus, Ohio: Fred J. Heer, 1904, pp. 13-14.

United Society of Believer's in Christ's Second Appearing. "Covenant of 1795," in Desroche, Henri., <u>The American Shakers: From Neo-Christianity to Presocialism</u>, trans. by John K. Savacool. Amherst, Massachusetts: University of Massachusetts Press, 1971, pp. 201-202.

Universal Friend. "Last Will and Testament," in Hudson, David. <u>Memoir of Jemima Wilkinson</u>. 2nd ed. Bath, New York: R. L. Underhill, 1844, pp. 287-288.

C. SECONDARY SOURCES

Albertson, Ralph. "A Survey of Mutualistic Communities in America," <u>Iowa Journal of History and Politics</u>, Vol. 34 (1936), 375-440.

Ancient and Mystical Order Rosae Crucis. <u>The Mastery of Life</u>. Official Publication No. 21. San Jose, California: AMORC, no date given.

Andrews, Edward Deming. <u>The People Called Shakers</u>. New York: Dover Publications, Inc., 1963.

Arndt, Karl J. R. <u>George Rapp's Harmony Society, 1785-1847</u>. Philadelphia, Pennsylvania: University of Pennsylvania Press, 1965.

Bole, John Archibald. <u>The Harmony Society</u>. Philadelphia, Pennsylvania: Americana Germanica Press, 1905.

Buckley, F. J. "Eunuch," <u>New Catholic Encyclopedia</u>, V (1967), 631.

Bushee, Frederick A. "Communistic Societies in the United States," <u>Political Science Quarterly</u>, XII (1905), 625-664.

Delhaye, P. "Celibacy, History of," *New Catholic Encyclopedia*, III (1967), 369-374.

Desroche, Henri. *The American Shakers: From Neo-Christianity to Presocialism*, trans. by John K. Savacool. Amherst, Massachusetts: The University of Massachusetts Press, 1971.

Dobbs, Catherine R. *Freedom's Will: The Society of the Separatists of Zoar*. New York: William Frederick Press, 1947.

Doll, Eugene E. *The Ephrata Cloister: An Introduction*. Ephrata, Pennsylvania: Ephrata Cloister Associates, Inc., 1958.

Durnbaugh, Donald F. *The Believers' Church: The History and Character of Radical Protestantism*. New York: MacMillan And Co., 1968.

_____. "Work and Hope: The Spirituality of the Radical Pietist Communitarians," *Church History*, Vol. 39, No. 1 (March, 1970), 72-90.

Ernst, James E. *Ephrata: A History*. Twenty-fifth Yearbook of the German Folklore Society. Allentown, Pennsylvania: Schlechter's, 1961.

Frank, G. "Labadie, Jean de, Labadists," *New Schaff Herzog Encyclopedia of Religious Knowledge*, VI (1910), 390-391.

Harmon, Nolan B. (ed.). *Corinthians, Galatians, Ephesians*. Vol. 10, *The Interpreter's Bible*. New York: Abingdon Press, 1953.

Holloway, Mark. *Heavens on Earth*. New York: Dover Publications, Inc., 1951.

Howe, Henry. "The Zoar Society," *Historical Collections of Ohio*, Vol. III. *An Encyclopedia of the State*. Columbus, Ohio: Henry Howe & Son, 1891, pp. 384-396.

James, Bartlett B. "The Labadist Colony in Maryland," *Johns Hopkins University Studies in Historical and Political Science*, XVII (1899), 277-315.

Johnson, Theodore E. *Life in the Christ Spirit: Observations on Shaker Theology*. Sabbathday Lake, Maine: United Society, 1969.

Kanter, Rosabeth Moss. "Commitment and Social Organization: A Study of Commitment Mechanisms in Utopian Communities," *American Sociological Review*, Vol. 33, No. 4 (August, 1968), 499-517.

Klatt, E., and G. Golze. *Langenscheidt's German-English, English-German Dictionary*. New York: Washington Square Press, 1952.

Landis, George B. "The Society of Separatists of Zoar, Ohio," *American Historical Association Annual Report* (1898).

Lea, Henry C. *History of Sacerdotal Celibacy in the Christian Church.* London: Watts and Co., 1932.

Randall, E. O. *History of the Zoar Society.* 3rd ed. Columbus, Ohio: Fred J. Heer, 1904.

Reibel, Daniel B. *A Guide to Old Economy.* Ambridge, Pennsylvania: Harmony Associates, 1969.

Reichmann, Felix, and Eugene Doll. *Ephrata as Seen by Contemporaries.* Seventeenth Yearbook of the German Folklore Society. Allentown, Pennsylvania: Schlechter's, 1952.

Sachse, Julius Friedrich. *The German Pietists of Provincial Pennsylvania, 1694-1708.* Philadelphia, Pennsylvania: printed for the author, 1895.

_____. *The German Sectarians of Pennsylvania, 1708-1742: A Critical and Legendary History of the Ephrata Cloister and the Dunkers*, I. Philadelphia, Pennsylvania: printed for the author, 1899.

_____. *The German Sectarians of Pennsylvania, 1742-1800: A Critical and Legendary History of the Ephrata Cloister and the Dunkers*, II. Philadelphia, Pennsylvania: printed for the author, 1900.

_____. *Justus Falckner: Mystic and Scholar.* Philadelphia, Pennsylvania: printed for the author, 1903.

_____. *The Music of Ephrata Cloister.* New York: reprinted by AMS Press, 1970.

Stoeffler, Ernest F. *Mysticism in the German Devotional Literature of Colonial Pennsylvania.* Fourteenth Yearbook of the German Folklore Society. Allentown, Pennsylvania: Schlechter's, 1949.

_____. *The Rise of Evangelical Pietism.* Leiden, The Netherlands: E. J. Brill, 1965.

Troeltsch, Ernst. *The Social Teaching of the Christian Churches.* New York: MacMillan and Co., 1931.

Webber, Everett. *Escape to Utopia.* New York: Hastings House Publishers, 1959.

Weigelt, Horst. "Interpretations of Pietism in the Research of Contemporary German Church Historians," *Church History*, Vol. 39, No. 2 (June, 1970), 236-241.

Weisenburger, Francis P. *The Passing of the Frontier: The History of The State of Ohio*, ed. Carl Wittke, Vol. II. Columbus, Ohio: Ohio State Archaeological and Historical Society, 1941.

Williams, John S. *Consecrated Ingenuity: The Shakers and Their Inventions*. Old Chatham, New York: The Chatham Courier Co., 1957.

Wisbey, Herbert A. *Pioneer Prophetess: Jemima Wilkinson, The Public Universal Friend*. Ithaca, New York: Cornell University Press, 1964.

APPENDIX

FRAKTURSCHRIFTEN AND OTHER ORNAMENTAL DESIGNS FROM EPHRATA CLOISTER

261

Pages from *The Christian ABC Book* a symbolic religious primer of drawings done in black ink, which have now faded to dull brown. This manuscript was also used as a pattern book in the writing school. Its complete title is *The Christian ABC is Suffering, Patience and Hope—Whoever has learned this has reached his goal.—Ephrata 1750.*[1]

---

[1] Eugene E. Doll, <u>The Ephrata Cloister: An Introduction</u> (Ephrata, Pennsylvania: Ephrata Cloister Associates, Inc., 1958), p. 28. The text and the Frakturschriften were reproduced from that page.

[2] Ibid., p. 25. The decorative piece was not identified as to source, but may have come from an Ephrata hymnal.

[3] Julius Friedrich Sachse, <u>The Music of Ephrata Cloister</u> (New York: AMS Press, 1970), p. 31. The decorative piece was not identified, but may have come from an Ephrata hymnal.